Global Business Intelligence

T0270865

Global Business Intelligence refers to an organization's ability to gather, process, and analyze pertinent international information in order to make optimal business decisions in a timely manner. With a challenging economic and geopolitical environment, companies and executives need to be adept at information gathering in order to manage emerging challenges and gain competitive advantages. This book, *Global Business Intelligence*, assembles a cast of international experts and thought leaders and explores the implications of business intelligence on contemporary management.

Global Business Intelligence will be a key resource for researchers, academics, students, and policy makers alike in the fields of International Business and Management, Business Strategy, and Geopolitics as well as related disciplines like Political Science, Economics, and Geography.

J. Mark Munoz is a US-based business author and Professor of International Business at Millikin University, Illinois, USA.

Routledge Studies in International Business and the World Economy

For a full list of titles in this series, visit www.routledge.com/Routledge-Studies-in-International-Business-and-the-World-Economy/book-series/SE0358

Global Business Intelligence

Edited by J. Mark Munoz

Routledge
Taylor & Francis Group

LONDON AND NEW YORK

First published 2018 by Routledge

2 Park Square, Milton Park, Abingdon, Oxfordshire OX14 4RN
52 Vanderbilt Avenue, New York, NY 10017

Routledge is an imprint of the Taylor & Francis Group, an informa business

First issued in paperback 2019

Library of Congress Cataloging-in-Publication Data
A catalog record for this book has been requested

ISBN: 978-1-138-20368-6 (hbk)
ISBN: 978-0-367-88981-4 (pbk)

Typeset in Sabon
by Apex CoVantage, LLC

Contents

Figures

Tables

Contributors

Jason Balogh is a Principal at the Hackett Group. Mr. Balogh has worked extensively in the consumer packaged goods, industrial manufacturing, and energy industry sectors. Formerly a Partner with Arthur Andersen, Mr. Balogh has multiple experiences in supporting clients with business transformations, operational improvements, and finance/back office improvements, with an emphasis on driving economic impact and effectively managing the change process.

Subhajit Chakrabarty is an Associate Professor with Narsee Monji Institute of Management Studies (NMIMS), Mumbai, India, with a PhD in international business from the Indian Institute of Foreign Trade (IIFT), New Delhi. He also has a background in computer science. His working experience spans over 23 years in multiple domains and he is also an alumnus of INSEAD. He has taught research methodology, marketing research, international business, statistics, data warehousing and mining, among other subjects.

Mohamed Z. Elbashir is an Associate Professor of Accounting Information Systems at Qatar University. He completed his PhD at the University of Melbourne and had worked at various universities in Australia and other countries. His research interests are in the management accounting and business intelligence systems in both private and public sector organizations. His publications have appeared in top-tier/international journals such as the *Accounting Review, International Journal of Accounting Information Systems*, the *Journal of Information Systems, Business Intelligence Systems*, and in the proceedings of international conferences.

Franziska Engelhard is a research and teaching associate in the Department of International Management at the Friedrich Alexander University of Erlangen-Nürnberg, Germany. Her research centers on biculturals, boundary spanning, multicultural group works and cultural intelligence. She is also actively involved with emerging markets, and has traveled to India and China for research and teaching activities. Two of her papers are currently under review in AMLE and IJCCM.

Andrew Gross has been on the faculty of Cleveland State University, Ohio, USA, for over four decades, but also served as a visiting professor, Fulbright Senior Scholar, or both in his native Hungary, across Canada, and in Australia; he also worked in industry and government. He was the first employee of Predicasts, Inc., a global market research firm, and now serves as a pro bono adviser to The Freedonia Group, a similar organization. He has published four books and over 100 refereed journal articles.

Dirk Holtbrügge is Professor of International Management at the School of Business and Economics, Friedrich-Alexander-University of Erlangen-Nürnberg, Germany. His main research interests are in the areas of international management, human resource management, and management in emerging markets. He has published seven books, eight edited volumes, and more than 70 articles in refereed journals such as *Academy of Management Learning & Education, European Management Journal, Human Resource Management, International Business Review, International Journal of Human Resource Management, Journal of Business Ethics, Journal of International Business Studies, Journal of International Management, Management International Review*, and *Thunderbird International Business Review*. He is also a member of the editorial boards of *International Journal of Cross Cultural Management, International Journal of Emerging Markets, Journal for East-European Management Studies*, and *Management International Review*.

Rajshekhar (Raj) G. Javalgi, Associate Dean and Professor of Marketing and International Business, is recognized as a leading scholar in the field of international business and international entrepreneurship. Dr. Javalgi has published over 125 articles in leading journals and several of his articles have received best paper awards.

Valtteri Kaartemo (DSc) acts as University Lecturer at Turku School of Economics (University of Turku, Finland), where he teaches a "Business Intelligence and the Global Business Environment" undergrad course. He also runs a master's level course on business intelligence at ESIEE, France. He has published academic articles, book chapters, and ebooks on various topics, such as big data.

Wiboon Kittilaksanawong is Professor of Strategy and International Business in the Graduate School of Humanities and Social Sciences, Faculty of Economics, Saitama University, Japan. He received PhD in Management from National Taiwan University. His research interests include global business and strategy, business strategies in emerging markets, and international entrepreneurship.

Sholape Kolawole is a Principal in the Hackett Group's EPM, ERP, and Enterprise Analytics Practice. With about 20 years of progressive experience through industry and consulting, Mr. Kolawole has led multiple global finance transformation and FP&A engagements at Fortune 500 companies in the US and elsewhere. His experience spans several industries including manufacturing, consumer products, technology, life sciences, retail, and financial services and his subject matter knowledge is in areas of finance transformation, enterprise performance management, finance system architecture, and organization design. Before joining the Hackett Group, Mr. Kolawole worked in various FP&A and decision support capacities at Sears Holdings Corporation and Whirlpool Corporation. He also worked at PricewaterhouseCoopers where he had responsibility for large audit engagement.

Marti Arran Masters is a global IT consultant with a master's degree in International IT and Management, backed by more than 20 years of work experience, including as a software engineer, IT manager, and director of R&D. Her primary interests include enterprise architecture and knowledge work informatics.

Nicholas Mathew is a doctoral candidate at Cleveland State University, Ohio, USA, specializing in global business and marketing. He received his undergraduate and graduate degrees in business from Cleveland State. In addition, he has conducted market research for organizations and institutes in fields such as manufacturing, healthcare, and nonprofit services.

J. Mark Munoz is a Professor of International Business at Millikin University in Illinois, USA, and a former Visiting Fellow at the Kennedy School of Government at Harvard University, USA. He is a recipient of several awards including four Best Research Paper Awards, an international book award, a literary award, and the ACBSP Teaching Excellence Award, among others. Aside from top-tier journal publications, he has authored/edited/co-edited fourteen books, namely *Land of My Birth*, *Winning Across Borders*, *In Transition*, *A Salesman in Asia*, *Handbook of Business Plan Creation*, *International Social Entrepreneurship*, *Contemporary Microenterprises: Concepts and Cases*, *Handbook on the Geopolitics of Business*, *Business Plan Essentials*, *Hispanic-Latino Entrepreneurship*, *Managerial Forensics*, *Strategies for University Management* (Vol 1 and 2), and *Advances in Geoeconomics*.

Al Naqvi is a big-data strategist and a finance expert. Former CFO of a healthcare system, entrepreneur, and Fortune 500 executive, he has developed over 100 use cases in big data. He is also an adjunct faculty member at Millikin University, USA, where he teaches an MBA Strategy course, and is a frequent speaker at conferences and the author of various articles and books.

Richard "RJ" P. Podeschi II is Assistant Professor of Information Systems and Director of Undergraduate Programs at Millikin University in Decatur, Illinois, USA. He has spent over ten years in industry as an Oracle database administrator and previously was co-owner of his own IT consulting firm. His primary research and teaching interests include database systems and business intelligence, specifically how best to build the necessary skills for a 21st-century workforce.

Zongqiang Ren is an Associate Research Fellow in business at The Research Center of the Wenzhounese Economy at Wenzhou University, China. He received his PhD from the School of Management, Zhejiang University. His research focuses on innovation networks, organizational mechanisms to leverage capabilities, and the social construction for man-machine coordination.

Satyendra Singh is a Professor of Marketing and International Business, and editor-in-chief of the *International Journal of Business and Emerging Markets* at the University of Winnipeg, Canada. Dr. Singh has published widely in reputed international journals such as *Thunderbird International Business Review, Industrial Marketing Management, Journal of Services Marketing, Services Industries Journal, Management Decision, Marketing Intelligence and Planning, Marketing Management Journal,* and *Journal of Global Marketing,* among others, and presented papers at international conferences such as AMA, EMAC, BAM, AMS, WMC, and ASAC, among others.

Tricia-Ann Smith DaSilva, BSC, CA, CPA, CISA, CRISC, CrFA, MBA, is a Senior Manager at PricewaterhouseCoopers Jamaica with over 11 years' experience in providing IT, internal, and financial audit services. She is also a Board Member of the American Board of Forensic Accounting and a Board Member of the local chapter of Information Systems Audit and Control Association (ISACA) for Kingston, Jamaica. She is the author of a number of articles that have been published in *The Jamaica Gleaner,* specifically on forensic accounting and cybersecurity, and has presented at numerous seminars on concepts surrounding IT audit and cybersecurity.

Duane Windsor (PhD, Harvard University) is Lynette S. Autrey Professor of Management in Rice University's Jones Graduate School of Business, USA. His research interests emphasize corporate social responsibility, stakeholder theory, and anti-corruption reform efforts. His research has appeared in various academic journals.

Jack G. Zheng is an Associate Professor of Information Technology in the College of Computing and Software Engineering at Kennesaw State University, USA. He received his PhD in Computer Information Systems from Georgia State University. His primary research and teaching interests include business intelligence, user interface design, data visualization, web/mobile application, and IT education. His extensive works and scholarship have appeared in the areas of information systems, information technology, and information design.

1 Introduction

J. Mark Munoz

Introduction

Globalization has redefined business and paved the way for the creation of new paradigms and operational models.

The evolution and proliferation of diverse technologies have forced organizations to think and operate in new ways. Companies are building their competitive advantages by utilizing and leveraging tools such as the internet, big data, web and social media analytics, among others. Business intelligence or the ability to gather and analyze information has become a critical tool for business success.

The abundance of gadgets and tools has accelerated a firm's ability to gather, assess, and explore voluminous information. Knowledge-capturing and disseminating tools are widely used by majority of corporate executives. One can marvel at the volume of data that are distributed daily though mobile phones, tablets, laptops and personal computers, sensor-based internet-enabled devices, and radio tags. The notion of the Internet of Things has well arrived and brought the level of human and corporate connectivity to unprecedented levels.

This connectivity redefined the notion of business intelligence and spurred new initiatives in e-commerce, e-government and politics, science and technology, health, safety and security, among others.

Business intelligence has grown in prominence in the field of business (Gartner Group, 2006). This heightened interest in business intelligence is anticipated to grow. Business intelligence software and services expenditures are in the vicinity of $16 billion in 2016 (Gartner Group, 2016).

Business intelligence may be viewed in at least two perspectives. It can be viewed in a very broad sense and encompassing all data-gathering initiatives of an enterprise. It can also be viewed in a narrow perspective entailing the information technology angle relating to software, services, or both. In this book, the broader notion is used. It is however evident that the information technology aspect of business intelligence, while a narrow definition, is an integral part of the overall concept of business intelligence.

The practice of business intelligence denotes an action orientation and quest for knowledge. It is grounded on data collection and its analysis (Chaudhuri, Dayal, and Narasayya, 2011). It is an innovative process that is driven by availability of data and the competitive terrain (Brignall and Ballantine, 2004; Klaves, 2003). It is a cyclical process that includes phases such as planning, collecting, analyzing, and distributing (Philips and Vriens 1999; Den Hamer 2005).

Gathering the right information is an important step of the process. However, the way in which information is captured, organized, analyzed, and cognitively interpreted is equally essential. Cognition refers to how an individual processes knowledge based on gathered facts or information (Schiffman and Kanuk, 2010). The cognitive abilities of individuals and companies can vary significantly. Confusion may also ensue since business intelligence has different stages of growth (Watson, Ariyachandra, and Matyska, 2001).

Due to the fact that technology, employee skills, and data gathering resources are different, information gathered are processed in distinctive ways. Companies such as Microsoft, IBM, and Oracle have been leading facilitators of business intelligence through data processing and analytics (Sallam, Richardson, Hagerty, and Hostmann, 2011).

The level of involvement of employees and corporate executives has been largely uneven. Certain executives, especially those designated as CIOs have proactively used business intelligence in recent years (Grajek and Pirani, 2012).

Business intelligence impacts business in profound ways. It has affected business planning, accounting, risk management, and management control systems (Vijayan, 2012; Elbashir, Collier, and Sutton, 2011; Nasar and Bomers, 2012; Robertson, Boehler, and Hansel, 2007). Business intelligence transcends mere data, process, and technologies and refers to organizational competencies relating to comprehension, problem-solving, and effective action (Wells, 2008).

The way a company distributes and captures information defines its communication strength. Blogs are popular forms of communication that spread ideas and information and can be an effective source of business feedback (Adar and Adamic, 2005; Liang, Tsai, and Kwee, 2009). Blogs facilitate understanding of the competitive terrain as well as the external operating environment (Chau, Xu, Cao, Lam, and Shiu, 2009; Chung, Chen, and Nunamaker, 2005).

Business intelligence is an excellent tool for executives to understand the market, competition, as well as other forces that can potentially affect their business. Intelligence can help identify emerging trends, competitive activities, as well as political and economic risks. Competitive intelligence comprises a set of initiatives designed to examine competitor activities (Wright, Eid, and Fleisher, 2009). It can take place through both formal and informal networks and facilitates decision-making (Jaworski, MacInnis, and Kohli, 2002).

When conducting business intelligence, the system and the process are key considerations. Information that is of quality would likely be utilized and translated into action (Maltz and Kohli, 1996). Relevance, credibility, and clarity of information gathered is essential (Yeoh and Koronios, 2010).

Understanding Business Intelligence

Outlined below are characteristics of the business intelligence practice:

Essential—business intelligence impacts organizations worldwide on a daily basis. An organization's ability to understand its market, customers, and competitors well determines its operational destiny and success. A small town grocery store whose owner learned through research that a truck stop is about to be built a few miles from his town might use this knowledge to open up a concession stand in the truck stop. Small and large businesses worldwide gather and act on information on a daily basis. The impact of this information depends on the action taken. For some, the selected action would mean a few thousand dollars in additional revenue; for others it can be millions of dollars. Yet, for others non-awareness or non-action would mean loss of potential income. The reality is, a multitude of information passes through each business enterprise each day. It is important for organizational members to proactively seek or capture valuable information.

Diverse Methodologies—organizations vary with regard to the technology and executive talent they possess. As a result, how they gather and process information can be very different. Consider this: Company A and Company B are both in the call center business. Both companies have a similar size and cater to the same market. Company A has a CIO and a team of research experts while Company B does not. This scenario demonstrates that Company A prioritizes information gathering and research. The breadth and quality of information gathered by Company A will likely be different from that of Company B. The intelligence gathering methodologies and its business impact would likely be different. A diversity of approach towards business intelligence would vary from one company to another.

Differentiator—a company's ability to gather and process information can be a business differentiator. Companies with a "passion for information" or ones having a "culture of research" can obtain unique advantages over its competitors.

Technology-Linked—the practice of business intelligence is often associated with technology. Innovative technologies have made the process of information gathering faster, better, and cheaper. Business intelligence software providers such as IBM, Oracle, SAP, SAS, Microsoft have products that are used by companies worldwide.

Infancy Stage—business intelligence, while widely used in the business community, is still in its early stages. Future innovation will likely make the information-gathering process even more convenient for companies. Numerous technological breakthroughs in the industry continue to emerge. Gartner Group (2016) pointed out the evolution in the contemporary business intelligence platforms: (a) data source (from upfront dimensional modeling to one that is not required), (b) data ingestion and preparation (from IT-produced to IT-enabled), (c) content authoring (from IT staff to business users), (d) analysis (from structured to free form), and (e) insight delivery (from the use of scheduled reports or portal to sharing and collaboration). Additional changes in the future may be expected.

Growing—the use of business intelligence in companies is on the rise. Gartner Group (2016) estimated that the global revenue in the business intelligence and analytics to increase by 5.2% in the period 2015–2016. Business Wire (2015) estimates the increase to be around 8.25% in the period 2014–2019.

International-Orientation—one defining nature of business intelligence is that it is not bounded by geography. As one does research over the web, information from all corners of the world can be accessed. This offers both opportunities and challenges. It is an opportunity since it casts a large net on information that can be acquired. It is a challenge since the information needs to be carefully vetted for accuracy, relevance, and reliability.

Cross-Industry—the practice of business intelligence is one where industry overlaps are common. With numerous data points worldwide, information across industries can easily be merged and combined. This is helpful in a sense that broader perspectives may be acquired. However, challenges can crop up when a very narrow or detailed set of information is required.

Inconsistent Interpretation—a serious challenge in business intelligence lies in the analysis and information of data gathered. Organizations have diverse skill sets and would therefore process information differently. The speed and the depth of information analysis would differ across organizations, departments, and individuals in organizations. Diversity of education, training, attitudes, and intelligence are key factors. Culture and geographic location are also factors to consider. Some countries for instance educate their students more extensively in the math and sciences. When processing high-level scientific information, some countries would be predisposed to perform better than others. It is also likely that in multinational organizations, there will be variances in business intelligence performance across countries.

Lack of Integration—in many organizations, business intelligence is gathered and used across units and not necessarily shared company wide.

There is much room for a more cohesive way of gathering and sharing business information in organizations.

Numerous Applications—business intelligence is used and applied in countless ways and for diverse purposes. Given that individuals, companies, countries, and technologies differ, a huge range of methodologies and styles are used for gathering and processing information.

The attributes mentioned above are snapshots of key characteristics of contemporary business intelligence. The system can be viewed and interpreted in many ways.

In this book, the practice of business intelligence is viewed in a global context. Challenges and opportunities are examined alongside its applicability within an international operational framework.

The Business Intelligence Advantage

Organizations that have a well-developed business intelligence process and structure can benefit in many ways.

Outlined below are a few benefits associated with effective business intelligence.

Value Creation—effective intelligence helps find value in the organization that the firm can leverage. Data collection is a source for building a competitive advantage (Power, 2008).

Market Comprehension—effective intelligence gathering offers important insights relating to trends and threats (Fitzpatrick, 2003). A keen understanding of the market and the changes taking place can help companies refine their strategies, products, and services to be even more relevant to their customers.

Customer Satisfaction—business intelligence is a tool that helps organizations better understand who their customers are as well as existing needs. It can be helpful in customer segmentation (Wixon, Watson, and Werner, 2011). Strong customer understanding can lead to better customer service and potentially increase patronage and sales.

Accurate Assessment—in an environment constrained by high volume of unverified and even fraudulent data, information accuracy is key. Business intelligence is helpful in the vetting process. Data warehouses and business intelligence applications offer a framework for analysis and decision-making (Kiron et al., 2012).

Business Improvement—there are several ways in which business intelligence can enhance business practices. It can support production efforts (Marin and Poulter, 2004). It facilitates information certainty within an operational environment (Vedder, Vanecek, Guynes, and Cappel, 1999).

Competitive Tools—gathering relevant data helps organizations develop unique assets in a competitive business environment (Huang, Liu, and Chang, 2012). With the right kind of information, companies can plan effective strategies in dealing with competition.

Revenue Generation—effective business intelligence can lead to identification of pathways for revenue generation. Business intelligence contributes to cost savings and revenue increases (Watson, Wixom, Hoffer, Anderson-Lehman, and Reynolds, 2006).

Strategic Planning—intelligence is important for strategic planning and anticipation of competitive moves (Vedder and Guynes, 2002). Companies that efficiently gather and process relevant business information can better respond to industry changes and competitive threats.

These mentioned benefits suggest that an organization that invests time and energy in carrying out effective business intelligence can transform their business.

Barriers to Business Intelligence

Several factors impede effective business intelligence.

Employee Biases—pre-conceived ideas and beliefs affect how data is gathered and processed. People have preconceived notions and biases when processing information (Clayton and Kimbrell, 2007). Hines (1987) alluded to the difference in thinking styles with some individuals tending to think in a logical left-brain mode while others in a right-brain mode. The status of the network can lead to biases (Jaworski et al., 2002). Organizational biases can impact the accuracy and reliability of business intelligence.

Inadequate Competency—the aptitude and skill of the person gathering and processing the data shapes its ultimate interpretation. Information processing abilities are limited (Miller, 1956). Cognitive biases often result from overestimation of accuracy, underestimation of the relevance of the information, or faulty judgment (Heuer, 1999). Analysis is not an easy task (Rhee and Honeycutt Sigler, 2010). Poor analysis is often a result of the inability to identify the root cause of the problem in time (Marr, 2006). Failure in intelligence is when unanticipated results are obtained due to incorrect or inadequate information, and erroneous hypothesis (Johnston, 2005). Skill in information location is essential (Shin, 2003).

Poor Comprehension—knowledge and skill gaps exist in organizations. Data users may not be experienced or may fail to see the relevance of information (Fisher, Smith, and Ballou, 2003). Users who do not comprehend the gathered data avoid its usage (Haley and Watson, 1998).

Inadequate Technology—lack of technological tools can derail business intelligence efforts. Disparity of technology infrastructure across companies and countries necessitates flexibility and resourcefulness. Less developed analytical technologies can impact business intelligence in developing nations (Bose, 2009).

Inadequate Utilization—in some cases, business intelligence applications have not been fully utilized (Giesen, Riddleberger, Christner, and Bell, 2010). It is likely that business intelligence is also unevenly processed and used throughout the organization with some departments doing more than others.

Poor Timing—excellent business intelligence gathered at the wrong time may end up worthless. It is critical that the right information is gathered and used at the appropriate time. It is important to consider how information gathered can be spread effectively throughout the organization (Crossan et al., 1999).

Limited View—a narrow view of business intelligence can lead to poor judgments and blunders. A broader view is often necessary incorporating important issues such as those pertaining to globalization, economic and political turbulence, risk management, and the growing complexity of business processes (Kemper, Mehanna, and Unger, 2004).

Unseen Value—organizational members may fail to see and appreciate the value of business intelligence. There is much more to be desired with regard to the understanding of the business value of business intelligence (Jourdan, Rainer, and Marshal, 2008).

With important barriers to overcome, organizations need to assess their organization's business intelligence competencies and plan out pathways toward improvement.

The Way Forward

Given its importance to business, business intelligence will continue to be implemented by organizations worldwide.

In an effort to uncover the best practices and viable steps forward, the editor assembled a cast of leading experts and thought leaders on the subject.

This book is a journey towards the understanding of business intelligence in a global context. Chapter 1 is the "Introduction" (*J. Mark Munoz*). Part I is about *Understanding Business Intelligence* and includes the topics "Executive Perspectives on Global Business Intelligence: Implications on Corporate Management" (*J. Mark Munoz*), "Beyond Adjustment: Cultural Boundary Spanning" (*Franziska Engelhard* and *Dirk Holtbrügge*), "Clustering Methods in Business Intelligence" (*Subhajit Chakrabarty*), and "Cybersecurity and the Importance of Business Intelligence" (*Tricia-Ann Smith DaSilva*). Part II is *Managing Business Intelligence* and covers "Data Visualization in Business Intelligence" (*Jack G. Zheng*), "Embedding Foresight in Business Intelligence" (*Marti Arran Masters* and *Valtteri Kaartemo*), "Inventing Consciousness: Beyond Business Intelligence" (*Al Naqvi*), "Corruption Intelligence and Analysis" (*Duane Windsor*), and "Enterprise Performance Management and Best Practices in Business Planning and Advanced Analytics" (*Jason Balogh* and *Sholape Kolawole*). Part III is *Strategies for Global Business Intelligence Success* and includes "Agility in Business Intelligence" (*Richard "RJ" P. Podeschi II*), "International Market Intelligence" (*Andrew Gross, Rajshekhar (Raj) G. Javalgi*, and *Nicholas Mathew*), "How Semiotic Analysis Generates Intelligence in Formulating Cross-Cultural Advertising Strategies" (*Satyendra Singh*), "Networks as Catalysts of Technological Intelligence: Cases of Chinese Small- and Medium-Sized Enterprises" (*Zongqiang Ren* and *Wiboon Kittilaksanawong*), "Creating Value From Business Intelligence Systems Investments" (*Mohamed Z. Elbashir*), and "Advanced Analytics: Moving the Needle of Business Performance" (*Jason Balogh*). The last chapter is the "Conclusion" (*J. Mark Munoz*).

This book is useful for students, educators, consultants, corporate executives, entrepreneurs, government officials, and policy makers worldwide. The intent of this book is to advance thinking, stimulate conversations, and encourage further research on the subject.

Global business intelligence can be viewed as a tool, a means, or strategy to optimize information gathering, processing, and analysis to improve business performance. It is the "brain" of the business enterprise. Through the following chapters in this book, the editor hopes to help readers unleash their "organizational brainpower" and achieve operational excellence.

References

Adar, E. and Adamic, L. A. (2005). Tracking information epidemics in blogspace. In *Proceedings of the 2005 IEEE/WIC/ACM International Joint Conference on Web Intelligence and Intelligent Agent Technology*, Compiègne, France, September 19–22.

Bose, R. (2009). Advanced analytics: Opportunities and challenges. *Industrial Management & Data Systems*, 109(2), 155–172.

Brignall, S. and Ballantine, J. (2004). Strategic enterprise management systems: New directions for research. *Management Accounting Research*, 15, 225–240.

Business Wire. (2015). *Research and Markets: Global Business Intelligence Market 2015–2019*. Accessed June 21, 2016. Available from: www.pcmag.com/article2/0,2817,2496370,00.asp

Chau, M., Xu, J., Cao, J., Lam, P., and Shiu, B. (2009). Blog mining: A framework and example applications. *IEEE IT Professional*, 11(1), 36–41.

Chaudhuri, S., Dayal, U., and Narasayya, V. (2011). An overview of business intelligence technology. *Communications of the ACM*, 54(8), 88–98.

Chung, W., Chen, H., and Nunamaker, J. F. (2005). A visual knowledge map framework for the discovery of business intelligence on the web. *Journal of Management Information Systems*, 21(4), 57–84.

Clayton, P. and Kimbrell, J. (2007). Thinking preferences as diagnostic and learning tools for managerial styles and predictors of auditor success. *Managerial Finance*, 33, 921–934.

Crossan, M.M., Lane, H.W. and White, R.E. (1999). An Organizational Learning Framework: From Intuition to Institution. *Academy of Management Review*, 24(3), 522–537.

Den Hamer, P. (2005). *De organisatie van Business Intelligence*. The Hague: Sdu Publishers.

Elbashir, M. Z., Collier, P. A., and Sutton, S. G. (2011). The role of organizational absorptive capacity in strategic use of business intelligence to support integrated management control systems. *The Accounting Review*, 86(1), 155–184.

Fisher, C. W., Smith, I. C., and Ballou, D. P. (2003). The impact of experience and time on the use of data quality information in decision making. *Information Systems Research*, 14(2), 170–188.

Fitzpatrick, W. M. (2003). Uncovering trade secrets: The legal and ethical conundrum of creative competitive intelligence. *SAM Advanced Management Journal*, 68(3), 4–13.

Gartner Group. (2006). *Gartner Survey of 1,400 CIOs Shows Transformation of IT Organisation is Accelerating*. Accessed June 19, 2006. Available from: www.gartner.com/press_releases/asset_143678_11.htm

Gartner Group. (2016). *Gartner Says Worldwide Business Intelligence and Analytics Market to Reach $16.9 Billion in 2016*. Accessed June 21, 2016. Available from: www.gartner.com/newsroom/id/3198917

Giesen, E., Riddleberger, E., Christner, R., and Bell, R. (2010). When and how to innovate your business model. *Strategy & Leadership*, 38(4), 17–26.

Grajek, S. and Pirani, J. A. (2012). Top-ten IT issues, 2012. *EDUCAUSE Review*, 47(3), 36.

Haley, B. and Watson, H. (1998). Managerial considerations. *Communications of the ACM*, 41(9), 32–37.

Heuer, J. R., Jr. (1999). *The Psychology of Intelligence Analysis*. Washington, DC: Center for the Study of Intelligence.

Hines, T. (1987). Left brain/right brain mythology and implications for management and training. *Academy of Management Review*, 12, 600–606.

Huang, T. C., Liu, C., and Chang, D. (2012). An empirical investigation of factors influencing the adoption of data mining tools. *International Journal of Information Management*, 32(3), 257–270.

Jaworski, B. J., Maclnnis, D. J., and Kohli, A. K. (2002). Generating competitive intelligence in organizations. *Journal of Market-Focused Management*, 54, 279–307.

Johnston, R. (2005). *Analytic Culture in the U.S. Intelligence Community*. Washington, DC: The Center for the Study of Intelligence.

Jourdan, Z., Rainer, R. K., and Marshal, T. E. (2008). Business intelligence: An analysis of the literature. *Information Systems Management*, 25, 121–131.

Kemper, H. G., Mehanna, W., and Unger, C. (2004). *Business Intelligence— Grundlagen und Praktische Anwendungen*. Wiesbaden: Vieweg.

Kiron, D., Shockley, R., Kruschwitz, N., Finch, G., & Haydock, M. (2012). Analytics: The widening divide. *MIT Sloan Management Review*, 53(2), 1–22.

Klaves, G. (2003). *Use of Business Intelligence in Telecommunication Companies*. Ljubljana: University of Ljubljana. (In Slovenian).

Liang, H., Tsai, F. S., and Kwee, A. T. (2009). Detecting novel business blogs. In *Proceedings of the 7th International Conference on Information, Communications and Signal Processing*, Macau, China, December 8–10.

Maltz, E. and Kohli, A. (1996). Market intelligence dissemination across functional boundaries. *Journal of Marketing Research*, 33(February), 47–61.

Marin, J. and Poulter, A. (2004). Dissemination of competitive intelligence. *Journal of Information Science*, 30(2), 165–180.

Marr, B. (2006). *Strategic Performance Management: Leveraging and Measuring Your Intangible Value Drivers*. Amsterdam: Butterworth-Heinemann.

Miller, G. A. (1956). The magical number seven, plus or minus two: Some limits on our capacity for processing information. *Psychological Review*, 63(2), 81–97.

Nasar, M. and Bomers, J. V. (2012). Data management and financial regulations: Using a big data approach to regulatory compliance. *Business Intelligence Journal*, 17(2), 34–40.

Philips, E. and Vriens, D. (1999). *Business Intelligence*. Deventer: Kluwer Bedrijfsinformatie.

Power, D. J. (2008). Understanding data-driven decision support systems. *Information Systems Management*, 25(2), 149–154.

Rhee, K. S. and Honeycutt Sigler, T. (2010). Developing enlightened leaders for industry and community: Executive education and service-learning. *Journal of Management Education*, 34(1), 163–181.

Robertson, B., Boehler, A., and Hansel, J. (2007). Sustainable performance improvement through predictive technologies. *Strategic Finance* (June), 57–64.

Sallam, R. L., Richardson, J., Hagerty, J., and Hostmann, B. (2011). *Magic Quadrant for Business Intelligence Platforms*. Stamford, CT: Gartner Group.

Schiffman, L. and Kanuk, L. (2010). *Consumer Behavior* (10th ed.). Upper Saddle River, NJ: Prentice-Hall.

Shin, A. (2003). An exploratory investigation of system success factors in data warehousing. *Journal of the Association for Information Systems*, 4, 141–170.

Vedder, R. G. and Guynes, C. S. (2002). Guynes CIOS' perspectives on competitive intelligence. *Information Systems Management* 19(4), 49–55.

Vedder, R. G., Vanecek, M. T., Guynes, C. S., and Cappel, J. J. (1999). CEO and CIO perspectives on competitive intelligence. *Communications of the ACM*, 42(8), 108–116.

Vijayan, J. (2012, September 12). *Finding the Business Value in Big Data Is a Big Problem*. CIO.com. Accessed June 21, 2016. Available from: www.cio.com/article/716102/Finding_the_Business_Value_in_Big_Data_is_a_Big_Problem

Watson, H. J., Ariyachandra, T., and Matyska, R. J. (2001). Data warehousing stages of growth. *Information Systems Management*, 18(3), 42–50.

Watson, H. J., Wixom, B. H., Hoffer, J., Anderson-Lehman, J., and Reynolds, A.-M. (2006). Real-time business intelligence: Best practices at Continental Airlines. *Information Systems Management*, 23(1), 7–19.

Wells, D. (2008). Business analytics—Getting the point. Accessed June 23, 2016. Available at: http://b-eye-network.com/view/7133

Wixon, B. H., Watson, H. J., and Werner, T. (2011). Developing an enterprise business intelligence capability: The Norfolk southern journey. *MIS Quarterly Executive*, 10(2), 25–35.

Wright, S., Eid, E. R., and Fleisher, C. S. (2009). Competitive intelligence in practice: Empirical evidence from the UK retail banking sector. *Journal of Marketing Management*, 25, 941–964.

Yeoh, W. and Koronios, A. (2010). Critical success factors for business intelligence systems. *The Journal of Computer Information Systems*, 50(3), 23–32.

Part I

Understanding Business Intelligence

2 Executive Perspectives on Global Business Intelligence

Implications on Corporate Management

J. Mark Munoz

Introduction and Rationale

Companies worldwide can benefit from additional literature on the impact of global business intelligence on the management of corporations. In this chapter, the author gathers the views of senior business executives in order to shed light on viable corporate approaches for global business intelligence.

Companies use business intelligence in different ways. Some firms prioritize data gathering and analysis; others ignore it. Multitudes of companies take the middle ground and use business intelligence in a specific business area or during occasions where competitive or market information is critically needed.

The convergence of the internet, computer and mobile phone technologies, software applications, and social media facilitates easy access to millions of global data. The challenge for individuals, companies, and governments is data management. Key issues to consider include: data acquisition and filtration, information reliability, data security, data analysis, efficiency in information processing, and workforce competence and preparedness, among others. With the global nature of data and information, the level of complexity expands.

This scenario offers both challenges and opportunities for companies. Managing, analyzing, and strategizing through a large pool of information can be a barrier for many firms. Some firms do not have the talent or the resources to be effective in business intelligence. While countless barriers exist, so do opportunities. Companies that do an excellent job in business intelligence can outsmart their competitors, delight their customers, and quickly respond to market changes.

In this chapter, the author gathers the views of three corporate leaders in order to gain clarity on the notion of global business intelligence, understand how it is applied in contemporary corporate management, and identify viable business practices. The author would like to thank Millikin University students Blake Davis and Rob Leonard for their assistance in the interview process.

Executive Interviews

The author developed a 12-item questionnaire for senior corporate executives to answer. The interviews were conducted in the period from May to September 2016. Highlights of the executive interviews are presented below.

John N. Lechman
President, Nova Solutions Inc.

Interview

1. What is global business intelligence in your viewpoint?
   Converting data into useful information to make informed business decisions.

2. Is there a need for companies to conduct business intelligence on a global level? Why or why not?
   Yes, there is a need. The internet and technology have provided access to global markets unlike any time in history. Any business transaction whether domestic or global should be executed utilizing the best available information.

3. What do you think are barriers to the effective practice of global business intelligence?
   The resources, know how, and capability to collect and analyze the appropriate information. This is especially true for small business.

4. Where do opportunities in the practice of global business intelligence exist?
   It appears that most companies offering global business intelligence services are large public accounting firms specializing in this area of consulting. At times, this concerns career opportunities. From a commerce perspective whether the opportunity is outsourcing goods and/or services or exporting the same, the transaction should be conducted utilizing the best available information.

5. What would be an example of a company that did their global business intelligence right? Why so?
   Apple! They have the resources to analyze emerging global opportunities whether it's the successful utilization of outsourcing or penetrating emerging and existing markets. They must be taking full advantage of the information they are converting into intelligence.

6. What attributes should companies possess in order to be effective in the practice of global business intelligence?
   Whether the organization is utilizing business intelligence software to analyze the data or they are outsourcing on a consulting basis, the key attribute is understanding the need of good information.

7. What are the implications of global business intelligence in the management function of Planning?

    Any good plan requires forecasting. A forecast requires a clear understanding of the market, external and internal capability, distribution channels, lead times, shipping, and the economic environment.

8. What are the implications of global business intelligence in the management function of Leading?

    A good leader should utilize the best information available to make the decision necessary to move their vision in the direction their cause requires.

9. What are the implications of global business intelligence in the management function of Organizing?

    Assuming organizing is referring to organizational development, the purpose of any organization is to fulfill the vision and purpose of the company. Having access to the best information is required to build an organization and even more critical to be sure it is efficient and profitable while achieving the vision and purpose.

10. What are the implications of global business intelligence in the management function of Controlling?

    A clearer understanding of the business cultures and the associated risks in the markets in which you are doing business.

11. What resources do you think companies need to excel in global business intelligence?

    The best alternative would be to professionally outsource the capability until the organization has a clear understanding of the benefit. Then resource allocation can be planned accordingly.

12. What do you think is the future of global business intelligence?

    Organizing and analyzing information to best serve the cause of any organization is the future. Our economy has become global and long-term stability and success will hinge on who wins the information assembled from the raw data.

William A. Rendina
Chief Executive Officer, Valor Systems, Inc.

Interview

1. What is global business intelligence in your viewpoint?

    Gathering and analyzing data for which a company can determine where strategic attention should be focused. Global intelligence is based on a company's product and service offerings, as well as their competitor's position in a particular market. For generations, companies considered demographics and consumer behavior for building their marketing plans. Today, demographics extend worldwide for many products.

2. Is there a need for companies to conduct business intelligence in a global level? Why or why not?

   I believe global business intelligence is paramount in developing strategic long-term plans for business. The internet has made our world even smaller, creating a need for understanding global consumer behavior, strategic growth, competition, procurement laws, and in our company's area of expertise, security.

3. What do you think are barriers to the effective practice of global business intelligence?

   Various countries have different procurement laws, and it's important to understand the practice prior to fully engaging in a particular region around the world. For example, where a US-based company may have a US-based customer who has facilities in China, it is not trivial to add on the China location on the existing US contract. The US-based solution provider must utilize a China agent or resource to procure and support the product under different Terms and Conditions. This practice may hinder the flow and control of intelligence back to the US.

4. Where do opportunities in the practice of global business intelligence exist?

   Where many companies depend on global business intelligence for developing marketing plans, delivery logistics, and financial projections, Valor Systems' solutions generates global business intelligence and helps companies protect their brand, assets, and people. Valor Incident Management System, (Valor IMS) is a software solution that helps companies manage security incidents around the world. Having global business/ security intelligence helps companies understand physical security vulnerabilities and allows them to prepare for incidents in a proactive manner. If a customer has a Global Security Operations Center (GSOC) in any given country, it may manage physical security incidents at multiple facilities across numerous countries. The GSOC can gather intelligence from all of the countries and determine where and when additional security resources are needed. Gathering global security intelligence allows a company to refine their security processes throughout various regions. A process may include response plans, Standard Operating Procedures, premise data, internal and external resources, and mass notification, all reducing on-scene arrival time with more information to minimize a would-be disaster. Global security intelligence illustrates incident trends at any level. Today's offender may have been yesterday's suspect. In summary, global business/security intelligence is the kernel for developing a company road map. Whether analyzing data for marketing purposes or security purposes, both have a direct effect on the future of the brand, assets, and people of that company.

5. What would be an example of a company that did their global business intelligence right? Why so?

   Steve Jobs once said the iPhone® should maintain a smaller screen size, and there would be no stylus. Some now say Steve was incorrect to maintain that mind-set. In reality, Steve was spot on for the era of which he was designing and developing. As technology and applications continued to evolve, the need for a larger screen became a demand that consumers lined up to buy. Apple certainly relied on global consumer-related business intelligence to develop their road map for larger iPhones and larger, yet lighter iPads® with a "great" stylus. It doesn't end there. With access to global business intelligence, Apple realized the entire world was not looking for a larger iPhone. In recent weeks, Apple announced a new iPhone with a form factor of their older, smaller-version iPhone. While most of the global market was waiting in line for a larger form factor, the Chinese consumer market wanted something smaller. These decisions are not made on a whim. They are decisions that are based on global business intelligence, and having the wherewithal to respond to consumer demands.

6. What attributes should companies possess in order to be effective in the practice of global business intelligence?

   A personal tag line I created for our company: We listen. We learn. We deliver. These attributes have helped our company understand customer needs from a marketing perspective, as well as a solution perspective. Companies must have access to global business intelligence, but they must also be immersed within their customer's environment to truly learn and deliver solutions that create a great user experience. It's not just about analytical numbers.

7. What are the implications of global business intelligence in the management function of Planning?

   In order to deliver, our company must produce realistic, forward-thinking product road maps.

8. What are the implications of global business intelligence in the management function of Leading?

   Our company must work as a team to execute on a vision to take solutions to the next level. There must be a leader who takes charge, and makes everyone on the team believe in this product road map as much as the leader. A leader must be capable of making adjustments along the way, while keeping the vision clear to all involved.

9. What are the implications of global business intelligence in the management function of Organizing?

   While the development of the product road map is in full motion, there must be organization among the entire team. Goals and objectives must be met along the way. Objectives may need to be altered along the way to stay on track of the ever-changing global business intelligence due to global economy, global behavior, and other competitive concerns.

10. What are the implications of global business intelligence in the management function of Controlling?

    As new product road maps are being developed, new ideas, functions, internal and external ideas based on global business intelligence will surely get in the mix. New ideas and global business intelligence may certainly force a company to reassess the goals and objectives along the way, but it is crucial to maintain control and avoid "scope creep," delaying the delivery date of a new product launch.

11. What resources do you think companies need to excel in global business intelligence?

    Companies need specialized, well-rounded team members who share in the company vision. Global business intelligence is gathering and analyzing data, but it is much more than statistical numbers and graphs. What are these numbers telling us? How do we respond to this intelligence, and better yet, how do we leap ahead of our competitors based on the global business intelligence? A company needs to be agile, and be capable of adapting within a day's notice. A company cannot control a global economy based on world events, but a company can control how it responds to a global economy and world events.

12. What do you think is the future of global business intelligence?

    Global business intelligence is far more advanced and available than it was 20 years ago. To learn about certain companies and markets, one method was to conduct research through Moody's Manual of Industrial and Miscellaneous Securities or Standard and Poor's, two-inch hard-bound books. Perhaps somewhat relevant, but quickly outdated. Today, the internet offers tremendous, virtually real-time data through various sources. Global business intelligence may be as simple as reviewing Google Analytics for your company's specific website hits, Google Scholar, and even tools with analytics for competitors' website activity. Online press releases notify us of current events within our competitive landscape. Online services are available to learn who is going out for bid in the next year. Social media such as LinkedIn offers industry specific links and related news, trends, and open conversation among strangers who are connected to industry groups. Much like the example sited earlier regarding security intelligence, companies may utilize internal applications to monitor company-specific data and trends through dashboards and reporting utilities. Internal applications may have the capability to create ad hoc queries and filters to gain a snapshot of global business intelligence to help define resources needed in a particular region of the globe, or to develop product road maps.

    The future of global business intelligence will continue to evolve as more disparate systems integrate. Linear data is limited in value, and must be enriched through association and relationship of integral data elements from multiple sources.

    A company needs to know how to take advantage of the available tools, decipher the information, and execute a plan based on global business intelligence.

    (Reference note: Apple, iPhone, and iPad are registered trademarks of Apple, Inc. The sited example of Apple-related products is based on the interviewee's perspective. Google Analytics and Google Scholar are registered trademarks of Google, Inc.)

Marty Schoenthaler
Chief Executive Officer, Tate Boys Tire & Service

1. What is global business intelligence in your viewpoint?

   It is the mining of global data to improve business decision-making.

2. Is there a need for companies to conduct business intelligence in a global level? Why or why not?

   Yes. If a company is a global company, then by definition a company should use BI globally. It has proven to be a very effective means of supporting improved and accelerated decision-making.

3. What do you think are barriers to the effective practice of global business intelligence?

   Clearly you have to have the data to practice BI. So, if you don't have access to the data, you're toast. Once you have the data, you must have the knowledge/skill to work with it to enable effective BI to take place. These skills are often hard to come by since so many companies are driving accelerated BI plans. Finally, you have to have the right tools to mine your data effectively as well.

4. Where do opportunities in the practice of global business intelligence exist?

   In my mind it's primarily in areas where having accurate or precise data can help drive more efficient or effective decisions along with allowing business leaders to do more analyzing and "what-iffing" their business lines.

5. What would be an example of a company that did their global business intelligence right? Why so?

   Wal-Mart. From the beginning, they have done a great job of capturing the appropriate data at the point-of-sale, then turning around and using it to drive and steer their future decisions. They have been doing this since before BI was in vogue.

6. What attributes should companies possess in order to be effective in the practice of global business intelligence?

   First of all they must have curiosity—wanting to know what is different and what decisions could be made differently. They also must have courage in order to do things differently, once their data tells them so.

7. What are the implications of global business intelligence in the management function of Planning?

   It needs to become a key function that is driven into all levels of global planning.

8. What are the implications of global business intelligence in the management function of Leading?

   It will undoubtedly cause changes to how things are looked at, run, etc. so business managers must be willing to lead change, otherwise BI will become irrelevant.

9. What are the implications of global business intelligence in the management function of Organizing?
BI can help organize functions more effectively by showing where there are logical connections, etc.

10. What are the implications of global business intelligence in the management function of Controlling?
Accelerated closing of books monthly/quarterly/annually as well as providing improved analysis of key business problems.

11. What resources do you think companies need to excel in global business intelligence?
People who have curiosity and people who can know where the data is and bring it to life.

12. What do you think is the future of global business intelligence?
It will quickly no longer become a function that is in vogue; it will become a required function for all companies and departments. Just like accounting, HR, etc.

Findings and Conclusions

The interview findings highlight important organizational standpoints and approaches. Noteworthy findings include:

Dimension	Perspectives
Perspective	Data conversion for informed decisions; gathering and analyzing data to determine strategic direction; mining global data to improve decision-making
Rationale	Utilize best available information; essential for long-term planning; improve and accelerate decision-making
Barriers	Resources and know-how; capability to collect and analyze information; reliable information; right data and accessibility; knowledge, skills, right tools
Opportunities	Leverage best available information; protection of brand, assets, people; security, resource optimization, timely action; strategy formulation; effective decisions through accurate and precise data; enhanced analysis
Success stories	Apple (conversion of information to intelligence, high response to consumer demand); Wal-Mart (data capturing that drive business decisions)
Key attributes	Understanding the need for good information; listening to customers and understanding their needs; focusing on solutions; curiosity; courage to do things differently

Dimension	Perspectives
Planning	Forecast alongside thorough market understanding; realistic, forward-thinking product road map; use as key function with a global approach
Leading	Utilize best information to make informed decisions; teamwork and collaboration; adaptation and adjustment; lead change and change perspectives
Organizing	Organize for efficiency and profitability; vision alignment; meet goals and objectives; change course as needed; global perspective and behavior; establish logical connections
Controlling	Clear cultural understanding and effective risk assessment; reassess goals and objectives; accelerate tasks and enhance analysis
Resources needed	Allocate appropriate resources; outsource to professionals and experts; specialized team members and consultants; skilled and curious team
Future trends	Organizing and analysis of information is the new competitive battlefield; winners extract the best information from raw data; growing analytical conveniences; importance of social media; innovative internal applications; continuous evolution; emergence of new data gathering and analytical tools; required function used in all companies

The findings suggest that corporations would be well served by pursuing a five-point strategy:

Acquisition and Application—organizations need to efficiently gather and analyze global business information. Acquisition of data is one thing, and how it is processed in a sensible and useful manner is another. Acquisition and application need to be planned in tandem.

Technological Assimilation—investing in technologies covers only one side of the equation. Effective global business intelligence entails matching up-to-date and relevant technologies with the appropriate organizational structure and framework. Organizations need to consider forming Geopolitical Strategy Teams, appointing a Geopolitical Strategy Officer, hiring consultants, or both to assist in geopolitically sensitive projects and endeavors.

Resource Preparation—corporations need to be prepared to develop their people and invest in appropriate technologies to get global intelligence done right. Effective intelligence is a product of combined access to talent and resources. It might make sense for companies to create Global Business Intelligence Teams, appoint a Global Business Intelligence Officer, or hire experts and consultants to move the agenda forward.

Rapid Intelligence—business intelligence has an expiration date. Great intelligence delivered after the time when it was needed is useless.

Acquiring, processing, and acting on gathered information in a timely manner is critical.

Strategic Integration—business intelligence must not be perceived as simply one facet of business. It has to be thought of holistically and integrated into the fabric of the organization. It needs to be ingrained in the culture and woven into the company's strategic plan.

Global business poses countless risks and challenges. However, companies out there are succeeding through effective global business intelligence and well-executed management functions of planning, leading, organizing, and controlling.

3 Beyond Adjustment

Cultural Boundary Spanning

Franziska Engelhard and Dirk Holtbrügge

Introduction: Cross-Cultural Adjustment—Limitations of a Common Concept

Since Black, Mendenhall, and Oddou (1991) published their seminal work on international assignments, cross-cultural adjustment has been regarded as a key concept in expatriate research. Cross-cultural adjustment refers to the degree of psychological comfort and the ease of stress that expatriates have with various dimensions of their host culture (Black, 1988). According to Black et al. (1991), adjustment can be regarded as a multifaceted concept that consists of three major dimensions, namely adjustment to the general environment, to the work situation, and to interacting with host nationals. The adjustment to the general environment delineates the psychological comfort with regard to the host culture environment, including weather, food, and living conditions. The second dimension of adjustment relates to the work situation, that is, the psychological ease with respect to dissimilar values, expectations, and standards at the foreign location of employment. The third dimension depicts the adjustment to socializing, the general interaction, the interacting outside of work, and speaking with host nationals.

Empirical studies and meta-analyses (Bhaskar-Shrinivas, Harrison, Shaffer, and Luk, 2005; Hechanova, Beehr, and Christiansen, 2003; Puck, Holtbrügge, and Raupp, 2017) discuss various individual, work-related, and environmental factors influencing cross-cultural adjustment (Figure 3.1). Moreover, positive effects of cross-cultural adjustment on job satisfaction, work performance, organizational commitment, and expatriate turnover have been revealed in numerous studies (see Froese and Peltokorpi, 2013; Takeuchi, Yun, and Tesluk, 2002).

While adjustment has often been stressed as a necessary behavior of expatriates, there is evidence that this concept no longer adequately reflects the challenges of globalization (Williams, 2002). One limitation of this concept is the unidirectional approach with regard to the actors involved in the adjustment process. Cross-cultural adjustment assumes that only expatriates have to adjust to the other culture and adapt their behavior by imitating the behavior of colleagues and other members of the respective culture. But

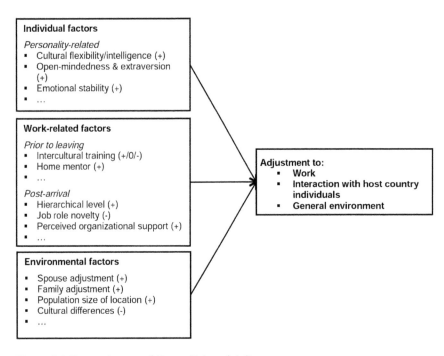

Figure 3.1 Determinants of Cross-Cultural Adjustment
Source: adapted from Puck et al. (2017)

in times of globalization, individuals are often interculturally experienced and therefore already gained a higher metacognitive capacity. For these individuals, the need to imitate behavior in order to adapt is not necessary as they are able to behave in a culturally competent manner based on the experiences gained in other cultures. Tung (1998) describes this phenomenon as cosmopolitanism and points to the fact that over-adaption may lead to difficulties. Instead, she proposes that expatriates have to balance the conflict between global integration and local responsiveness and calls for a reorientation of the expatriate literature.

Given these limitations of the cross-cultural adjustment concept, researchers increasingly propose boundary spanning as alternative conceptualization of expatriate behavior (Au and Fukuda, 2002; Barner-Rasmussen, Ehrnrooth, Koveshnikov, and Mäkelä, 2014). Boundary spanning is different from adjustment as it not only produces consistent behavior with one foreign culture, but rather involves bridging and linking processes such as information gathering, interacting with other assignees, and connecting previously unconnected people (Barner-Rasmussen et al., 2014; Reiche, 2011). Moreover, boundary spanning enables assignees to adapt and interact more effectively in multiple cultures and to develop cultural intelligence.

In the following, the concept of boundary spanning will be introduced in general. This is followed by a review of existing boundary spanning literature in the context of expatriation. In a next step, the cultural boundary spanning construct is introduced and its proposed beneficial effect on cultural intelligence and other outcomes will be discussed alongside a conceptual research framework. In the last section, practical implications for multinational corporations (MNCs) will be derived.

Boundary Spanning—A Multifaceted Concept Still Neglected in the Context of Expatriation

Boundary Spanning Literature—A Short Overview

According to Thomas (1991), the concept of boundary spanning is rooted in open systems theory (Katz and Kahn, 1978) and role theory (Kahn, Wolfe, Quinn, Snoek, and Rosenthal, 1964; Katz and Kahn, 1978). Aldrich and Herker (1977) are often cited as the first in mentioning boundary spanning roles as links between the environment and the organization. Thus, early boundary spanning literature portrays boundary spanners as individuals engaging in significant transactions with external agents (Adams, 1976; Aldrich and Herker, 1977) and as individuals coping with environmental constraints. The first role of boundary spanners according to Aldrich and Herker (1977) is information processing. Since boundary role incumbents are exposed to a mass of information and are also able to actively search for it, they should have expertise in information selection and processing and be able to protect themselves and the organization from information overload. Boundary spanners are therefore information transmitters, acting as filters and facilitators at the same time (Aldrich and Herker, 1977).

The second role according to Aldrich and Herker (1977) is external representation which includes resource acquisition and disposal, political legitimacy and hegemony, and a residual category of social legitimacy and organizational image. Some of the functions mentioned by Aldrich and Herker (1977) are also reflected in the items of Ancona and Caldwell (1992) who measured external boundary spanning activities in a team. Scott (1995) defines boundary spanners as bridge-builders between organizations and external needs, and providers of information for internal use. Fennell and Alexander (1987) describe four different kinds of boundary spanning activities: two buffering strategies and two bridging strategies, both including external linkages.

Building on the common factors above, the authors define boundary spanning as an activity in which not only information is transmitted; mediating, linking, and facilitating also take place between relevant actors in and outside the organization in a foreign context. In following Vora, Kostova, and Roth (2007), boundary spanners can act as bi-directional interpreters, enabling information flows. Finally, they may assist in maintaining cultural consistency and facilitate significant interactions between two different organizational units (Ancona and Caldwell, 1988, 1992).

The literature on boundary spanning is currently fragmented in the field of international management. While one strand of research examines boundary spanning inside teams (Ancona and Caldwell, 1992; Dau, 2016; Golden and Veiga, 2005; Marrone, 2010), including informational and representational roles, another strand focuses on the context of expatriation and inpatriation which is gaining more and more prominence (Au and Fukuda, 2002; Barner-Rasmussen et al., 2014; Johnson and Duxbury, 2010; Reiche, 2011; Vora et al., 2007). A third avenue of research talks about cultural boundary spanning (Di Marco, Taylor, and Alin, 2010; Holtbrügge and Engelhard, 2016) and involves the active facilitation of cross-cultural interactions. In the following section, the authors review the existing boundary spanning literature in the field of expatriation and discuss current limitations of these studies.

Expatriate Boundary Spanning Literature—Fragmented and Isolated Research Ignoring Cultural Aspects

Expatriates are assignees that hold top management positions or key positions in functional departments of a foreign subsidiary. Thus, they play a very prominent role in MNCs today (Harzing, 2001). Expatriates are able to act as links between subsidiary and headquarters and obtain useful resources for both. Unfortunately, little attention has been paid to the expatriates' facilitating (Fang et al., 2010) and boundary spanning roles (Barner-Rasmussen et al., 2014).

One of the first empirical studies analyzing boundary spanning of expatriates has been conducted by Au and Fukuda (2002). Based on the theoretical propositions of Thomas (1991), they reveal that boundary spanning is performed by many expatriates and that the activities are multifaceted (e.g. task coordinator, ambassador, and scout). Boundary spanning activities of expatriates are measured by the ten most robust out of the 24 external boundary spanning activity items of Ancona and Caldwell (1992). Those capture some aspects of boundary spanning, especially externally focused activities in a team, but do not cover all activities undertaken by an expatriate to span boundaries. For example, there are also boundary spanning activities inside the organization, such as social and networking activities (Reiche, 2011), and between headquarters and subsidiary (Vora et al., 2007), which are not addressed in this study.

The exploratory case study of Johnson and Duxbury (2010) does also relate to the team roles of Ancona and Caldwell (1992). Based on qualitative telephone interviews, the authors reveal that these roles only partially capture the dimensions of the expatriate's boundary spanning roles. In contrast to Ancona and Caldwell's (1992) four team roles, nine dimensions emerged in interviews of 79 expatriates. This result stresses again the manifold facets of the expatriates' boundary spanning roles which are still not captured in the international management literature.

A new measure was introduced by Reiche (2011) who examined the role of inpatriates' boundary spanning in the knowledge transfer process in MNCs. In a study of 269 inpatriates (i.e. assignees sent from the subsidiary to the headquarters of the company) he found that boundary spanning is positively related to inpatriates' individual efforts to transfer knowledge and their perceptions of headquarters' staff efforts to acquire subsidiary-specific knowledge. For his study, he developed a scale with six items measuring the boundary spanning function of inpatriates. Thus, Reiche (2011) focuses specifically on the knowledge transfer of individuals through social interaction (Felin and Hesterly, 2007). While this aspect is new and interesting, only focusing on sharing contacts in one unit with individuals from other units, Reiche (2011) ignores other aspects of inpatriate boundary spanning especially in the knowledge transfer position between headquarter and subsidiary. Although he includes other variables such as mentoring by headquarters staff or perceived absorptive capacity, the concept of the boundary spanning role is only partly applied. Moreover, the scale of Reiche has not yet been validated in other studies.

Kostova and Roth (2003) see boundary spanning mainly rooted in social networks and social capital theory (e.g. Krackhardt and Stern, 1988; Tsai and Ghoshal, 1998) and propose two factors influencing the formation of a boundary spanner's social capital, namely the extent and efficacy of the individual's interactions with the headquarters. In their conceptual paper, they stress the importance of social capital in foreign sub-units of MNCs and argue that the required levels and forms of social capital are determined by the nature of interdependence between headquarters and sub-units. Furthermore, they propose dividing social capital into private (Leana and Van Buren, 1999) and public elements (Bourdieu, 2011). Boundary spanners who gain private social capital will transform it into public social capital of the sub-unit depending on the extent of the interactions with headquarters and the efficacy of their interactions with it.

These and other studies try to capture and highlight important aspects of boundary spanning, such as boundary spanning as a function of social capital in form of networking, boundary spanning as an interpreter function between two different units, and boundary spanning in the form of information and knowledge exchange. Besides the importance of these roles, one major shortcoming is the lack of reliable measures and the comprehensive test of different expatriate boundary spanning roles in one single study.

Lastly, the influence of culture on expatriates' behavior is not adequately addressed. While the international education literature already identified the importance of this construct for study abroad stays and the development of cultural intelligence (see Holtbrügge and Engelhard, 2016), the expatriation literature still neglects the importance of cultural influences on boundary spanning.

Why and How Could Cultural Boundary Spanning Affect Cultural Intelligence—A Conceptual Framework

In this section, the authors present a conceptual framework which proposes different antecedents and outcomes of cultural boundary spanning that have not been part of empirical examination yet. The conceptual model is based on the idea of the nomological network of cultural intelligence by Ang and Van Dyne (2008). The authors adapted the structure of this network to a conceptual framework because the main purpose is to understand the role of cultural boundary spanning better by developing a holistic framework that includes all relevant antecedents, correlates, and outcomes. The main proposition is hereby the positive influence of cultural boundary spanning on cultural intelligence.

Earley and Ang (2003) conceptualized cultural intelligence as a multi-dimensional construct by drawing on Sternberg and Detterman's (1986) multidimensional perspective of intelligence. This perspective views intelligence not only in cognitive patterns, but defines cultural intelligence as an "individual's ability to grasp and reason correctly in situations characterized by cultural diversity" (Ang and Van Dyne, 2008, p. 4). Therefore, cultural intelligence as a multifactor construct includes a metacognitive, cognitive, motivational, and a behavioral dimension. According to Ang and Van Dyne (2008), CQ is a specific and individual capability that should be related to other indicators of intercultural competence while remaining conceptually and empirically distinct. The authors argue that the various components of CQ will be positively influenced by cultural boundary spanning behavior.

Cultural boundary spanning involves bridging processes, including gaining information, achieving influence, exchanging with others, and cooperating with host nationals with respect to resources and networking (Holtbrügge and Engelhard, 2016). It is conceptualized as a mediator and influenced by different individual (demographic, psychographic) and organizational antecedents. Boundary spanners can be seen as cultural brokers who empathize with others and respect their values and perspectives (Trevillion, 1991). Thus, cultural boundary spanning differs from boundary spanning in general as it describes the behavior in culturally heterogeneous environments. Figure 3.2 illustrates the antecedents and determinants of cultural boundary spanning and the effects on cultural intelligence and other related outcomes.

Possible antecedents are demographic factors, such as age, gender, experience, or language. For example, Barner-Rasmussen et al. (2014) found that intercultural and language skills are important resources of boundary spanning within MNCs. In addition, psychographic determinants could be of relevance, as Holtbrügge and Engelhard (2016) revealed intrinsic motivation to affect cultural boundary spanning behavior. Further antecedents are personality traits, such as low ethnocentrism, self-monitoring, and cultural flexibility. The study of Luo (2001), for example, found personal attachment to

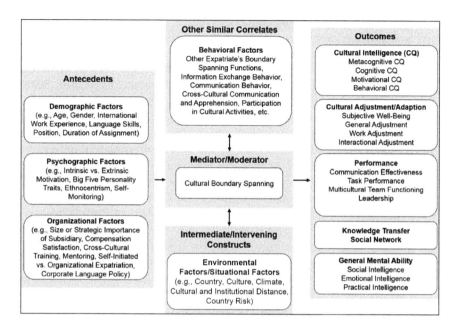

Figure 3.2 Conceptual Framework of Cultural Boundary Spanning

Source: partly based on the Nomological Network of Cultural Intelligence of Ang and Van Dyne, 2008

be an important antecedent of boundary spanning. Besides these, the big five personality traits could influence cultural boundary spanning as they already do largely affect general adjustment (Bhatti et al., 2013). A third group are organizational factors, such as the size and strategic importance of the subsidiary, the compensation system, the organization of the international assignment, and the corporate language strategy. Reiche (2011), for example, found mentoring as a moderating influence on the relationship between inpatriate boundary spanning and knowledge transfer. Additional factors derived from the expatriation literature are pre-departure training and the impact of work roles (Osman-Gani and Rockstuhl, 2009; Peltokorpi and Froese, 2009).

Several behavioral factors are argued to influence cultural boundary spanning as well. These involve, for example, complementary expatriate boundary spanning functions as well as cross-cultural communication and apprehension (Barner-Rasmussen et al., 2014). Finally, environmental and situational determinants could influence cultural boundary spanning behavior, such as climate (e.g. humid vs. dry), cultural distance (Caligiuri, Lazarova, and Zehetbauer, 2007), institutional distance (Noble and Jones, 2006), or country risk (Bader and Schuster, 2015). As illustrated in a study by Leifer and Huber (1977), boundary spanning was found to be an important variable to reduce perceived environmental uncertainty and supported the assumption that boundary spanning can be seen as an intervening variable. Other studies in the expatriation context revealed that perceived and objective cultural distance have effects on expatriate adjustment (Jenkins and Mockaitis, 2010).

With regard to outcomes, cultural boundary spanning has a positive relationship with all four dimensions of CQ (Holtbrügge and Engelhard, 2016). But cultural boundary spanning may also be positively related to cultural adjustment. In following Black et al. (1991), who suggest to look at the role transition literature and how an individual adjust to work role change, individuals can actively adjust by changing the new environment to correspond to their needs and abilities, or they can reactively adjust by changing themselves (Dawes and Lofquist, 1984). Only in the latter case, an individual's energies are devoted to the task of adapting new skills and social behaviors to meet the requirements of the new situation (Nicholson, 1984). While reactive adjustment is generally regarded to be imperative for expatriate success, the authors assume that cultural boundary spanning may have an impact on the active adjustment process as it involves behaviors that facilitate individuals to handle environmental constraints before adjustment takes place.

In general, there have already been a number of attempts to empirically examine the influence of boundary spanners on performance. Ancona and Caldwell (1992) found that teams with boundary-spanning capabilities are perceived as more effective and are more likely to achieve their final goals. Aldrich and Herker (1977) revealed that boundary spanners can increase the chance of success in inter-organizational collaboration. Di Marco et al. (2010) were the first to examine cultural boundary spanning and its influence on collaboration effectiveness. They found that cultural boundary spanners communicate more frequently. Moreover, cultural boundary spanning has a positive effect on initial performance and adaption performance in multicultural project networks (Di Marco et al., 2010).

Moreover, as cultural boundary spanning involves active information seeking and the ability to explain subjects to other colleagues, it could also reveal a positive effect on knowledge transfer (Reiche, 2011). As cultural intelligence is only one facet of the whole intelligence construct, it is yet to be examined which effect cultural boundary spanning has on general mental ability, such as social intelligence, emotional intelligence, and practical intelligence. Previous studies already found emotional intelligence to be important in the context of expatriation (Koveshnikov, Wechtler, and Dejoux, 2014).

Discussion—Time to Define, Delimit, and Further Develop the Concept of Cultural Boundary Spanning

The main objectives of sending expatriates on foreign assignments are to perform given tasks and ensure a continuity of operations. Thus, the significance of expatriates' ability to interact across countries and cultures and span boundaries at the same time has considerably increased (Korschun, 2015; Schotter and Beamish, 2011). In line with this, organizations need to predict and identify the relevant factors that could maximize expatriates' performance. While there is still no consensus in the expatriation literature on the relationship between adjustment and performance stressing the stagnation in this question (Puck et al., 2017), the authors propose cultural boundary spanning as mediating construct impacting performance and cultural intelligence.

Based on a comprehensive literature review, the authors developed an inclusive model of the antecedents, correlates, and outcomes of expatriate cultural boundary spanning. While this model is primarily based on theoretical considerations, further research is needed in order to test this model. Future studies should hereby focus on the mediating and intervening role of cultural boundary spanning. In the context of expatriation, cultural intelligence is an outcome of high importance as it helps expatriates to behave more adequately in the foreign market. A higher cultural intelligence could have positive effects on the individual level, such as higher job satisfaction or well-being, and on the organizational level, like higher multicultural leadership effectiveness.

While the majority of studies in the expatriation context are still focused on the adjustment and adaption process as the most important outcome, the authors propose cultural boundary spanning as a more adequate concept in the context of foreign assignments in the globalized era. While adjustment stresses the reactive part of role behavior when being abroad, the cultural boundary spanning function is an active behavior to encounter situations characterized by cultural diversity (Holtbrügge and Engelhard, 2016). Future studies should take this distinction into account and explore different effects of cultural boundary spanning and adjustment behavior on performance outcomes in the context of international assignments. Moreover, further research should test cultural boundary spanning alongside complementary or additional expatriate boundary spanning roles. This could help to further define, delimit, and develop the constructs of expatriate and cultural boundary spanning.

Practical Implications for MNCs

The concept of cultural boundary spanning has several implications for international assignments. First, human resource departments could restructure their assessment center and selection criteria to secure a better selection process and, for example, pay more attention to cultural intelligence and cultural boundary spanning capabilities. Similarly, expatriates with distinctive boundary spanning skills could be appointed as leaders of multicultural teams as their international experience in combination with their cultural boundary spanning behavior could be particularly beneficial in this context (Stahl, Maznevski, Voigt, and Jonsen, 2010).

As recent research (Schotter and Beamish, 2011) proves that the presence of boundary spanners reduces dysfunctional conflict and leads to better overall performance, the formalization of the expatriate boundary spanning role inside the organization is another useful measure. Being officially entitled as boundary spanner will increase the status of the expatriate in the entire organization. This formalization could have beneficial effects on the overall acceptance and the awareness of cultural boundary spanning for future international assignments.

Finally, the role of trust should not be neglected in the context of expatriate boundary spanning as trust turned out to be important for boundary spanning (Perrone, Zaheer, and McEvily, 2003; van Meerkerk and Edelenbos, 2014). The strategic identification of trustful persons in different divisions and departments could build the foundation of a possible pool of expatriates to choose from.

References

Adams, J. (1976). The structure and dynamics of behavior in organizational boundary roles. In M. D. Dunnette (Ed.), *Handbook of Industrial and Organizational Psychology* (pp. 1175–1199). Chicago: Rand McNally College Publishing Company.
Aldrich, H. and Herker, D. (1977). Boundary spanning roles and organization structure. *Academy of Management Review*, 2(2), 217–230.
Ancona, D. G. and Caldwell, D. F. (1988). Beyond task and maintenance: Defining external functions in groups. *Group & Organization Management*, 13(4), 468–494.
Ancona, D. G. and Caldwell, D. F. (1992). Bridging the boundary: External activity and performance in organizational teams. *Administrative Science Quarterly*, 37(4), 634–665.
Ang, S. and Van Dyne, L. (2008). Conceptualization of cultural intelligence. In S. Ang and L. Van Dyne (Eds.), *Handbook of Cultural Intelligence: Theory, Measurement, and Applications* (pp. 3–15). New York: Sharpe Inc.
Au, K. Y. and Fukuda, J. (2002). Boundary spanning behaviors of expatriates. *Journal of World Business*, 37(4), 285–296.
Bader, B. and Schuster, T. (2015). Expatriate social networks in terrorism-endangered countries: An empirical analysis in Afghanistan, India, Pakistan, and Saudi Arabia. *Journal of International Management*, 21(1), 63–77.
Barner-Rasmussen, W., Ehrnrooth, M., Koveshnikov, A., and Mäkelä, K. (2014). Cultural and language skills as resources for boundary spanning within the MNC. *Journal of International Business Studies*, 45(7), 886–905.
Bhaskar-Shrinivas, P., Harrison, D. A., Shaffer, M. A., and Luk, D. M. (2005). Input-based and time-based models of international adjustment: Meta-analytic evidence and theoretical extensions. *Academy of Management Journal*, 48(2), 257–281.
Bhatti, M. A., Battour, M. M. and Ismail, A. R. (2013). Expatriates adjustment and job performance: An examination of individual and organizational factors. International Journal of Productivity and Performance Management, 62(7), 694–717.
Black, J. S. (1988). Work role transitions: A study of American expatriate managers in Japan. *Journal of International Business Studies*, 19(2), 277–294.
Black, J. S., Mendenhall, M., and Oddou, G. (1991). Toward a comprehensive model of international adjustment: An integration of multiple theoretical perspectives. *Academy of Management Review*, 16(2), 291–317.

Bourdieu, P. (2011). The forms of capital. In I. Szeman and T. Kaposy (Eds.), *Cultural Theory: An Anthology* (pp. 81–93). West Sussex: Wiley-Blackwell.

Caligiuri, P., Lazarova, M., and Zehetbauer, S. (2007). Top managers' national diversity and boundary spanning: Attitudinal indicators of a firm's internationalization. *Journal of Management Development*, 23(9), 848–859.

Dau, L. A. (2016). Biculturalism, team performance, and cultural-faultline bridges. *Journal of International Management*, 22(1), 48–62.

Dawes, R. V. and Lofquist, L. H. (1984). *A Psychological Theory of Work Adjustment*. Minneapolis: University of Minnesota Press.

Di Marco, M. K., Taylor, J. E., and Alin, P. (2010). Emergence and role of cultural boundary spanners in global engineering project networks. *Journal of Management in Engineering*, 26(3), 123–132.

Earley, P. C. and Ang, S. (2003). *Cultural Intelligence: Individual Interactions Across Cultures*. Stanford: Stanford University Press.

Fang, Y., Jiang, G.-L. F., Makino, S. and Beamish, P. W. (2010). Multinational Firm Knowledge, Use of Expatriates, and Foreign Subsidiary Performance. *Journal of Management Studies*, 47(1), 27–54.

Felin, T. and Hesterly, W. S. (2007). The knowledge-based view, nested heterogeneity, and new value creation: Philosophical considerations on the locus of knowledge. *Academy of Management Review*, 32(1), 195–218.

Fennell, M. L. and Alexander, J. A. (1987). Organizational boundary spanning in institutionalized environments. *Academy of Management Journal*, 30(3), 456–476.

Froese, F. J. and Peltokorpi, V. (2013). Organizational expatriates and self-initiated expatriates: Differences in cross-cultural adjustment and job satisfaction. *The International Journal of Human Resource Management*, 24(10), 1953–1967.

Golden, T. D. and Veiga, J. (2005). Spanning boundaries and borders: Toward Understanding the cultural dimensions of team boundary spanning. *Journal of Managerial Issues*, 17(2), 178–197.

Harzing, A. (2001). An analysis of the functions of international transfer of managers in MNCs. *Employee Relations*, 23(6), 581–598.

Hechanova, R., Beehr, T. A., and Christiansen, N. D. (2003). Antecedents and consequences of employees' adjustment to overseas assignment: A meta-analytic review. *Applied Psychology–An International Review* [*Psychologie Appliquee–Revue Internationale*], 52(2), 213–236.

Holtbrügge, D. and Engelhard, F. (2016). Study abroad programs: Individual motivations, cultural intelligence, and the mediating role of cultural boundary spanning. *Academy of Management Learning and Education*, 15(3), 435–455.

Jenkins, E. and Mockaitis, A. (2010). You're from where? The influence of distance factors on New Zealand expatriates' cross-cultural adjustment. *The International Journal of Human Resource Management*, 21(15), 2694–2715.

Johnson, K. L. and Duxbury, L. (2010). The view from the field: A case study of the expatriate boundary-spanning role. *Journal of World Business*, 45(1), 29–40.

Kahn, R. L., Wolfe, D. M., Quinn, R. P., Snoek, J. D., and Rosenthal, R. A. (1964). *Organizational Stress*. New York: Wiley.

Katz, D. and Kahn, R. L. (1978). *The Social Psychology of Organizations*. New York: Wiley.

Korschun, D. (2015). Boundary-spanning employees and relationships with external stakeholders: A social identity approach. *Academy of Management Review*, 40(4), 611–629.

Kostova, T. and Roth, K. (2003). Social capital in multinational corporations and a micro-macro model of its formation. *Academy of Management Review*, 28(2), 297–317.

Koveshnikov, A., Wechtler, H., and Dejoux, C. (2014). Cross-cultural adjustment of expatriates: The role of emotional intelligence and gender. *Journal of World Business*, 49(3), 362–371.

Krackhardt, D. and Stern, R.N. (1988). Informal networks and crisis: An experimental simulation. *Social Psychology Quarterly*, 51(2), 123–140.

Leana, C.R., and Van Buren, H.J. (1999). Organizational social capital and employment practices. *Academy of Management Review*, 24(3), 538–555.

Leifer, R. and Huber, G.P. (1977). Relations among perceived environmental uncertainty, organization structure, and boundary-spanning behavior. *Administrative Science Quarterly*, 22(2), 235–247.

Luo, Y. (2001). Antecedents and consequences of personal attachment in cross-cultural cooperative ventures. *Administrative Science Quarterly*, 46(2), 177–201.

Marrone, J.A. (2010). Team boundary spanning: A multilevel review of past research and proposals for the future. *Journal of Management*, 36(4), 911–940.

Nicholson, N. (1984). A theory of work role transitions. *Administrative Science Quarterly*, 29(2), 172.

Noble, G. and Jones, R. (2006). The role of boundary-spanning managers in the establishment of public-private partnerships. *Public Administration*, 84(4), 891–917.

Osman-Gani, A.M. and Rockstuhl, T. (2009). Cross-cultural training, expatriate self-efficacy, and adjustments to overseas assignments: An empirical investigation of managers in Asia. *International Journal of Intercultural Relations*, 33(4), 277–290.

Peltokorpi, V. and Jintae Froese, F. (2009). Organizational expatriates and self-initiated expatriates: Who adjusts better to work and life in Japan? *The International Journal of Human Resource Management*, 20(5), 1096–1112.

Perrone, V., Zaheer, A., and McEvily, B. (2003). Free to be trusted? Organizational constraints on trust in boundary spanners. *Organization Science*, 14(4), 422–439.

Puck, J., Holtbrügge, D., and Raupp, J. (2017). Expatriate adjustment: A review of concepts, drivers, and consequences. In B. Bader, T. Schuster, and A. K. Bader (eds), *Expatriate Management* (pp. 297–336). London, UK: Palgrave Macmillan.

Reiche, B.S. (2011). Knowledge transfer in multinationals: The role of inpatriates' boundary spanning. *Human Resource Management*, 50(3), 365–389.

Schotter, A. and Beamish, P.W. (2011). Performance effects of MNC headquarters—subsidiary conflict and the role of boundary spanners: The case of headquarter initiative rejection. *Journal of International Management*, 17(3), 243–259.

Scott, W.R. (1995). *Institutions and Organizations*. Thousand Oaks, CA: Sage Publications.

Stahl, G., Maznevski, M.L., Voigt, A., and Jonsen, K. (2010). Unraveling the effects of cultural diversity in teams: A meta-analysis of research on multicultural work groups. *Journal of International Business Studies*, 41(4), 690–709.

Sternberg, R.J. and Detterman, D.K. (1986). *What Is Intelligence? Contemporary Viewpoints on Its Nature and Definition*. New York: Ablex Publication Corporation.

Takeuchi, R., Yun, S., and Tesluk, P.E. (2002). An examination of crossover and spillover effects of spousal and expatriate cross-cultural adjustment on expatriate outcomes. *Journal of Applied Psychology*, 87(4), 655–666.

Thomas, D.C. (1991). Boundary spanning behavior of expatriates: A model of internal exchange in the multinational corporation. *Academy of Management Proceedings*, 1991(1), 110–114.

Trevillion, S. (1991). *Caring in the Community*. London: Longman.

Tsai, W. and Ghoshal, S. (1998). Social capital and value creation: The role of intrafirm networks. *Academy of Management Journal*, 41(4), 464–476.

Tung, R. L. (1998). American expatriates abroad: From neophytes to cosmopolitans. *Journal of World Business*, 33(2), 125–144.

van Meerkerk, I. and Edelenbos, J. (2014). The effects of boundary spanners on trust and performance of urban governance networks: Findings from survey research on urban development projects in the Netherlands. *Policy Sciences*, 47(1), 3–24.

Vora, D., Kostova, T., and Roth, K. (2007). Roles of subsidiary managers in multi-national corporations: The effect of dual organizational identification. *Management International Review*, 47(4), 595–620.

Williams, P. (2002). The competent boundary spanner. *Public Administration*, 80(1), 103–124.

4 Clustering Methods in Business Intelligence

Subhajit Chakrabarty

Introduction

Clustering is the art of finding groups in data (Kaufman and Rousseeuw, 2005). The basic problem is: given a set of data points, partition them into a set of groups which are as similar as possible (Aggarwal, 2014). Clustering refers to grouping of data when the groups are unknown beforehand. In classification, the groups (categories or classes) are known and there is a need to identify which group (category or class) each data belongs to (supervised learning). But in clustering, the groups are unraveled from the data (unsupervised learning). Quite often, using known groups could be arbitrary. Clustering is more useful because it can potentially find hidden groups. For example, in the case of customers of cars, grouping based on income categories, horse-power desired, or fuel-efficiency could be visible. But what may not be apparent is a combination such as "rich customers needing high horse-power" or "middle-income and low-income needing high fuel-efficiency." What could be even more challenging is when the variables also are not known and feature extraction becomes an added task. Clustering is a broad term for several methods and approaches.

The broad approaches to clustering are named as Partition clustering, Hierarchical clustering, Density-based clustering, Grid-based clustering, Graph clustering, Time series clustering, Semi-supervised clustering, Spectral clustering, and Manifold clustering. Further, different domains may have different methods of clustering—such as Document clustering, Stream clustering, Multimedia data clustering, and High-dimensional data clustering. Various kinds of metrics have evolved, such as metrics for finding distance between points and metrics for validation of clustering results. Given the strong potential to discover hidden information from data, the study of clustering is of immense significance in business intelligence.

The purpose of this chapter is to discuss clustering methods, the circumstances in which specific methods apply to global business intelligence, and the impact of these methods on global business intelligence. The layout of the remaining part of this chapter is as follows. The nature of data (variables) is a key factor in the choice of method. This is discussed first. In grouping each data point, distance is measured from other points using various metrics, which is discussed next. The various clustering approaches follow. The next section describes various methods of clustering with respect to specific domains. Feature selection is discussed next, as clustering may encounter a number of candidate features. The results of clustering need to be validated against the ground truth—a discussion of validation metrics follows subsequently.

Basic Considerations

Nature and Participation of Variables

Variables are basically of three types—Interval (scaled), Ranked (ordered), and Categorical (nominal). For scaled variables, the distance measures between two points are meaningful whereas for nominal variables the standard distance measures such as in L_k norm bear no meaning. Methods such as K-means clustering do not work properly on categorical data because they use distance measures such as centroid which is meaningless for categorical data. As an example, Latent Class models can work on clustering discrete or categorical data efficiently. For mixed data, methods such as spectral clustering can be applied because they can consider distance between records. Each method prefers an underlying estimation method. In the above example, K-means uses the Sum-of-Squared-Errors (SSE) estimation while the Latent Class Analysis (LCA) uses Maximum Likelihood Estimation (MLE). MLE is a point estimate and hence justified for use with categorical data.

Participation of variables may be partial, so that the latent variable may have proportions of participating variables. In the case of Principal Component Analysis (PCA), orthogonal components are derived from the variables and the components have partial participation of the variables. But PCA does not work on categorical data.

Ranked data can be converted to scaled data (albeit with some limitations). Even categorical data can be converted to a form (such as dummy variables) which takes binary values and can be used in scalar data analysis. But for better analysis, categorical data do need separate methods which are discussed subsequently.

Measures of Distance

Distance measures are among the key elements in data mining and particularly for clustering tasks (Wang and Sun, 2012). For scaled data, a generalized distance measure is the Minkowski distance which is the following.

$$d_{i,j} = \left(\sum_{i=1}^{n} |x_i - y_i|^p \right)^{1/p}$$

When p =1, it is called the Manhattan distance and when p = 2, it is called the Euclidean distance.

For clustering of scaled data, specific measures of distance may be used such as Single linkage (nearest neighbor method), Average linkage (minimum variance method), Weightage average linkage, Complete linkage (furthest neighbor method), and Ward's linkage (minimizes within-cluster variance as opposed to between-cluster variance). In Single linkage one drawback is the "chaining effect"—a few points that form a bridge between two groups merges the two groups into one. Average linkage may cause elongated clusters to split. Complete-linkage clustering methods usually produce more compact clusters and more useful hierarchies than the Single-link clustering methods.

For ranked data, a simple measure could be to use standardized scores for each rank observation as follows.

$$z_i = \frac{rank_i - 1}{maximum\_rank_i - 1}$$

For categorical data, identifying a distance measure is more challenging but a simple distance measure could be Hamming distance (the number of coefficients in which two vectors differ). For two bit strings (having 0s and 1s indicating presence or absence), the Hamming distance could be calculated simply using an eXclusive OR operation.

$$d_{A,B} = XOR(A,B)$$

Some probabilistic measures assign higher similarity to infrequent matches under conditions that there are also other categories, which are even less frequent than the examined one. Such probabilistic measures include Goodall measure, Smirnov measure, and Anderberg measure. There are information-theoretic measures such as Burnaby measure and Lin measure. The Lin measure assigns higher weights to more frequent categories in case of matches and lower weights to less frequent categories in case of mismatches. There could also be context-based similarity measures. Therefore, the choice of variables and the choice of distance measures require careful decisions.

Clustering Approaches

The basic clustering approaches which have been developed are listed in Figure 4.1.

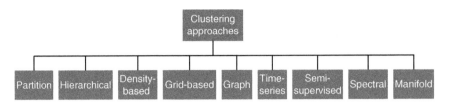

Figure 4.1 Clustering Approaches

Partition clustering relocates points from one partition to another. The advantage is that the quality of clustering can be improved with iterative optimization (Berkhin, 2006). Typically, the number of partitions is pre-defined. So, if three clusters are known and information on customer data is available, for example, then data points of each customer can be relocated so that optimum quality of clusters (to be validated) is obtained. The measures of quality are mentioned under the "Clustering Validation" section. The relocation of points is done over many iterations.

Hierarchical clustering recursively groups in a bottom-up (agglomerative) or top-town (divisive) manner. This does not require a user-defined number of clusters (Jain, Murty, and Flynn, 1999). So, in the example of customer data, each data point is grouped with a similar data point (based on distance measure) and these smaller groups are grouped together to form larger groups recursively. From the top of this tree-like structure, one can see the required grouping of the customer data at the desired level of grouping.

Density-based clustering basically groups based on threshold density of points (Ester, Kriegel, Sander, and Xu, 1996). So, for the example of customer data, the adjacent data points in a particular cluster may have distances less than a threshold.

Grid-based clustering uses grids for faster computation (Wang, Yang, and Muntz, 1997). Taking the example of customer data, assuming that the data is uniform, it can be partitioned into a given number of cells and the cells may be sorted according to their densities (here this method overlaps with density-based method). Then, the partition centers can be identified. The challenge is to determine the grid.

Graph clustering uses the connectedness within sub-graphs to group them (Schaeffer, 2007). So, if customer data can be represented in the form of a connected graph such as a social media network of online customers, then one can find clusters of these online customers such as college students and working professionals (each grouped based on connectedness).

Time series clustering does groupings of series having similar trends or series having similar shapes (Yi et al., 2000; Liao, 2005). The customer data may represent monthly sales of several products over 15 years. Some product groups may have seasonality (e.g. selling more during winter) and some product groups may be selling together having a long-run relationship.

Semi-supervised clustering does grouping by using information such as labels for seeds (initializing), pairwise constraints, active learning, and user feedback (Chapelle, Scholkopf, and Zien, 2006). In the example, when clusters from the customer data are sought, some prior information such as initial identification of few clusters (labels) or expert feedback on identification of clusters for particular points, could help in the effort.

Spectral clustering uses the spectrum (eigenvalues) of the similarity matrix of the data to perform dimensionality reduction before clustering in fewer dimensions (Filiponne, Camastra, Masulli, and Rovatta, 2008). The customer data could be in high dimensions (substantial number of variables). Sometimes, the dimensions are so many that one can only deal with subspaces (subspace clustering) though subspaces may be different among themselves. Dimensionality reduction is a better idea. This could be done with particular matrix operations in the process of spectral clustering.

Manifold clustering uses nonlinear dimensionality reduction (such as using Kernel Principal Component Analysis or Locally Linear Embedding) on the data before clustering in fewer dimensions (Roweis and Saul, 2000). Nonlinear dimensionality reduction manages the "curse of dimensionality" (data becomes increasingly sparse and creates new problems in high dimensions) to some extent.

The above are broad approaches. Overlap of the above approaches is possible, as shown in the case of grid clustering. Other generalizations of types of clustering approaches are possible—such as, based on whether the underlying data representation is feature-based (vector of features) or graph-based (similarity graph between data points). K-means is an example of a feature-based approach, while spectral clustering is an example of a graph-based approach.

A Clustering Algorithm Example—K-means

To explain the algorithmic process of clustering, take the example of the most popular clustering algorithm: K-means algorithm (MacQueen, 1967; Lloyd, 1982). In K-means, each observation is grouped based on the nearest mean. The algorithm is as follows.

1. Initialization: place K points into the space represented by the objects that are being clustered. These points represent initial group centroids or an initial set of K-means.
2. Assignment: assign each observation to the group that has the closest centroid or K-mean.
3. Update: update the positions of the K centroids or K-mean.
4. Repeat Steps 2 and 3 until the centroids or K-means no longer move or are based on convergence criterion.

It is important to note that K-means is an optimization problem and cannot guarantee a global optimum solution. A major drawback of the K-means algorithm is that it is highly sensitive to the initial K-means. One popular option for initialization is to use random values in the partitions and another of the options is to draw from some distribution (such as normal distribution).

In Figure 4.2, one sees the results of K-means run over the Iris dataset (UCI Machine Learning Repository). The classes are the three types of flowers—Iris Sentosa, Iris Versicolor, and Iris Virginica. These are plotted against two principal components. The classification ground truth is on the left and the comparison with K-means clusters is on the right.

There are many adaptations of the K-means algorithm, such as K-medians, K-medoids, Fuzzy C-means, and K-modes. "Mean" has no meaning for categorical data. For example, K-modes algorithm can work in categorical data. The K-modes algorithm is given below.

1. Initialization: select K initial modes;
2. Assignment: assign each observation to the group that has the closest mode using a matching metric;
3. Update: update the K-modes of the clusters;
4. Repeat Steps 2 and 3 until the K-modes no longer move or are based on convergence criterion.

So, as compared with K-means, K-modes use modes (frequencies of mismatches or a matching metric).

Using a generalization of K-means, one can use a model-based clustering method called the Expectation-Maximization (EM) algorithm (Dempster, Laird, and Rubin, 1977). EM finds clusters by determining a mixture of Gaussians that fit a given set of observations. The parameters can be initialized randomly or by using the output of K-means. It has two steps, the Expectation step in which the expected value of log likelihood is calculated, and the Maximization step in which parameters maximizing the expected value are calculated and fed into the Expectation step iteratively.

In the process, clustering algorithms can have variants which can be adapted to given circumstances/conditions. To this end, it is important to identify the underling nature of data and to understand the underlying domain.

Clustering in Specific Domains

The broad types of domain-specific clustering are listed in Figure 4.3.

Document Clustering

The additional challenges in document clustering are that documents are sparse (compared to the dictionary, many words are unused), that it has a high-dimensional corpus (dictionary) and that words can be correlated. Text can be viewed as a bag of words. A document can be viewed as a

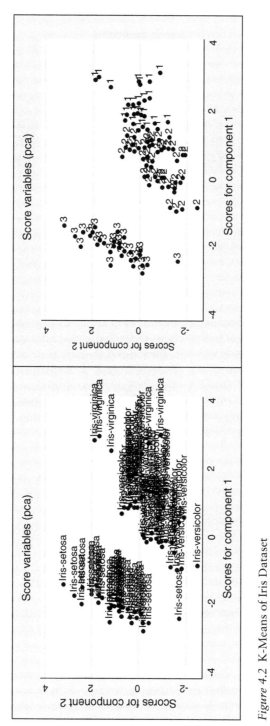

Figure 4.2 K-Means of Iris Dataset

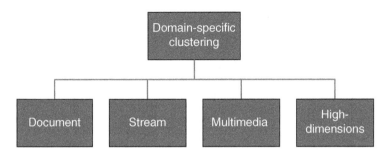

Figure 4.3 Domain-Specific Clustering

term-frequency vector where f_i is the term-frequency (or inverse-frequency) of the ith term in the document.

$$d_f = \left(f_1, f_2, \ldots, f_n\right)$$

For the analysis of documents, instead of the frequency, the inverse-frequency is often used because less frequent terms have more discriminatory power. The length of the document is normalized to consider documents of varying lengths. The words are processed using stemming or lemmatization. Stemming cuts off word endings while lemmatization finds synonyms or common words from lexical databases. Word sequence and sentence structure can be modeled using n-gram models (Manning, Raghavan, and Schutze, 2008; Porter, 1997).

Stream Clustering

The key challenges in stream clustering are the massive volume of online data (which often cannot be stored in a single disk) and the continually evolving patterns of online data streams. The components in handling stream clustering are called online micro-clustering and offline macro-clustering. Micro-clusters are cluster feature vectors with timestamps. The purpose of micro-clustering is to store summary statistics from a fast data stream. Offline macro-clustering utilizes these summary statistics along with other inputs to interpret the clusters (Aggarwal, Han, Wang, and Yu, 2003).

Multimedia Data Clustering

Clustering has been applied to a wide variety of multimedia data such as image and video/audio. For example, image segmentation can be done by minimizing an energy function—measure of smoothness of labeling plus measure of agreement between labeled pixels and labeling functions

(Boykov, Veksler, and Zabih, 2001). Face clustering (Guillaumin, Verbeek, and Schmid, 2009) and photo album event recognition (Tsai, Cao, Tang, and Hunag, 2011) are some other applications of clustering on image data. For video data, video summarization, video event detection, and video story clustering have evolved. For example, in video story clustering, a story is linked to keyframe clusters and textual keywords associated with them, based on frequency of keywords and story (Gong and Liu, 2000).

Clustering High-Dimensional Data

High-dimensionality brings in a special kind of challenge called the "curse of dimensionality" (a term coined by Ricard E. Bellman) in which the data becomes increasingly sparse and presents various problems—such as, global optimization difficulty increases exponentially, similarity measures such as L_p norm become less useful and irrelevant attributes arise. There are two basic approaches in clustering high-dimensional data—projected clustering (Aggarwal, Procopiuc, Wolf, Yu, and Park, 1999) and subspace clustering (Agrawal, Gehrke, Gunopulos, and Raghavan, 1998). Projected clustering partitions the dataset in such a way that each point belongs to exactly one cluster by projecting on the attributes of the cluster. In subspace clustering a point may belong to more than one cluster (partial membership and overlaps are allowed). Subspace clustering finds all clusters in all subspaces. There are also hybrid approaches. It is important to note that there is no general solution to clustering on high-dimensional data. So, some algorithms work on interesting subspaces, some try to build hierarchically, some try to optimize locally, and so on.

Feature Selection

The concept of feature selection is slightly different from traditional feature extraction. In feature extraction, the features are projected into new space with lower dimensionality. Examples of feature extraction methods include Principal Component Analysis, Linear Discriminant Analysis, and Singular Value Decomposition. In feature selection, a small subset (variables) of features is selected which minimizes redundancy and maximizes relevance to the class label. Examples of feature selection methods include Information Gain, Relief, and Fischer Score. Feature selection may be considered superior to feature extraction because it maintains the original feature values (in reduced space) and hence is easy to interpret. In contrast, the new features through feature extraction are in new space; such features cannot easily be linked to features in the original space (Liu and Motoda, 2007).

Feature selection can be considered to consist of four basic steps— variable generation (based on a search strategy), variable evaluation (based on an evaluation criterion, the better variable is selected over iterations), stopping criterion (when variable generation and evaluation are stopped) and result validation with respect to the ground truth. The variable search may be a complete search, incremental search (not all possible variables considered), or a random search. The variable evaluation may be based on distance measures (features which separate classes as far as possible), information measures (choosing features with more information gain), dependency measures (choosing features having more correlation with a class), and consistency measures (finding a minimum number of features which perform consistently in separating the classes) (Liu and Yu, 2005).

Do feature selection and clustering represent a chicken-and-egg dilemma as to which is required first? Well, basically feature selection comes earlier and serves requirements of clustering. Ideally, clustering inputs (class labels) may not be used for feature selection—clustering methods may only guide the variable search process (Alelyani, Tang, and Liu, 2014).

Clustering Validation

Clustering validation makes an evaluation about how good the clustering results are. Although this has been examined in literature for a prolonged period, there is no conclusive universal solution to this. Different validation measures seem to be appropriate for different clustering algorithms.

There are basically two types of clustering validation discussed in literature—internal validation and external validation, depending on whether external information is used for the validation. External validation knows the true class labels in advance, unlike internal validation. So, external validation mainly evaluates clustering results with respect to the ground truth (if the information is available). Internal validation mainly evaluates choice of algorithms and optimum number of clusters. Popular internal validation criteria include Sum of Square Errors (SSE), Maximum Likelihood Estimation (MLE), and Scatter matrix (such as Trace, Determinant, and Invariant). Other internal cluster validation measures include Modified Hubert statistic, Calinski-Harabasz index, I index, Dunn's indices, Silhouette index, Davies-Bouldin index, Xie-beni index, SD validity index, S_Dbw validity index, and CV NN^2 index. Popular external validation criteria include Rand index (ratio of agreements over total pairs for two clusters) and Precision-Recall. Precision is the ratio of true positives over total positives, while Recall is the ratio of true positives over the sum of true positives and false negatives. The harmonic mean of Precision and Recall is known as the F measure. Other external cluster validation measures include Entropy, Purity, Variation of Information, Mutual Information, Jaccard Coefficient, Fowlkes-Mallows index, Hubert statistic, Minkowski score, van Dongen criterion, Goodman-Kruskal coefficient, and Mirkin metric (Xiong and Li, 2014).

To give an example of clustering customer data, results could be represented as per Table 4.1.

Table 4.1 Precision and Recall

		Predicted		
		Positive	Negative	
Ground Truth	True	True Positive (TP)	False Negative (FN)	**Recall = TP/(TP+FN)**
	False	False Positive (FP)	True Negative (FN)	
		Precision = TP/(TP+FP)		

So, if the class labels are known or if an expert can identify the clusters, then it is best to use metrics such as Precision and Recall for external validation.

Some methods (like K-means) require prior specification of the number of clusters. So, in the case of clustering customer data, it makes sense to specify the number of customer groups before running the K-means algorithm to find which point belongs to which customer group. What is the correct number of clusters? This is generally considered in internal validation. One method is to plot the variance explained against the number of clusters and choose a number at which the slope becomes relatively flat. Another method is known as Silhouette, which measures the distance between and within clusters. This can be applied in the validation process—say, based on average Silhouette width. Statistical measures such as maximization of the Bayesian Information Criterion (BIC) are quite useful in determining the optimum number of clusters.

Summary

To summarize, clustering is the grouping of data when the groups themselves are not known in advance. It offers a powerful range of techniques to uncover hidden groups in business data. The underlying nature of variables, choice of distance measures, and feature selection are key parameters in the clustering process. Several generic clustering approaches have evolved and some are specific to domains. Internal and external validation metrics are available. Indeed, clustering has evolved towards a comprehensive range of tools and techniques. Clustering is also an art—as it involves understanding the underlying data, choosing the right clustering method, choosing the number of clusters, interpreting the clusters, and understanding the dynamic nature of the grouping.

As the clustering methods are core methods of analysis, the choice of the methods would clearly impact the results in the processes of global business intelligence, namely data discovery, data analysis, data transformation, and data reporting (Figure 4.4).

Figure 4.4 Impact of Clustering Methods in Business Intelligence (BI)

In data discovery for global business intelligence, clustering methods are powerful in finding unknown groups and hidden relationships. In data analysis for business intelligence, better competitive analysis and data mining can be done because the techniques present generic methods as well as domain-specific methods. The improved insights through use of the clustering tools may indicate requirement of better data representation in the data warehouses and requirement data transformation. In data reporting, several types of clusters can be visualized. Good visualizations may also lead to visual discovery of latent clusters, not easily found through the other methods. It is important to notice that the clusters can capture the dynamic nature of global business intelligence—clusters would continuously keep changing and new clusters would emerge as the dynamics of the global business change.

References

Aggarwal, C. C. (2014). An introduction to cluster analysis. In C. C. Aggarwal and C. K. Reddy (Eds.), *Data Clustering: Algorithms and Applications* (pp. 1–27). Boca Raton, FL: CRC Press.

Aggarwal, C.C., Han, J., Wang, J., and Yu, P. (2003). A framework for clustering evolving data streams. In *VLDB Conference* (pp. 81–92), Berlin, Germany: VLDB Endowment.

Aggarwal, C.C., Procopiuc, C.M., Wolf, J.L., Yu, P.S., and Park, J.S. (1999). Fast algorithms for projected clustering. In *Proceedings of* the 1999 *ACM* SIGMOD *International Conference on Management of Data* (pp. 61–72), NY, USA: ACM New York.

Agrawal, R., Gehrke, J., Gunopulos, D., and Raghavan, P. (1998). Automatic subspace clustering of high dimensional data. In *Proceedings of* 1998 *ACM* SIGMOD *International Conference on Management of Data* (pp. 94–105), NY, USA: ACM New York.

Alelyani, S., Tang, J., and Liu, H. (2014). Feature selection for clustering: A review. In C.C. Aggarwal and C.K. Reddy (Eds.), *Data Clustering—Algorithms and Applications* (pp. 29–60). Boca Raton, FL: CRC Press.

Berkhin, P. (2006). A survey of clustering data mining techniques. In J. Kogan, C. Nicholas, and M. Teoulle (Eds.), *Grouping Multidimensional Data* (pp. 27–71). Berlin Heidelberg: Springer.

Boykov, Y., Veksler, O., and Zabih, R. (2001, November). Fast approximate energy minimization via graph cuts. *IEEE Transactions on Pattern Analysis and Machine Intelligence*, 29(11), 1222–1239: IEEE.

Chapelle, O., Scholkopf, B., and Zien, A. (2006). *Semi-Supervised Learning*. Cambridge, MA: MIT Press.

Dempster, A.P., Laird, N.M., and Rubin, D.B. (1977). Maximum likelihood from incomplete data via the EM algorithm. *Journal of the Royal Statistical Society*, 39(1), 1–38.

Ester, M., Kriegel, H.P., Sander, J., and Xu, X. (1996). A density-based algorithm for discoverng clusters in large spatial databases with noise. In *ACM KDD Conference* (Vol. 96, No. 34, pp. 226–231). http://130.238.12.100/edu/course/home-page/infoutv2/vt14/dm2-litterature/KDD-96.final.frame.pdf

Filiponne, M., Camastra, F., Masulli, F., and Rovatta, S. (2008). A survey of kernel and spectral methods for clustering. *Pattern Recognition*, 41(1), 176–190.

Gong, Y. and Liu, X. (2000). Video summarization using singular value decomposition. In *Proceedings of* IEEE Conference on Computer Vision and Pattern Recognition, 2000 (pp. 174–180): IEEE.

Guillaumin, M., Verbeek, J., and Schmid, C. (2009). Is that you? Metric learning approaches for face detection. In 2009 IEEE 12th International Conference on Computer Vision (pp. 498–505): IEEE.

Jain, A.K., Murty, M.N., and Flynn, P.J. (1999). Data clustering: A review. *ACM Computing Surveys (CSUR)*, 31(3), 264–323.

Kaufman, L. and Rousseeuw, P.J. (2005). *Finding Groups in Data—An Introduction to Cluster Analysis*. Hoboken, NJ: John Wiley & Sons, Inc.

Liao, T. (2005). Clustering of time series data—A survey. *Pattern Recognition*, 38(11), 1857–1874.

Liu, H. and Motoda, H. (2007). *Computational Methods of Feature Selection*. Boca Raton, FL: CRC Press.

Liu, H. and Yu, L. (2005, April). Towards integrating feature selection algorithms for classification and clustering. *Knowledge and Data Engineering, IEEE Transactions on*, 17(4), 502: IEEE.

Lloyd, S. (1982). Least squares quantization in PCM. *IEEE Transactions on Information Theory*, 28(2), 129–137: IEEE.

MacQueen, J.B. (1967). Some methods for classification and analysis of multivariate observations. In Lucien Lecam and Jerzy Neyman (Eds.), *Proceedings of 5th Berkeley Symposium on Mathematical Statistics and Probability* (pp. 281–297). Berkeley: University of California Press.

Manning, C. D., Raghavan, P., and Schutze, H. (2008). *Introduction to Information Retrieval*. Cambridge: Cambridge University Press.

Porter, M. F. (1997). An algorithm for suffix stripping. In K. S. Jones and P. Willett (Eds.), *Readings in Information Retrieval* (pp. 313–316). San Francisco, CA: Morgan Kaufmann Publishers Inc.

Roweis, S. T. and Saul, L. K. (2000, December). Nonlinear dimensionality reduction by locally linear embedding. *Science*, 290(5500), 2323–2326.

Schaeffer, S. (2007). Graph clustering. *Computer Science Review*, 1(1), 27–64.

Tsai, S.-F., Cao, L., Tang, F., and Hunag, T. S. (2011). Compositional object pattern: A new model for album event recognition. In MM '11 Proceedings of the 19th *ACM* International Conference on *Multimedia*, 1361–1364, NY, USA: ACM New York.

Wang, F. and Sun, J. (2012). Distance metric learning in data mining. In *SDM12 Conference (Tutorial)*: SIAM. https://www.siam.org/meetings/sdm12/wang_sun_part1.pdf

Wang, W., Yang, J., and Muntz, R. (1997). Sting: A statistical information grid approach to spatial data mining. In *VLDB 1997 Conference*: VLDB Endowment. http://suraj.lums.edu.pk/~cs536a04/handouts/STING.pdf

Xiong, H. and Li, Z. (2014). Clustering validation measures. In C. C. Aggarwal and C. K. Reddy (Eds.), *Data Clustering—Algorithms and Applications* (pp. 571–605). Boca Raton, FL: CRC Press.

Yi, B. K., Sidiropoulos, N. D., Johnson, T., Jagadish, H., Faloutsos, C., and Biliris, A. (2000). Online data mining for co-evolving time sequences. In 16th International Conference on Data Engineering, 2000: IEEE. doi: 10.1109/ICDE.2000.839383.

5 Cybersecurity and the Importance of Business Intelligence

Tricia-Ann Smith DaSilva

Over the years, cyberspace has become an essential element in virtually every facet of contemporary society. A number of institutions have portals which customers use to transact business. These portals contain an increasing amount of sensitive data, including names, addresses and credit card information. As such, persons appreciate the advantages of utilizing information technologies. However, unfortunately, cybercrime has resulted in undesirable consequences. News on cyberfraud, intellectual property theft, the compromise of personal data and hacker attacks are recurrent in the news. Hence, protection against cyberattacks is an imperative component in ensuring that entities can shield their economic interests, reputation, intellectual property rights, and their information assets. By the end of this chapter, readers will be able to:

- obtain an overview of Information Technology (IT) risks;
- learn about various cyberattacks and how to mitigate against them;
- understand the importance of business intelligence in the modern world; and
- understand the role of the board and senior management in identifying, assessing, and managing the risk.

Cybersecurity is defined as the IT infrastructure that has been implemented to protect computer networks and data from unauthorized access. Principles have been established to permit entities to practice safe security techniques to facilitate a reduction in the number of successful cybersecurity attacks. With the increased volume of cyberattacks, business intelligence is an important tool for entities to minimize cyber-risk. Business Intelligence (BI) comprises the set of strategies, processes, applications, data, technologies, and technical architectures which are used by enterprises to support the collection, data analysis, presentation, and dissemination of business information (Stanier, 2016).

BI can be used for generating business strategies. However, gathering data has amplified the quantity of security risks. Once an entity identifies the various threats impacting their business, it provides them with the opportunity to organize an effective defense against cybercrime. As mentioned previously, cyberattacks can damage a business in numerous ways. For instance, there may be a loss of data, customer trust, and resources. Szoldra (2015) highlighted several instances of high-profile cyberattacks in recent years. For instance:

- In 2015, financial institutions across several countries were infiltrated by an unknown group. At least 100 banks in 30 countries were affected. In many cases, the criminals used their computer exploits to dispense cash from Automated Teller Machines or to execute digital transfers to their personal accounts.
- Subsequent to the breach of the credit-checking company, Experian, millions of T-Mobile customers had their information stolen.
- A breach of Vtech, a manufacturer of children's toys, caused the unauthorized publication of records on millions of parents and kids.
- The US government agency in charge of background checks was breached, exposing information on virtually every federal employee since the year 2000.
- More than 200,000 users of WhatsApp's messenger, a web-based messaging service, were affected by a cyberattack that allowed hackers to compromise individuals' personal data.

  In a more recent case, there was a hack on the Ukrainian power grid on December 23, 2015, which resulted in the blackout of power supplies to more than 225,000 people and affected three regional electronic power distribution companies within 13 minutes of each other (*The Japan Times*, 2016). Furthermore, the governing body of global athletics (IAAF) suffered a cyberattack which compromised information about athletes' medical records (Eyewitness News, 2017).

According to the 2016 Global Economic Crime Survey, 61% of respondents in the capacity of CEO were noted to be anxious about cybersecurity threats than in the previous 12 months (PwC, 2016). The overwhelming number of cybercrime incidents has forced the Boards of Directors (BoD) to become more educated about the topic and ask strategic and thoughtful questions directed toward management. In The Institute of Internal Auditor's (IIA's) Audit Executive Center (2014) survey, participants responded that the BoDs are thinking about cybersecurity. When asked, "How would you characterize the board's perception of cybersecurity risks over the last one to two years?" more than 65% of BoD respondents indicated that the cybersecurity risks had increased. As such, the Federal Bureau of Investigation (FBI) has implemented procedures to expose and inspect web-based intrusion attacks and established a team of trained computer scientists capable of extracting hackers' digital signatures from malicious code (FBI, n.d.).

To this end, executives need to understand and approach cybersecurity as an enterprise-wide risk management issue, not just an IT issue. Directors should therefore understand the legal implications of cyber-risks as they relate to their company's specific circumstances. With cybersecurity there is increased damage to an entity's reputation. As such it is imperative that senior management and executives are kept up to date with the potential risk exposure of the entity to cyberattacks including details of risks that have been identified, mitigated, or risk accepted. Members of the BoDs should have adequate access to cybersecurity expertise. Furthermore, discussions about cyber-risk management and ways to utilize business intelligence to minimize cyber-risks should be included on the agendas of the meetings of BoDs. Directors should set the expectation that management will establish an enterprise-wide risk management framework with adequate staffing and budget. Refer to Appendix 5.1 for a number of areas of consideration for executives.

Hence, there are a number of IT risks, both operational and financial in nature, that are on the Boards of Directors' and the Audit Committees' agendas. There has been growth with the utilization of mobile computing as customers' needs for on-demand access to information and services have increased. Furthermore, entities have greater focus on increasing the effectiveness and efficiency of their business processes and as such have introduced business process automation. Business process automation is defined as the strategy a business uses to automate processes in order to contain costs through integrating applications, restructuring labor resources, and using software applications throughout the business. Since technology is at the forefront of business development for sustainable growth, various risks such as access, integrity, and availability risk have been introduced within the business environment. These risks are defined as follows:

Table 5.1 Definition of IT Risks

Risk	Definition
Access Risk	The risk that there may be unauthorized access to systems.
Availability Risk	The risk that systems, information, and data may be lost.
Integrity Risk	The risk that an application may not function as intended.

Currently, companies are using online services to improve the effectiveness and efficiency of their operations. However, these emerging technologies also potentially increase an entity's exposure to access, availability, and integrity risk. As such, management should seek to understand these technologies in the context of the risk exposures that may be created. A few of the emerging technologies utilized by organizations include:

- Cloud computing, which is defined as the centralization of computing resources.
- Social technologies, which is defined as a range of software programs that are often web based and allow users to interact and share data with other users.

It should be noted that the contemporary digital environs make gathering information easier. Firewall logs and digital records provide entities with information that they may analyze using business analytics software (Radak, 2017). This assists to position entities to detect or prevent instances of cybercrime within their organizations.

The benefits and risks of the aforementioned technologies are of utmost importance to executives and are highlighted in Tables 5.2 and 5.3:

Table 5.2 Cloud Computing

Benefits	Risks
Rapid placement of IT infrastructure and hence a reduction of the initial investment costs.	Increased third party risk as there may be inappropriate security, governance, and IT controls at the service provider.
The ability to access the cloud via various devices and hence the establishment of facilities to allow for central storage, simultaneous editing, and offline editing.	Issues with capacity utilization and speed due to inappropriate bandwidth at the third party.

Sources: Queensland Government, 2016 and Beckham, 2011

Table 5.3 Social Technologies

Benefits	Risks
Increased use of the technology to promote organizations' products and services.	The utilization of corporate email by employees to register on sites such as LinkedIn and Facebook resulting in increased spam to corporate email.
The utilization of the platform to send out general messages, news, and other information to key stakeholders.	An increased risk that viruses may be embedded in user posts which may put the corporate network at risk.
	An increased likelihood of the disclosure of private company information allowing hackers to be able to build a database of information to carry out attacks.

Sources: DeMers, 2014 and Siciliano, 2014

Professionals need to be able to identify and assess IT security risks within organizations. A key question is—"Where to begin with cybersecurity Risk?"

The United States' Securities and Exchange Commission's (SEC) formal jurisdiction over cybersecurity is directly focused on the integrity of market systems, customer data protection, and disclosure of material information (Roth et al., 2014). SEC's Division of Corporate Finance issued guidance on existing disclosure obligations related to cybersecurity risks and incidents to assist public companies in framing disclosures of cybersecurity issues. The guidance clearly stated that material information regarding cybersecurity risks and cyber-incidents should be disclosed. SEC has also focused on cybersecurity risk issues for registered investment advisers, broker-dealers, and funds, including, for example data protection and identity theft vulnerabilities. In this area, the Commission adopted regulations, which requires certain regulated financial institutions and creditors to adopt and implement identity theft programs. Cybersecurity at SEC-registered entities has become an area of focus for the SEC inspections and enforcement division. SEC-registered firms should anticipate the SEC's increasing obligation to regulating cybersecurity. This means investigating data security incidents above all else, with independence and neutrality, a notion the SEC in particular respects and appreciates (Stark, 2016).

As an organization establishes its cybersecurity strategy, there are guiding principles that should be considered. The potential impact of cybercrime including the potential damage and the consequences of cyberattacks on an enterprise should be established. Furthermore, an entity should seek to understand end users, their cultural values, and their behavior patterns. This would allow for the assessment of the influence of these factors on an organization's strategic, tactical, and operational security measures. In addition, through this assessment a business case for cybersecurity, the associated risk appetite, the governance infrastructure, and a cost-benefit analysis based on risk and potential impact should be developed.

Cyber-breaches serve as a warning for executives to remain focused. When implementing the aforementioned guiding principles, discussions amongst executive members surrounding cyber-risk should include the identification of which risks to avoid, accept, mitigate, or transfer through insurance, as well as specific plans associated with each approach. Furthermore, other areas of consideration may be assessed as outlined in Table 5.4.

As mentioned previously, it is essential for entities to improve their cybersecurity and reduce any related risk. Areas that companies should focus on to facilitate the development of an effective cybersecurity strategy include

1. Understanding and evaluating the critical business operations and systems and the possible cybersecurity risks. This includes identifying the acceptable level of risk and the various areas of investment that may be required to mitigate cybersecurity risk (Sharma, n.d.).

Table 5.4 Key Areas for Cybersecurity Consideration in Corporations

Key Area	Items of Consideration
Security framework	Assess if the organization utilizes a security framework such as the Control Objectives for Information and Related Technology framework.
Top risks	Identify the top risks that may affect the organization as it relates to cybersecurity. Instances of potential areas of risk include disaster recovery and business continuity and user access.
Security awareness	Examine employee roles relating to cybersecurity. For instance, check if a security-awareness training program and an annual test have been implemented.
External and internal threats	Investigate any external and internal threats when planning cybersecurity program activities.
Security governance	Validate if appropriate security governance has been established within the organization. It is vital for the executive team to understand how the governance activities of the IT department complement those of Internal Audit.
Response protocol	Ensure that management has developed a robust response protocol in the event of a serious security breach.
Involvement of Board of Directors (BoD)	Engage with the BoD. The BoD should examine the organization's data management policy on a periodic basis. For instance, the BoD may consider the following suggestions: • Policies on cybersecurity and the procedures established to monitor compliance should be examined on a periodic basis, • The BoD and key executives should obtain training on cybersecurity issues, • The BoD should consider whether a committee should be established to assist with the oversight of cybersecurity, and • Given the potential risk exposure, the BoD should work with the general counsel to determine the extent to which existing insurance coverage provides protection.

2. Integrating cybersecurity strategy across personnel in various lines of services such as information technology, finance, operations, and physical security. An effective cybersecurity strategy must work across an organization's security measures (Sharma, n.d.).

3. Establishing preventive and detective controls to deter possible threat. This approach also assists companies to address the threat of employees perpetrating or facilitating an attack (Sharma, n.d.).
4. Accepting that some attacks will breach an entity's security measures (Sharma, n.d.).

Within companies, it is imperative to assess level of readiness with regard to a number of components. Data classification can be defined as a device for categorization of data to help companies identify the data types available within their business and their location. This will allow entities to assess the access levels that have been implemented over sensitive data and to ensure that there is appropriate security over these critical data sources. The utilization of a data classification process will also assist an entity to determine the time and cost required to secure the most critical information assets of the organization. This will guide managerial decisions to facilitate effective security expenditures based on the business value of the data that is being protected. Data has value, either by the creation of competitive advantage or the costs related with unauthorized disclosure of that data. An effective data classification initiative will determine the intrinsic value of an entity's data framework.

Data analytics assists entities with the creation of a single-screen dashboard that can assist a business prepare a snapshot of a company's firm-wide information security environment including key cybersecurity indicators. An information security dashboard can be personalized to show data in a form that is easy to comprehend (Dr. Ramon Barquin, 2012). As such, an IT manager's job may become easier with such a tool. The utilization of the above-described dashboard can effectively guide the decisions of the Board of Directors and key management in the organization.

When dealing in the cybersecurity domain, it is necessary to keep data on the types of attacks, the malware, and the categories of hackers. Information such as the URLs of both the attackers and the attacked, and the time of the incident will allow management to perform analysis on this data to attain valuable business intelligence (Barquin, 2012).

Cybersecurity controls go beyond IT General Controls which includes change management and user access reviews. As such entities should seek to implement a cybersecurity control framework such as ISO 27001 or SANS Critical Security Controls. ISO 27001 is a specification for an information security management system. The ISO standard sets out the process that an organization should follow when managing information security. On the other hand, the SANS Institute prioritizes security functions with an emphasis on "What Works" and defines the top 20 control areas for enhancing cybersecurity. On a periodic basis, an entity should assess their security controls to attain assurance over cybersecurity control effectiveness. The process includes defining the actions a business should follow when developing the plan. A cybersecurity response plan includes critical events such as:

- Identifying the key contact personnel in the event of a cybersecurity breach.
- Establishing a response team of team members from various key business units. This would aid in ensuring that decisions affecting key business processes within the entity are considered during a cybersecurity attack.
- Implementing protocols to detect, monitor, and track intruder activity. This should also include establishing procedures to prevent and reduce cyberattacks.
- Notifying key stakeholders such as the Board of Directors, regulatory bodies, legal authorities, and possibly security forces.
- Estimating the extent of the compromise, to facilitate discussions with legal counsel and insurance carriers.
- Analyzing root cause and implementing security remediation. Remediation may include performing periodic simulations to ensure that an entity is able to respond to cybersecurity breaches within an effective and efficient manner.

As mentioned earlier, high-profile cyberattacks demonstrate that companies suffer breaches even though they have comprehensive security processes in place. As such it is imperative that companies understand their financial exposure relative to a compromised dataset. This will allow an entity to evaluate the effectiveness of its cybersecurity process and choose whether to accept, mitigate, or reduce that risk possibly through a cyber-liability policy. American International Group has recently commenced offering cyber security insurance plans to individuals. This demonstrates that cyber security risk has escalated and is not only an issue for companies but also individuals (Baker Tilly, 2014).

According to State of Cybersecurity, Implications for 2016—An ISACA and RSA Conference Survey, cybersecurity threats continue to affect enterprises. Seventy-four percent of participants anticipate to be impacted by a cyberattack in 2016 (ISACA and RSA, 2016). However, respondents appeared to have an understanding that cybersecurity incidents could have a significant impact on a business. Executives should, therefore, be aware of the looming threats that exist in the cyberworld. Global corporations should be better prepared to look at cybersecurity as a business issue and should seek to manage cybersecurity and create comprehensive policies to proactively address risk in both domestic and international fronts. Businesses must assiduously manage cybersecurity due to the importance of business intelligence in the modern world including creating wide-ranging policies to address risk for 2017 and beyond. Some of the key takeaway messages are as follows:

- Information Technology (IT) risks such as access, availability, and integrity. Management needs to utilize Business Intelligence to analyze data and minimize the aforementioned risks. This would aid to prevent or detect cybercrime more efficiently and effectively.
- There have been numerous cyberattacks. For instance users of WhatsApp have been impacted by a cyberattack that compromised their personal data.
- The utilization of business intelligence in the modern world may assist an entity to understand trends based on analyzing data from their security systems. An understanding of vulnerabilities may assist an entity to prepare the company to design appropriate cybersecurity policies.
- The Board of Directors should examine the organization's data management policy on a periodic basis.

The combination of business intelligence and cybersecurity has proven to aid organizations managing cybersecurity risk as entities have now started to incorporate such dashboards into their boardroom meetings. Each organization is a distinctive entity with unique metrics and indicators. As such the utilization of cybersecurity dashboards is the key to data business intelligence (Barquin, 2012).

References

Baker Tilly. (2014, November 30). *Implementing an Effective Cybersecurity Management Program.* Accessed March 30, 2017. Available from: www.bakertilly.com/insights/implementing-an-effective-cybersecurity-management-program/

Beckham, J. (2011, May 3). *Small Business—The Top 5 Security Risks of Cloud Computing.* Cisco Blogs. Accessed March 30, 2017. Available from: http://blogs.cisco.com/smallbusiness/the-top-5-security-risks-of-cloud-computing

DeMers, J. (2014, August 11). Entrepreneurs. *Forbes.* Accessed March 30, 2017. Available from: www.forbes.com/sites/jaysondemers/2014/08/11/the-top-10-benefits-of-social-media-marketing/#232cb4392a4d

Eyewitness News. (2017, April 3). Accessed March 30, 2017. Available from: http://ewn.co.za/2017/04/03/coe-apologises-after-iaaf-suffers-cyber-attack

FBI. (n.d.). *FBI.* Accessed March 30, 2017. Available from: www.fbi.gov/

(IIA), T.I. (2014). Pulse of the profession 2014. In *IIA's Audit Executive Center "Pulse of the Profession 2014."* Accessed October 17, 2017. Available from: https://www.theiia.org/centers/aec/Pages/2014-global-pulse-of-internal-audit.aspx

ISACA and RSA. (2016, March). *State of Cybersecurity Implications for 2016.* ISACA. Accessed March 30, 2017. Available from: https://cybersecurity.isaca.org/csx-resources/state-of-cybersecurity-implications-for-2016

The Japan Times. (2016, February 27). U.S. studying sophisticated cyber attack on Ukraine power grid. Accessed March 30, 2017. Available from: www.japantimes.

co.jp/news/2016/02/27/business/tech/u-s-studying-sophisticated-cyberattack-ukraine-power-grid/#.WMV639LbKUk

PwC. (2016). *Global Economic Crime Survey 2016*. PwC Global. Accessed March 30, 2017. Available from: www.pwc.com/gx/en/services/advisory/forensics/economic-crime-survey/cybercrime.html

Queensland Government. (2016, May 4). *Cloud Computing for Business*. Accessed March 30, 2017. Available from: www.business.qld.gov.au/business/running/technology-for-business/cloud-computing-business/cloud-computing-benefits

Radak, D. (2017, May 19). *How Business Intelligence Affects Cyber Security?* My Digital Shield. Accessed March 30, 2017. Available from: www.my digitalshield.com/business-intelligence-affects-cyber-security/

Ramon Barquin, S. G. (2012, July 17). *Cybersecurity: The Role for Data Analytics*. Beye Network. Accessed March 30, 2017. Available from: www.b-eye-network.com/view/16206

Roth, A., Stefanak, C., Van Dorn, W., and Walker, J. (2014, May 13). *United States: SEC (OCIE) Cybersecurity Initiative*. Mondaq. Accessed March 30, 2017. Available from: www.mondaq.com/unitedstates/x/313100/Securities/SEC+OCIE+Cyb ersecurity+Initiative

Sharma, N. N. (n.d.). *Helping Organisations to Develop an Effective Cyber Security Strategy*. Paconsulting.com. Accessed March 30, 2017. Available from: www.paconsulting.com/insights/developing-an-effective-cyber-security-strategy/

Siciliano, R. (2014, February 24). *The Blog*. The Huffington Post. Accessed March 30, 2017. Available from: www.huffingtonpost.com/robert-siciliano/7-small-business-social-m_b_4846083.html

Stanier, D. N. (2016). Measuring the success of changes to existing business intelligence solutions to improve business intelligence reporting. *Lecture Notes in Business Information Processing*. Basel, Switzerland: Springer International Publishing.

Stark, J. (2016, June 14). *LinkedIn*. Accessed March 30, 2017. Available from: www.linkedin.com/pulse/key-takeaways-from-sec-morgan-stanley-cybersecurity-action-stark

Szoldra, P. (2015, December 29). *Business Insider*. Tech Insider. Accessed March 30, 2017. Available from: www.techinsider.io/cyberattacks-2015-12

Appendix 5.1

Key Considerations for the Board of Directors, the Audit Committee, and Other Executives

Areas of consideration	Illustrative responses
Whether a security framework has been established	For example ISO 27001 or COBIT framework (Governance, Risk, and Control).
Risks within the entity that may be related to cybersecurity	Instances of potential areas of risk include unauthorized program changes, changes to user access, the inability of the company to resume operations upon a disaster due to poor disaster recovery, business continuity procedures, and changes to audit logs that reduces an entity's ability to detect compromise of data. Furthermore sensitive client data or financial data may be compromised.
The basis on which employees are made aware of their role related to cybersecurity	Security awareness training program may be conducted upon employment and an ongoing basis. Furthermore team members may be required to complete a periodic test to assess their knowledge of cybersecurity, the associated risks, and potential responses to attacks.
Determining whether potential threats are considered when planning cybersecurity program activities	This could be included as a standard agenda item for discussion in management meetings. This should cover potential internal and external threats.
The understanding of the process of managing security governance within the organization	In response to cybersecurity, it is important for the Board of Directors and the Audit Committee to understand how the governance activities of the IT department complement those of internal audit and other key functions.
Whether management has developed a robust response protocol, in the event of a serious breach	This should also be another area of discussion at meetings of executives to confirm whether a response protocol has been established. In addition, management should be encouraged to perform periodic simulations to test the adequacy of the response protocol.

(Continued)

(*Continued*)

Areas of consideration	Illustrative responses
Whether measures have been established in the event of a cybersecurity attack	A number of measures should be established in the event of a cyberattack. Often times, cyberattacks may result in the loss of mission critical data. As such it is important to have backup management processes for data and systems. In addition other items of consideration should include • utilization of antivirus software—to mitigate the possibility of viruses affecting a company's network, • implementation of strong passwords on systems and portals—to reduce the extent of compromise of systems once a hacker accesses a company's IT infrastructure, • enforcement of secure connections to access company resources, • periodic review of security settings on computers and firewalls.
Ways to reduce cybersecurity attacks	• disable remote connectivity, • consider encrypting websites using Secure socket layer to encrypt data, • read privacy policy before submitting data over the Internet.

Case Study

Description of control/issue	Does this pose a cybersecurity risk?	Mitigating controls that may need to be implemented
CyberStars has a Chief Information Officer that has overall responsibility for information security within the organization.		
There is no comprehensive Information Technology Policy. A draft policy has been established and is currently stored on an unsecured drive.		
Security configurations have been documented for all critical systems and are kept on the Intranet.		
Access to mission critical applications, databases, and operating systems is restricted to IT security personnel.		

Description of control/issue	Does this pose a cybersecurity risk?	Mitigating controls that may need to be implemented
Employees do not receive training on cloud computing, social networking, and general security matters when hired.		
Tools are available for manipulating data and use of the tool is not closely controlled.		
Initial access to the operating systems is granted based on an employee's job title and department.		
Sensitive access must be approved by the Chief Security Officer. There are however no periodic user access reviews.		
On a periodic basis, IT receives a notification from the Human Resources department of all terminations. This allows the IT personnel to disable user accounts and physical access cards within three weeks of notification.		
Segregation of duties are enforced through roles and responsibilities and logical access.		
All facility doors and data center doors are secured by a keycard access system.		
Data center access request forms must be completed and approved by the Chief Security Officer.		

Part II

Managing Business Intelligence

6 Data Visualization in Business Intelligence

Jack G. Zheng

Introduction

Business Intelligence (BI) is a set of methods, processes, architectures, applications, and technologies that gather and transform raw data into meaningful and useful information used to enable more effective strategic, tactical, and operational insights and decision-making to drive business performance (Evelson and Nicolson, 2008). A general BI process covers a number of sub-processes or phases including data gathering, data cleanse, data storage, data analysis, data presentation and delivery (Zheng, Zhang, and Li, 2014). In the phase of data presentation, query or analysis results are presented and delivered in various human comprehendible formats (such as tables and charts) which directly supports sense-making and decision-making. Data presentation also includes interactive queries and data explorations that help users find useful information. Correspondingly in the technology stack, BI systems include various data visualization and interaction forms and techniques through reports (static and interactive reports), digital dashboards, and more complex analytical visual tools (Chiang, 2011).

Data visualization has been rising rapidly for the past a few years in the BI and analytics industry, as part of the modern BI movement which emphasizes on self-service (Parenteau et al., 2016). It is also a big part of data science which has gained wide popularity recently. There have a been a plethora of tools and systems that feature their data visualization solutions. As an interdisciplinary field, data visualization brings together psychology, technology, art, and decision science to deliver the last mile of the complete BI and analytics capability to users. Compared to other types and applications of visualization, business data visualization, particularly concerns about the visualization of business data, is mainly for the purpose of communication, information seeking, analysis, and decision support.

One of the key questions in business data visualization is how, and in what form, data visualization contributes to the overall business intelligence process and system. This chapter provides a comprehensive high-level view of different types of data visualizations that can be used in the business environment, and to provide a guidance of technology and system selection. The chapter starts with defining business data visualization and comparing it to other common types of visualizations and their applications, then provides a comprehensive review and analysis of common tools and applications of business data visualizations used in business intelligence, and concludes with a brief overview of recent trends and prospects.

Background

What Is Business Data Visualization?

The term "business" in "business data visualization," as well as in "business intelligence," has a broader meaning than just commercial activities. It generally refers to many human and organizational activities and operations that keep a system running. This can include commerce, education, sports, entertainment, government, and many others. In these business activities and processes, data are produced and recorded to reflect all aspects of the business (human or organizational activities), and then it is analyzed and reported at various levels. Business intelligence is about transforming raw data into meaningful and useful information that is consumed by humans. Business data or information is different from other types of data (Tegarden, 1999). In the context of business intelligence, business data has the following features:

- Abstract: most business data describes abstract activities and processes (e.g. product sales, member registration, product or user movement, etc.). The data does not describe or is not directly used to create real-life entities (objects, models) or phenomenon. The visual representation of this kind of data is also abstract by using metaphors.
- Quantitative: although qualitative data also offers great insights and has a lot of values today especially in the artificial intelligence discipline, quantitative data is the focus of business data. In many cases, qualitative data is quantified in business intelligence analysis and business data visualization.
- Structured or semi-structured: most data is structured and shares common attributes with clearly defined metadata.
- Multidimensional: facts or measures can be viewed and analyzed through different perspectives and levels. This is particularly common in business analysis.
- Atomic: most business activities are based on business transactions; each raw data record represents a transaction and can be viewed and understood independently.
- Comprehendible: data and results can be directly understood by human users (assuming with domain knowledge) in a short time.

The BI process typically consists of data management (also including data gathering, cleanse, storage), data analysis, and data presentation. The term data presentation describes the interfacing layer between data and human. In this layer, data (can be raw, aggregated, or any types of analysis results) are presented to users in their desired forms and formats. In the statistics discipline, the three basic categories of data presentation are commonly summarized as textual, tabular, and graphical. These categories can also apply to BI data presentation methods. Data visualization is the graphical or visual method of presenting data. In the context of business intelligence, it can also be called business data visualization or business information visualization to distinguish other types of visualization.

In general, visualization is the process of forming a concrete and direct vision-perceivable image in a human mind by utilizing a combination of visual elements (shapes) and variables like color, positions, etc. Things that can be visualized include visible reality that people can see (person, world, nature), hidden reality that normally be hidden (earth core, blood, universe), invisible reality (wind, air, heat, electron, sound, smell), and abstract things (data, idea, hierarchy, process, relationship).

Data visualization is the visual and interactive exploration and graphic representation of data of any size, type (structured and unstructured) or origin. The purposes of visualizing data are multifold, ranging from general comprehension and understanding of ideas, supporting information behaviors (analysis and decision support, information seeking, browsing, navigation), to artistic (beauty) expression and appreciation (Viégas and Wattenberg, 2007), and even just for fun or storytelling. In contrast, the goals of visualizing business data are focused on human information seeking and decision-making behaviors, particularly in two broad goals: (a) visualizing key metrics for easy and fast comprehension which directly facilitates decision-making; (b) providing a visual and interactive way to explore data. Such visualizations often use simple, standard, and abstract charts or diagrams, and utilize data binding techniques at the back end.

Both research and practices have shown data visualization's value and contribution to the decision process (Vessey, 1991) and information-seeking process (Shneiderman, 1996). Visualization generally helps data comprehension and enhances problem-solving capabilities. More specifically:

- Visualization eases the cognitive load of information processing, and it helps one recall or memorize data easily because of the perceivable image (Borkin et al., 2013).
- Data visualization techniques provide a visual overview of complex data sets to identify patterns, structures, relationships, and trends at a high level.
- Visualizations provide visual cues that draw people's attention to quickly focus on areas of interest or areas of difference (can be an anomaly). This allows decision makers to use their natural spatial/visual abilities

to determine where further exploration should be done (Tegarden, 1999).

• Visualization exploits the human visual system to extract additional (implicit) information and meaning, sometimes referred to as intuition.

Business Data Visualization vs. Other Types of Visualization

Business data visualization has some unique features compared to some related fields or methods that also utilize general visualization techniques. These related fields or methods mainly include: information visualization, illustration, scientific visualization (discussed together with computer graphics and VR), and simulation. Their differences can be best illustrated in their content (what is to be visualized), visual forms/tools (how they are visualized), and purposes. The comparison is summarized in Table 6.1.

Information visualization is a very close field to data visualization. In fact, the term is often used as the synonym to data visualization if data is used in a more general sense (in contrast to business data). They share many common features, principles, and methods. However, information can be generally more qualitative and less structured, for example, information about workflows, structures, concepts, and ideas. The visualization of information utilizes more free forms of visual diagrams or illustrations

Table 6.1 Comparison of Related Visualization Fields

	Content	Visual Forms/Tools	Purpose
Business data visualization	Quantitative data, metrics, key performance indicators (KPIs)	Charts, diagrams, dashboards	Data exploration, analysis, decision-making
Information visualization	All kinds of information, quantitative and qualitative	Infographics, illustrational diagrams	Information seeking, artistic illustration, casual communication, storytelling
Illustration	Processes, structures concepts, ideas	Diagram, image, graphics	Making the content more vivid and engaging, easier to understand the complexity
Scientific visualization	Real-world object or phenomenon, mathematical functions and formulas	Computer-generated graphics, 3D virtual reality	Recreate or simulate the real-world object or phenomenon, or visualize an algorithm effect
Simulation	Calculated data based on formulas or rules	Animated diagram or virtual reality	Demonstrate the effect of scenarios under certain rules

(illustrational diagrams) that are not specifically for quantitative data, for example, network graphs and workflow charts.

Information graphics or infographics are a common tool for information visualization especially in a more casual context. An infographic is commonly a mixture of different forms of information (text and numbers) and multiple visual forms (charts, diagrams, images, tables, maps, lists, etc.) to quickly and vividly communicate a good amount of information in an engaging manner (Harrison, Reinecke, and Chang, 2015). Many infographics have a typical format characterized by large typography and long vertical orientation (Lankow, Ritchie, and Crooks, 2012). They are gaining popularity in online marketing over the years and their use has expanded in many occasions where communication to the public is important. Some examples can be found at dailyinfographic.com and cooldaily-infographics.com.

Information visualization is more casual (Pousman, Stasko, and Mateas, 2007), general, and subjective than business data visualization whose purpose is more for decision support or data exploration. It is intended for a wider and casual audience with a focus on storytelling or narrative visualization (Segel and Heer, 2010). Because of this, information is presented with stronger artistic expression than that found in typical business data visualizations (Hagley, n.d.), sometimes with overuse of artistic design, often referred to as visual embellishment (Bateman et al., 2010).

Illustration, as a term, is a little different than visualization. Illustration often is used to explain ideas or concepts with the help of diagrams or even general pictures and graphs. It materializes abstract ideas using more concrete and directly perceivable images for explanation, or uses simplified diagrams for explaining more complex situations (processes or structures). Most importantly in the context of business, illustrations are not necessarily data driven.

Scientific visualization, commonly used in science, is "primarily concern[ed] with the visualization of three-dimensional phenomena (architectural, meteorological, medical, biological, etc.), where the emphasis is on realistic renderings of volumes, surfaces, illumination sources, and so forth" (Friendly and Denis, 2006). Examples include physical science visualization, visualization (simulation) of reality (universe, sun, explosion, atom, climate, etc.), and mathematical model/algorithm visualization. The visual output can be a virtual replica creation based on real data, or computer-generated data based on algorithms and imaginary creation. Scientific visualizations often make use of computer graphics and virtual reality technologies to recreate the visual scene.

Simulation is somewhat related to scientific visualization and is specifically used to demonstrate motion-based visuals. It can utilize complex computer graphics to generate realistic scenarios. On the other hand, it also can create simple scenarios using animated diagrams or simple graphics (e.g. http://setosa.io/bus/).

Business Data Visualization Forms

With the increasing recognition of data visualization's roles and values in a business intelligence system, tools and applications that specifically target business data visualization solutions have become widely available. This section will review some most common types of data visualization forms and tools used in BI.

Categorizing Business Data Visualization Forms

Typically, BI results are presented in the form of reports, dashboards, and analytical tools. Among these, dashboards are mostly data visualization driven. Reports are traditionally static and non-interactive, and they present more detailed data. Modern reports add a lot of elements of visualization (either embedded visuals or charts/diagrams) and interaction, which enhance reports' readability. Analytical tools are also becoming more visually oriented. Some analytical tools, labeled as visual analytical tools (or analytical dashboards), are also driven by visualizations.

There are several commonly used visualization forms and tools in BI reporting and analytics. There are three basic categories of visual forms based on how visualizations are presented on screen: embedded visuals, block visuals, and standalone visuals. Table 6.2 summarizes features and examples of each one.

Table 6.2 Common Forms of Business Data Visualization

Form/Style	Description	Typical Types and Examples
Embedded visual	It is embedded in, or directly on top of, texts and other forms of data presentation (tables, graphics, etc.).	• Conditional formatting • Inline chart (Sparkline)
Block visual	It is displayed as an independent visual unit and occupies a larger space. It is often a part of a report or dashboard, appearing together with other content. But sometimes it can become a standalone visual with many data points or enough complexity.	• Chart • Illustrational diagram • Map (smaller) • Data table (usually with embedded visuals)
Standalone visual	It is a standalone application and is not mixed with other types of content or tools. Most interactions are within the visual. It may consist of a combination of different types of visuals.	• Dashboard • Visual analysis tool (or an analytical dashboard) • Map (bigger or full screen)

Embedded Visuals

Embedded visuals are visual effects embedded in another form of presentation. They are not independently presented but always used on top of other presentation forms. Embedded visuals include two major forms: conditional formatting and inline mini charts (or Sparkline).

Conditional formatting refers to the direct formatting or styling of text, numbers, shapes, and other contents utilizing visual variables like color, size, etc. (Bertin, 2010). Conditional formatting does not significantly change the layout and flow of contents, thus it is less intrusive to the content. Instead, it provides a decorative effect that reveals more meaning or highlights selected content from the data or text.

A Sparkline is a small minimized chart embedded in the context of text paragraphs, tables, images, or other type of information. It presents the general data pattern (variation, trends, differentiations, etc.) in a simple and highly condensed way (Tufte, 2006). Interpretive and supporting information like title, label, data point, legend, are omitted from the chart. A miniature line chart (hence called Sparkline) is most commonly used, but it can be of other chart types, including bar charts, bullet graphs, etc.

Charts and Diagrams

A block visual occupies a larger space but still part of a report or dashboard, appearing together with other content. It is a more independent and self-contained visual unit. Sometimes it can become a standalone visual if there are many data points or enough visual and interaction complexity. Charts and diagrams are the two most common forms of block visuals.

Charts are a visual combination of symbols (visual elements of point, line, and area) and visual variables (color, shape, size, etc.) which are directly associated with data. The terms of chart and diagram can sometimes be used interchangeably without any explicit differences. More often, diagrams are considered to include charts. In the context of business data visualization, a chart is more abstract and focuses on visualizing quantitative values (e.g. business performance measures and indicators), while a diagram can also visualize qualitative information as well to illustrate structures, relationships, sequences, etc. Charts and diagrams are the major forms of business data visualizations used in BI. They are the fundamental piece to present data in many reports and presentations.

Basic types of charts include line charts, bar charts, pie charts, etc., and examples of diagrams include organization structure diagrams, tree diagrams, network diagrams, workflows diagrams, etc. Abela (2008) provides a basic categorization of charts by purpose; the visual guide has been widely used for guiding chart choices (Table 6.3). Another purpose, profiling, is also added to the table for a more complete comparison. Profiling can be seen as a special case of comparison among multiple data items.

Table 6.3 Chart Chooser by Abela (2008)

Purpose	Meaning	Example Charts
Comparison	Comparing and sorting data points	Bar/column chart, line chart, radar chart
Composition	Showing part-to-whole comparisons	Stacked column/area chart, pie chart
Distribution	Aggregated value (usually count) of data points placed in categories; the category can be value ranges or time (trend)	Histogram, scatter plot, bubble chart
Relationship	How things (data items) are related or positioned in a bigger context	Scatter plot, bubble chart
Profiling*	Comprehending things through visual shapes and patterns	Radar chart, parallel coordinates

* Added by the author to enhance Abela's version

Other more specific types of charts are used in different business contexts for more specific purposes. These charts are based on the more generic chart types like bar charts and line charts, and add more specific visual elements, or arrange the elements in a specific way to represent domain-specific meanings. For example, bullet charts (based on bar charts) are used in performance measuring; perceptual maps (based on scatter plots) are used in marketing; waterfall or bridge charts (based on column charts) are used in driving factor analysis; Gantt charts (based on data tables and bar charts) are used in project management; funnel charts are used in sales; candlestick charts are used in stock technical analysis.

Location-Based Visuals

Location as a dimension plays an important role in many areas of business data analysis and decision-making. Many business activities are associated with locations. It has been gaining increased attention especially with the wide adoption of location sensors (like GPS and other location capture technologies) which generate location data. Location-based visuals, commonly based on a map, provide a background or a context that is familiar to the users and make the location-related data more comprehendible and perceivable. A 2015 yearly survey (Dresner, 2015) finds

> map-based visualization of information as the top priority, and more than 95 percent of respondents rank it as at least somewhat important. More than 60 percent report that the functionality for layered visualizations is "very important" or "critical" for their organization.

The location-based visuals involve three basic factors: type of location data, visual forms, data points representation on the map.

The types of location data are directly associated with a business and its analysis. One major type of location data is geo locations that come with real-world maps. Many places and regions are based on geospatial mapping, such as political regions (country, state, city, etc.), various types of real estate properties or areas (park, campus, road), or any other arbitrary locations determined by businesses (postal ZIP area, sales region, service district). A second type of location data is local contextual locations which do not directly rely on geo coordinates. These locations are relative locations within in a confined area, such as inside a park, campus, building, room, court, bus/subway line, or even as small region such as a shelf, body, etc. For example, many sports-related analytics analyze the data related to locations on playing fields; stadium and airlines analyze seating data which relates to locations; mall, hospitals, universities, and apartments analyze room/facility usages which are also related to locations. The last type of locations is associated with more abstract ideas like processes, computer networks, organization structures, etc. These abstract locations can also be visualized on an abstract map (or more like an illustration diagram).

The visualization forms for location data is how the background layer of the map is presented. There are two broad categories: (a) real-world maps are used as the background layer, then points, paths, and areas are displayed accurately or closely proximate to the background (Figure 6.1a); (b) a more abstract map (either geo location or non-geo location), sometimes just an illustrational diagram, is used as the background layer, and positioning of objects are based on relative position (e.g. X/Y coordinates) in the map context. The positions or areas on the map are for illustration purpose only, and not corresponding to their real-world locations or sizes (Figure 6.1b).

Figure 6.1b shows a type of abstract map called tile grid map (Shaw, 2016). Tile grid maps abstractly use similar-sized tiles to represent geo regions with irregular sizes. It has several visual advantages in some cases when location precision is not important:

- Eliminate map distortions on some real-world map projections. For example, avoid the Alaska effect on US maps (Taylor, 2017).
- Provide a more consistent view of places of irregular shape and different sizes. In some cases, it makes smaller areas more visible.
- Provide a more modern and consistent look and feel.

Dashboards

Standalone visuals are more like applications than visualizations. They occupy even larger space or even full screens. They also contain multiple types of content as well as interaction controls. A digital dashboard is a major type of standalone visual. A dashboard is "a visual display of the

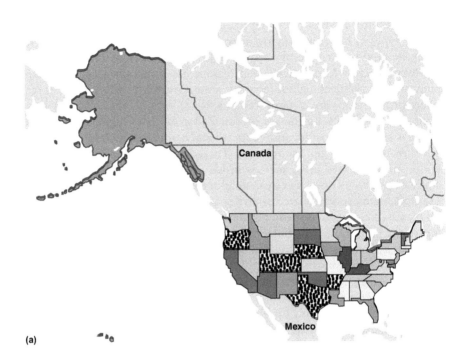

(a)

(b)

Figure 6.1 Business Measures Visualized on Maps
Source: created following Taylor, 2017

most important information needed to achieve one or more objectives; consolidated and arranged on a single screen so the information can be monitored at a glance" (Few, 2004). The term dashboard originally came from operational status monitoring on machines which provides visual display for quick reading. Its use has been expanded to visualization of digital data associated with business performance on screens. A dashboard (at the front end) is basically an integrated application of data (content), visual views, and user interface/interaction (UI).

$$Dashboard = Data + Visualization + UI$$

The data on the dashboards primarily consists of metrics, Key Performance Indicators (KPIs), and textual information. Metrics (or measures, indicators) are numerical values that measure various aspects of the business activities. A KPI is a metric that compares to its target (goal) and other comparable benchmarks (performance intervals, historical periods, or industry averages) (Barr, 2009). KPIs are used intensively in performance-focused dashboards. Other common data on a dashboard include a set of values to reflect history, trends, distributions, breakdowns, forecasts, or other kinds of comparisons and relationships. Textual information is not typically on many dashboards but it can be included depending on the purpose of the dashboard.

The data on the dashboard are presented via a variety of views or visualization forms discussed earlier, including charts, diagrams, tables (with conditional formatting or other embedded visuals), and styled standalone numbers (usually KPIs).

Last, a dashboard is a business application with a rich user interface for users to interact with data. The key UI elements considered in dashboard include layout (arrangements of data and visualizations, following human information behavior best practices), overall formatting/styling components (which can be visuals themselves) such as title and background, and user interaction controls such as command buttons and navigational controls (menus, tabs).

Traditional BI reports contain detailed data in a tabular format (or pivot tables) and typically display numbers and text only. The two main purposes of reports are printing (with styling) and exporting (raw data). It is geared towards people who need detailed data rather than direct analysis and understanding of data. Modern BI reports can be interactive and visual, but the focus is still on presenting detailed data. The distinction is a bit blurred between reports and dashboards in some practical cases. For example, the IT spending dashboard (www.itdashboard.gov/drupal/summary/006i) is more like a report (a visual-intensive interactive report).

Compare to reports, dashboards are more focused on data visualizations arranged in a single screen, or with limited scrolling and panning. Textual information and detailed data tables can be part of a dashboard only if they are necessary and important to user needs. Even so, it is better to present detailed data through interactive means like pop-ups, tooltips, or in separate screens via details-on-demand designs (Shneiderman, 1996).

A well-designed dashboard allows decision makers to see the most relevant data that reflects business status and supports decisions. It is a highly summarized and centralized snapshot that saves a user's time by eliminating the need to run multiple reports or get data through different sources. It should allow the user to quickly understand data and respond promptly at one place (bidashboard.org, n.d.).

As the use of dashboards grew, they have expanded into three basic types of dashboard: overview, operational, and analytical. Each of them share common attributes of dashboards (data + visualization + UI), but each of them has some different purpose, data, and design best practices. Operational dashboards display data that facilitate the operational side of a business, monitoring operational activities and statuses as they are happening. They provide views of important operational indicators, often based on real-time or near real-time data; they focus on current performance and are action-oriented. Summary/overview dashboards provide high-level summary of business performance represented by KPIs. A strategic dashboard is a typical example of a summary/overview dashboard at the strategic or executive level, which specifically concerns the state of the overall business against strategy goals.

Analytical dashboards, or visual analysis tools, focus on interactive exploration or analysis (visual analysis) of a large amount of data. They allow users to investigate trends, predict outcomes, and discover insights. This kind of use is a bit different from traditional dashboards, which are primarily used for quick scanning and understating of key metrics. Some people specifically categorizes them as "visual analysis tools" (Chiang, 2011) rather than a type of dashboard. Nonetheless, the design of analytical dashboards is similar to general dashboards with a focus on data, visualization, and UI design. Analytical dashboards usually visualize patterns, trends, and other complex relationships among a large amount of data, without a significant focus on a few metrics. The purpose is to explore data and analyze patterns through an interactive process. They contain abundant parameter settings, selections, filters, and other controls to manipulate the main visualization. The main visualization is usually a single (or very few) visual component that occupies a big portion of the screen as the main UI component, with a large number of data points displayed on it. Users' major activity will be repeatedly setting parameters and examining the generated visuals. This type of dashboard often supports ad hoc querying, dynamic visualization generation, common OLAP operations like drill down. It is primarily used for intensive data exploration or analysis, used by data analysts and researchers.

Trends and Prospects

Data visualization has been one of the growing forces driving the BI industry. As an important part of modern BI systems and platforms, business data visualization closely follows or even impacts the general BI and analytics trends. Some of the notable trends are presented below.

Personal or self-service BI: Self-service BI features control in the hands of users, especially power users. This group of people is highly skilled in using technology applications in business tasks, and they often need instant results. They are able to use computer tools and languages to get what they want with little assistance from their IT departments. Some of the tools like Tableau and Power BI have quickly risen to satisfy this need using a visualization-driven approach and gained wide recognition (Sallam, 2017).

Embedded BI: Personal BI tools are usually standalone tools which need a separate data connection or import process. Embedded BI emphasizes the analytics and data presentation as an integral part of an application, instead of using an independent tool or system. Embedded BI or visualization has an advantage in local data modeling and integration, thus delivers standard reports and dashboards in a more efficient way to satisfy the most common needs. The analytics component has become a competitive component of many business systems. However, in many systems, the module is often seen as a separate module which requires businesses to pay separately (for example, Brightspace Insights).

Mobile BI: Mobile computing also drives the evolvement of BI and data visualization to be more accessible and usable on multiple devices with different screen sizes and interaction techniques. Although not typically for mobile phones, access to dashboards though tablets or tablet-like devices is increasing in many business environments where people move around regularly, such as sales, field support, sports, and hospitals. The major influence from mobile computing is the interaction method of touch-oriented interfaces, which requires some new design principles and best practices on dashboard interactions.

The job market and career development related to data analysis and visualization have seen an increasing demand over recent years. Preferably, data visualization development requires skills from a number of fields, including information design, UI design, human information behavior and cognition, interaction design, artistic design, programming, data processing, and business domain knowledge. The demand for multi-skill and interdisciplinary experience will continue to grow.

Conclusion

The shifting focus on end users with better and more effective data presentation and visualization is a global phenomenon. Business data visualization has an increasing importance in the complete BI process and is becoming an integral part of any BI system. Various forms of data visualization, each with their unique features, help BI users and decision makers at different levels from different perspectives. BI managers and developers should understand their features, strengths and weakness, and use them together to create a good mix that satisfies different types of users with different needs. This chapter provides a comprehensive review of these visualization forms and tools, which will help BI managers, decision makers, analysts, and developers better select and utilize them. The perception of visualization is common across all cultures and business environment, but the meaning delivered through visualizations may be affected by a number of factors like color and orientation. Adapting data visualization solutions in local culture is also important in the global business environment.

References

Abela, A. (2008). *Advanced Presentations By Design: Creating Communication that Drives Action* (1st ed.). San Francisco: Pfeiffer. Available from: https://extremepresentation.com/design/7-charts/

Barr, S. (2009, November 23). *What Does "KPI" Really Mean?* Dashboard Insight. Available from: www.dashboardinsight.com/articles/digital-dashboards/fundamentals/what-does-kpi-really-mean.aspx

Bateman, S., Mandryk, R. L., Gutwin, C., Genest, A., McDine, D., and Brooks, C. (2010). Useful junk? The effects of visual embellishment on comprehension and memorability of charts. In *Proceedings of the SIGCHI Conference on Human Factors in Computing Systems* (pp. 2573–2582). New York, NY: ACM. Available from: https://doi.org/10.1145/1753326.1753716

Bertin, J. (2010). *Semiology of Graphics: Diagrams, Networks, Maps* (1st ed.). Redlands, CA: Esri Press.

bidashboard.org. (n.d.). *Dashboards Benefits.* Accessed July 10, 2017. Available from: www.bidashboard.org/benefits.html

Borkin, M. A., Vo, A. A., Bylinskii, Z., Isola, P., Sunkavalli, S., Oliva, A., and Pfister, H. (2013). What makes a visualization memorable? *IEEE Transactions on Visualization and Computer Graphics*, 19(12), 2306–2315. Available from: https://doi.org/10.1109/TVCG.2013.234

Chiang, A. (2011, November 28). *What Is a Dashboard?* Accessed July 10, 2017. Available from: www.dashboardinsight.com/articles/digital-dashboards/fundamentals/what-is-a-dashboard.aspx

Dresner, H. (2015, May 25). *IoT and the Growing Use of Location Features in Business Intelligence Software.* Sand Hill. Available from: http://sandhill.com/article/iot-and-the-growing-use-of-location-features-in-business-intelligence-software/

Evelson, B. and Nicolson, N. (2008). *Topic Overview: Business Intelligence—An Information Workplace Report.* Forrester. Available from: www.forrester.com/report/Topic+Overview+Business+Intelligence/-/E-RES39218

Few, S. (2004, March 20). *Dashboard Confusion.* Retrieved July 10, 2017, from www.perceptualedge.com/articles/ie/dashboard_confusion.pdf

Friendly, M. and Denis, D. (2006). *Milestones in the History of Thematic Cartography, Statistical Graphics, and Data Visualization.*

Hagley, J. (n.d.). *What's the Difference Between an Infographic and a Data Visualization.* Accessed July 10, 2017. Available from: www.jackhagley.com/What-s-the-difference-between-an-Infographic-and-a-Data-Visualisation

Harrison, L., Reinecke, K., and Chang, R. (2015). Infographic aesthetics: Designing for the first impression. In *Proceedings of the 33rd Annual ACM Conference on Human Factors in Computing Systems* (pp. 1187–1190). New York, NY: ACM. Available from: https://doi.org/10.1145/2702123.2702545

Lankow, J., Ritchie, J., and Crooks, R. (2012). *Infographics: The Power of Visual Storytelling.* Hoboken, NJ: Wiley.

Parenteau, J., Sallam, R.L., Howson, C., Tapadinhas, J., Schlegel, K., and Oestreich, T. W. (2016). *Magic Quadrant for Business Intelligence and Analytics Platforms*. Available from: http://get.tableau.com/gartner-magic-quadrant-2016.html

Pousman, Z., Stasko, J., and Mateas, M. (2007). Casual information visualization: Depictions of data in everyday life. *IEEE Transactions on Visualization and Computer Graphics*, 13(6), 1145–1152. Available from: https://doi.org/10.1109/TVCG.2007.70541

Sallam, R. (2017, February 16). *Magic Quadrant for Business Intelligence and Analytics Platforms*. Accessed July 10, 2017. Available from: www.gartner.com/doc/3611117/magic-quadrant-business-intelligence-analytics

Segel, E. and Heer, J. (2010). Narrative visualization: Telling stories with data. *IEEE Transactions on Visualization and Computer Graphics*, 16(6), 1139–1148. Available from: https://doi.org/10.1109/TVCG.2010.179

Shaw, T. (2016, April 27). *Good Data Visualization Practice: Tile Grid Maps*. Accessed July 10, 2017. Available from: https://forumone.com/ideas/good-data-visualization-practice-tile-grid-maps-0

Shneiderman, B. (1996). The eyes have it: A task by data type taxonomy for information visualizations. In *IEEE Symposium on Visual Languages* (pp. 336–343).

Taylor, K. (2017, January 13). *Viz Variety Show: Use Hex-Tile Maps to Eliminate the Alaska Effect*. Accessed July 11, 2017. Available from: www.tableau.com/about/blog/2017/1/viz-whiz-hex-tile-maps-64713

Tegarden, D. P. (1999). Business information visualization. *Communications of the AIS*, 1(4), 1–38.

Tufte, E. R. (2006). *Beautiful Evidence* (1st ed.). Cheshire, CT: Graphics Press.

Vessey, I. (1991). Cognitive fit: A theory-based analysis of the graphs versus tables literature. *Decision Sciences*, 22(2), 219–241.

Viégas, F. B. and Wattenberg, M. (2007). Artistic data visualization: Beyond visual analytics. In *Proceedings of the 2nd International Conference on Online Communities and Social Computing* (pp. 182–191). Berlin, Heidelberg: Springer-Verlag. Available from http://dl.acm.org/citation.cfm?id=1784297.1784319

Zheng, G., Zhang, C., and Li, L. (2014). Bringing business intelligence to health information technology curriculum. *Journal of Information Systems Education*, 25(4), 317–325.

7 Embedding Foresight in Business Intelligence

Marti Arran Masters and Valtteri Kaartemo

Introduction

Nobody knows the future, but everyone wants a slice of the pie. Back in 1985, before the popularity of personal computers as business machines, the idea of a paperless office was just a glimmer on the distant horizon. At a fledgling company in America, an ambitious young executive with a hunch decided that paper should be handled electronically, but he did not have ten million dollars to spend on R&D. He had guessed correctly that in a world of mainframes, where microcomputers were still being viewed as novelties, this view would change in the near future and impact global commerce. Armed with the knowledge that being first to market often translates into competitive advantage, he hired a small team of software engineers on a shoe string budget. Six months later, the paperless office system went online in Chicago, Detroit, and Los Angeles. Within a year, it was implemented in all the company's regional offices scattered throughout the USA. Today, the firm is a multinational corporation enjoying a formidable market share.

The lessons learned from this story are two-fold: (a) with electronic files of customer data at their fingertips in an information system (IS) that was fast and easy to use, office personnel viewed the personal computer as a useful tool on their desks. The IS had no special status and did not burden the workers with extra tasks. Hence, it became embedded in their work roles, providing the human actors with a rich data source and the means to communicate about complex business processes between all levels of the organization. As a result, the firm was able to offer superior customer service, resulting in an annual 45% increase in revenues, which continued over the years, propelling the firm to the ranks of a Fortune 500 Company. (b) Saving money by investing in a cheap new technology was a risk, but the potential benefits outweighed the opportunity cost. The young executive's idea that an agile company can adapt to change and transform it into competitive advantage suggests that foresight, which involves viewing the future to support long-term planning, is a desirable business activity that firms should adopt.

Empowered by these ideas, the authors conducted a systematic literature review of studies that combine foresight and BI in four databases (Academic Search Premiere, Business Source Complete, Springer Link, and ScienceDirect) and arrived at the first conclusion of this study: peer-reviewed research combining foresight and BI is extremely scarce. Instead of leaving it there, the authors decided to continue with a conceptual study by taking a closer look at these studies to answer the following research questions:

Q1: How do companies conduct BI foresight activities?

Q2: How do companies recognize subtle changes in the external environment, which could impact their long-term planning or disrupt their position in the marketplace at some point in the future?

Q3: Is there a way to implement BIS and embed foresight across an entire organization to facilitate the detection of future changes and support long-term strategic decision-making?

By reviewing the initial findings on the topic, the authors contribute to the BI literature by showcasing how foresight can be embedded in BI, what the requirements are from a management perspective, and how business intelligence systems (BIS) can be designed to effectively enable analyzing future events impacting a company.

The authors present the results of the literature review and their answers to the research questions in the succeeding sections. First, they discuss how companies conduct BI and foresight activities, and present potential sources of failure to do those successfully. Second, they share insight on how companies can collect data to identify changes in the external environment. Third, the authors move on to discuss how foresight can be embedded in the mind-set of a firm using BI and IT tools to facilitate the detection of future changes and support long-term strategic decision-making. In the conclusions section, the authors sum up the findings of their literature review, and identify the themes that are crucial to the success of BI foresight activities in the firm.

Business Intelligence and Foresight in the Firm

In order for a company to sustain growth in the post-modern world of global commerce, discerning trends and areas for future expansion are critical to support decision-making and prevent the loss of market share. Köseoglu, Ross, and Okumus (2016) provide a summary of definitions and for the purposes of this study, the authors will adopt the viewpoints that perceive BI as a strategic tool, which enables management to identify propulsive forces and foresee changes in the external environment by transforming of raw data into competitive intelligence to support business decisions, have been adopted.

Table 7.1 Potential Value Contributions of Strategic Foresight Activities

Group	Potential
Perception	• Gaining insights into changes in the environment • Contributing to a reduction of uncertainty (e.g. through identification of disruption)
Interpretation and usage (for strategic management)	• Fostering conversations about the overall strategy of the company • Support the adjustment of the company in situations of uncertainty • Improving the coordination of business objectives • Creating the ability to adopt alternative perspectives
Interpretation and usage (for innovation management	• Reducing the level of uncertainty in R&D projects • Enhancing the understanding of customer needs • Identifying potential customers • Enhancing the understanding of the market • Identification of the opportunities and threats regarding our product and technology portfolio
Overall	• Facilitating organization learning • Shaping the future (e.g. though influencing other parties, such as politics and other companies)

Source: Rohrbeck and Schwarz (2013), p. 8

Rohrbeck and Schwarz (2013) identify three foresight activities that translate into competitive advantage for the firm, described in Table 7.1.

BI foresight activities begin with management requiring intelligence data for long-term strategic planning. Project parameters define what type of external data should be collected, for example, patent data to support decisions regarding product innovation or market data to look for emerging consumer-buying habits. Once the parameters have been established, the data can be collected and analyzed. Based on the analysis, there may be recommendations for making changes within the company, such as scaling back or gearing up product development in one area to prepare for shifts in the marketplace. The final step is the dissemination of the recommendations to executive management for decision support.

In some companies, decision makers participate in the entire process. These BI foresight activities in the firm comprise the entire field of *corporate foresight*, which is an emerging field in the peer-reviewed literature. According to a survey by Hammoud and Nash (2014, p. 11), "The top five ways participants mentioned that foresight helped the corporation were in shaping the future, improving corporate changeability or flexibility, enhancing organizational alignment, improving the customers' perception of the company, and creating an awareness of new opportunities."

As far back as 1979, Fowler realized that the role of the IT department in Decision Support Systems should be providing inquiries, not answers. They illustrate an HMO executive, who delighted in querying the database, and conclude that filtering data should be done by the decision maker because only he/she can correlate subtle relationships. Patton (2005) likewise confirms that a leader in top management should focus on continuous scanning of the environment and participate in decision-making. More recently, Mayer, Steinecke, Quick, and Weitzel (2013) propose incorporating the use of IT for gathering raw data, then disseminating the resulting information to executive decision-making.

Eastburn and Boland (2015) caution against becoming too comfortable with ways of analyzing big data when looking for subtle clues to changes in the environment. They report that overreliance on IS causes people to miss clues in the data representing circumstances that they are not prepared to deal with. In their case study of the banking industry, two key factors associated with intelligence failure were uncovered:

- **Organizational mindlessness,** defined as the tendency of management to engage in routine activities, wrongly attributing data anomalies as normal variations, and failure to think outside the box.
- **Rigidity of organizational routines,** where enterprises fail to incorporate creativity because the established structure does not allow flexibility.

They recommend instilling a policy of *mindfulness* to reduce the frequency and likelihood of *surprise* catching a firm completely off guard.

Numerous studies indicate that without the organized support involving specific stakeholders, BI foresight activities may be conducted sporadically, which can result in failure. Urbany and Montgomery (1998) report that proactive firms improve their success rate through the practice of adopting competitors, where the adoption team is a group of executives tasked with studying the competitor and assessing risks or threats. Membership on the team continues throughout the executives' careers in order to provide a steady stream of insight about the competitor's behavior.

The inability to prepare for change is another type of BI foresight failure associated with insufficient organizational support and it primarily occurs in firms which lack agility. Rohrbeck and Schwarz (2013) found that scenario planning and road mapping are activities which can foster collaboration within a firm to facilitate change. In large organizations with complex internal business processes, change usually requires a shift to new procedures, which middle managers may resist as they cling to legacy incentive systems. Research findings indicate that companies enjoy improved performance in foresight initiatives when middle managers are included (Rohrbeck and Schwartz, 2013) and communication between employees is supported (Muntean, Cabău, and Rînciog, 2014).

A good example of how communications failure can lead to disaster is described by Cunha, Clegg, and Kamoche (2012) in their study of real-time foresight. They found that valuable insights can originate with employees at any level of the organization and this information should not be overlooked by management, who may be focused on a single area and not paying attention to other external forces. Communication and collaboration within a firm as a pillar of intelligence success was also studied by Hammoud and Nash (2014), who published the top methods used by foresight practitioners in a variety of enterprises. See Table 7.2.

Firms adopting an enterprise-wide holistic approach empower key stakeholders with new ways of thinking to expand the firm's memory of the future (Rohrbeck, Thom, and Arnold, 2015). Scenario planning and constructing road maps are participatory exercises which identify possible futures that people remember. Altogether, this becomes the firm's collective future memory. Rohrbeck and Schwartz (2013, p. 16) conclude: "The more memories of the future that are stored, the more receptive can an individual be to signals from the outside world."

In support of a holistic approach that embeds foresight in BI, Graefe, Luckner, and Weinhardt (2010) advocate developing "a continuous observation of possible future developments, challenges and opportunities" (p. 395), which requires a shift in how companies manage their strategy portfolio. Their study concludes that one-off activities, such as forecasting, strategic planning, or scenario techniques, must be replaced by comprehensive foresight with a timely response in order to achieve competent strategic issues management.

Table 7.2 Top Interview Responses for Method

Codes/ Subthemes	Example Responses
External experts	Outside consultants conduct primary research and develop trends; moving company from understanding future to actually making investment decisions; serve department-specific needs.
Scenario	"Creating Leading Questions" to identify key topics; Deductive Scenarios for strategy; Inductive Scenarios for research; develop a story describing the future based on identified signals of change.
Trends	Trends Monitoring (or scouting) to understand developments in macroenvironment; Big-Trends: clusters of smaller trends (5–10) with significance; Trend Analysis projects only 2–3 years.
Scanning	Looking for signals of change (new developments, directional, trends, and discontinuity on the horizon).
STEEP	Gauging aging external environments; VSTEEP: STEEP factors-emergent activities across the factors become a Big-Trend.
Workshop	Facilitate ideation (internal for discovery or presentation); or innovation: held in various locales/customer sites around globe.

Source: Hammoud and Nash, 2014, p. 6

The argument for developing a comprehensive and effective means of instilling foresight systematically throughout an enterprise is compelling. Research indicates that BI foresight has given rise to the terminology of competitive intelligence (CI), which is gaining a strong foothold in large commercial enterprises as a result of leadership recognizing how actionable intelligence enhances a firm's competitive advantage (Prescott and Miree, 2015).

Collecting Data to Identify Changes in the External Environment

Fundamental to the concept of BI foresight is the analysis of data from external sources which should include a wide range of industries because game-changing events often come from a different industrial sector than what the company is currently engaged in, particularly in the area of technological change (Du Preez and Pistorius, 1999). Table 7.3 summarizes the type of external data companies typically collect:

Table 7.3 Examples of the Sources of Information

Published sources
Annual company reports
Articles in the business press/technical journals
Electronic databases
Company brochures and internal newsletters
Announcements of new equipment, facilities, or other resource commitments
Patent awards
Advertising literature
Symposium of conference proceedings
Reports of government agencies
Processional society reports
Internet homepages of organizations
Other internet resources

Unpublished sources
Speeches by management or other role players
Expert opinions
Reverse engineering and benchmarking
Industry contacts and friends
Trade shows, exhibition, tours, or conferences
Court appearances, testimony, lawsuits, and antitrust information
Customers
Suppliers
Unions
Subcontractors

Source: Du Preez and Pistorius, 1999, p. 222

BI professionals and organizations who engage in foresight activities must be vigilant in discerning information from the periphery because it is here that warnings and environmental shifts, that is, weak signals, may be detected (Calof and Wright, 2008). Patton (2005) identifies six characteristics associated with weak signals:

- Signals of change;
- Discontinuities;
- Outliers (events or developments that are off the current trend line);
- Items that defy conventional wisdom;
- Inflection points;
- Disruptive developments or technologies.

In their literature review of scanning systems, Mayer et al. (2013) summarize three models: early warning systems (Cohen, Zinbarg, and Zeikel 1967); weak signals (Ansoff, 1975); and second generation environmental scanning systems (ESS) (Davies, Studer, Sure, and Warren, 2005). Our research suggests that contemporary methods employ all three models.

Palomino, Taylor, and Owen (2013) conclude that organizations need to develop ways to automate scanning for better performance. They developed and tested a semi-automated horizon scanning system, which provides daily scans and a feedback loop to improve quality (see Figure 7.1).

Mayer et al. (2013), in turn, developed the 360° corporate radar which scans all aspects of the horizon to zero in on specific target areas with the greatest potential impact. The external environment is split into two parts: (a) the task environment, generally associated with a value chain consisting

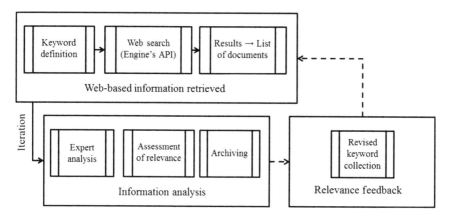

Figure 7.1 A Generalized Web-Based Horizon Scanning Approach Using Relevance Feedback

Source: Palomino et al. (2013, p. 358)

of suppliers, customers, and competitors; and (b) the general environment, which focuses on indirect impacts over the long term by detecting changes in the economic, political, social, and legal or regulatory climate, along with nascent developments in the technology sectors. When signals are detected, indicators, based on lead time, clarity, and cost/impact ratio are identified using an IS to perform analysis by incorporating semantic search and data mining.

Patton (2005) found that most companies have insufficient expertise and resources to perform the actual task of scanning, yet it is precisely this task and the ability of an organization to embrace rapid change which are essential for survival in a highly competitive global marketplace. He concludes that consulting firms may facilitate the scanning process and describes a case study of the SRI Consulting Business Intelligence (SRIC-BI), which hosts periodic meetings where the participants examine 100 abstracts created by experienced SRIC-BI employees. These abstracts contain indicators of change not on any known development trajectory, which participants are free to discuss without feeling restricted by a specific company culture. SRIC-BI publishes monthly reports that provide a "push-pull" mechanism intended to spur BI activities in the companies who receive them by providing data on an as-needed basis, along with information not usually on the corporate radar.

Despite the critical importance of environmental scanning, this research indicates that companies struggle to achieve good results because organization competence in detecting weak signals is dismal (Petrişor and Străin (2013). Less than 40% of surveyed corporate respondents reported satisfaction with *external* data reliability and consistency, compared to 75% who mined *internal* data (Isik, Jones, and Sidorova, 2011).

The failure of an organization's ability to accurately detect changes in the environment and use BI foresight to improve competitive advantage occupies a small space in the literature. The definitive study by Fleisher and Wright (2010) identifies four levels of failure concerning data gathering and analysis within the firm as well as external environmental failure. The authors suggest the model proposed by Fleisher and Wright correlates to the four domains identified by Lyytinen and Hirschheim (1987) in their seminal study of general IS failure. Yet, research integrating these concepts is not prevalent in the BI foresight or CI literature.

Carlof and Wright (2008) suggest that recognizing CI as separate field of research warrants a more thorough approach. They observe how many of the concepts overlap other heavily researched areas, including knowledge management, foresight, strategy, and business analytics.

Petrişor and Străin (2013) also confirm that BI foresight studies which focus on competitive advantage for the firm are sparse. They suggest that insight is a core competency of the intelligence domain, but areas including risk assessment, war gaming, state-gate analysis, blue ocean strategy, and early warning are not fully integrated in the academic literature. Their recommendation that both practitioners and academic researchers need to include *intelligence* in their concept of using CI is supported by Harvey and Jones (1992), who blame the focus of business schools and the lack of courses which teach intelligence as the main reason companies cannot stay afloat in the global marketplace.

Finding ways to improve the performance of environmental scanning and analyzing data to support decision-making in order to react to changes in the rapidly changing global marketplace requires a multi-level approach. In the foregoing discussion, two themes emerged which empower these activities: (a) *support of top management, along with active participation at all levels within the organization* and (b) *the IS must be positioned to avoid overreliance on IT, which can result in mindlessness.*

The argument for developing a comprehensive and effective means of instilling BI foresight systematically throughout an enterprise is compelling. With the advent of knowledge and expert systems to facilitate communication and information sharing, the authors endeavored to find out whether specially designed IT tools can also support BI foresight activities to produce more positive outcomes and reinforce a state of mindfulness throughout an organization.

Embedding Foresight in the Mind-Set of a Firm Using Business Intelligence and IT Tools

According to Rohrbeck, Thom, and Arnold (2015), companies are scrambling to evolve their information and communications technology (ICT) in order to take advantage of their data assets to aid in decision-making. They surmise that the volume and diversity of data is large, but the most effective interpreters of this data are top managers, whose time constraints do not allow them to analyze raw data. This view is supported by Kuilboer, Ashrafi, and Lee (2016, p. 4), who conclude,

> To optimize benefits, BI solutions have to be aligned with the organization's goals and deployed properly. In addition, the structure of the organization needs to allow data-driven decision-making. Otherwise, the results extracted from BI solutions will not make a difference and the organization will resist the suggested course of action.

A study by Grublješič and Jaklič (2015) confirms that unless computer support for BI foresight activities is viewed as an embedded tool by decision makers, it will not be effectively utilized. They suggest that firms which are market-oriented tend to use these tools more readily as their focus is on growth and rewarding employee performance encourages personal innovation. Their study reinforces prior research by Shanks, Bekmamedova, Adam, and Daly, (2012, p. 1), who found that an organization should strive for "BI-driven decision-making routines and BI-enabled organizational processes that take managerial decision making to new levels of understanding and foresight."

In this study, two views on embedding BIS were discovered: (a) developing BI activities throughout the firm in a creative manner to encourage employee participation and (b) reinforcing foresight activities within the business information system (BIS). Based on these findings, the authors consider that a BIS which successfully supports BI activities must include both views.

Grublješič and Jaklič (2015) found that in order for a BIS to be effective, three dimensions must be present:

- **Intensity:** what a person thinks when using the BIS and how absorbed he/she in this activity;
- **Extent:** how the user engages the BIS to perform work and to what extent;
- **Embeddedness:** the person uses the BIS as a tool to perform work, that is, the BIS has no special status and the purpose of the BIS is to facilitate the person in his/her work role.

Furthermore, a culture of information openness must exist at all levels of the enterprise. This requires transparency in gathering and disseminating information along with reporting errors and failures. Quality of the data and ease of use play important roles in determining whether people will use the BIS or try to avoid it. Critical to user acceptance is the design and capability of the user interface, for example, dashboards and the ability to print custom reports. Finally, companies who actively seek competitive advantage are more likely to embed BIS because they place a high value on CI.

Although the contemporary marketplace offers a rich variety of software tools for big-data analytics, which are useful in short-term forecasting, user-friendly apps which combine foresight with the powerful data manipulation of BIS seem to be missing from the pack. According to von der Gracht, Bañuls, Turoff, Skulimowski, and Gordon (2015, p. 1), "The foresight discipline applies more than 30 different techniques to obtain valid and profound conclusions about future developments and scenarios. Until now, only a few of these techniques have been transferred into reliable software applications." Five objectives of a foresight support system (FSS) are identified in Table 7.4 below.

Rather than encouraging custom applications, von der Gracht et al. (2015) advocate selecting individual software modules from commercially available FSS so organizations can implement those most appropriate for their specific needs. This kind of BIS is already is already in use at Deutsche Telecomm and is showcased in the following.

In a case study of Deutsche Telecomm, Rohrbeck, Thom, and Arnold (2015) identified barriers in the BI foresight process that inhibit change.

Table 7.4 FSS Attributes: Objectives and Required Actions

Objective	Required Action
Identify changes in the business environment	Ensure transparency and consistency of foresight results
Utilize large volumes of statistical and qualitative data	Support efficient handling and assessment
Convince decision makers about the relevance of changes	Facilitate communication that enables collaboration
Plan strategies	Provide a structure for decision modeling
Act in the changing business environment	Provide rules of order in foresight processes

Source: von der Gracht et al. (2015)

These barriers are largely focused on collecting external data and recognizing indicators of forthcoming environmental shifts. The BI foresight activities and human actors associated with each barrier are illustrated in Figure 7.2.

Their study concludes that an IS designed to overcome the barriers of data collection, recognition of key indicators, and facilitate enterprise-wide BI foresight activities should incorporate three *enablers*:

- **Data gathering**: enabling a large number of contributors from inside and outside the organization to share information (ideas, observations, insights, etc.), the IT tools being particularly useful for handling a large quantity of information;
- **Interpretation**: enabling multiple stakeholders to assess and judge information from their perspectives and to participate in a dialogue with other stakeholders;
- **Organizational response**: enabling follow-up activities, particularly with innovation management through a direct process link.

They describe a working solution at Deutsche Telecomm built on a tri-tier ICT platform that satisfies all three enablers:

- **A database and workflow tool** *for scouting and assessment of developments and trends coming from markets and technology (PEACOQ Scouting Tool);*
- **An idea generation and management system** *building on impulses coming from technology and market intelligence (PEACOQ Gate 0.5);*
- **An Intranet portal** *for making insights available to every DT employee and for crowd sourcing additional information and opinions (Foresight Landing Page).*

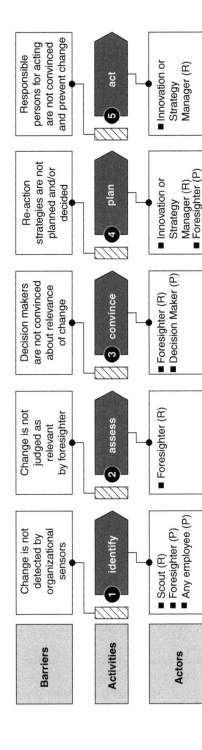

Figure 7.2 Foresight Process With Barriers, Activities, and Actors

Source: Rohrbeck, Thom, and Arnold (2015, p. 5)

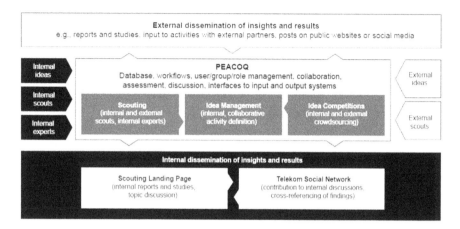

Figure 7.3 Purposes and Interfaces of T-Labs Foresight Tools
Source: Rohrbeck, Thom, and Arnold (2015), p. 17

The system interfaces are illustrated in Figure 7.3.

The system design encourages collaboration, which improves the detection and management of weak signals, fosters creative thinking and continuity throughout the BI foresight process, provides formal tools for decision-making, enriches archiving knowledge by linking first detection of a signal to future outcomes as users add their updates, and potentially bridges the gap between the planned outcome and the actual response taken by the firm. Rohrbeck, Thom, and Arnold observe that when these activities generate enough "noise" in the organization, it gets the attention of top management. They conclude that employee participation in the steps which leads to decision-making spurs motivation and commitment. Finally, because the system is used as part of the daily work routine, the BI foresight activities become fully embedded in the mind-set and operations of the firm.

Concluding Remarks

The literature specific to BI and corporate foresight is scarce. The majority of research focuses on competitive advantage in specific areas, such as technological forecasting, or simply lacks any mention of foresight. On the other hand, scholars and practitioners who view corporate foresight as an emerging field include Ruff (2006), Colakoglu, T. (2011), Rohrbeck, Battistella, and Huizingh (2015), and Köseoglu et al. (2016),

By putting all the pieces of the puzzle together from the articles in the literature review, the authors identified two themes crucial to the success of BI foresight activities in the firm:

- Support of top management and active participation in BI activities throughout the enterprise;
- The IS must be positioned to avoid overreliance on IT and a mindless approach to data analysis.

Empowered by these observations, the authors investigated how BI foresight may be embedded in a company culture, utilized in daily activities by human actors in their work roles, and determined whether specially designed IT tools past the experimental stage can be successfully implemented in the firm. One system meets these criteria: the case study by Rohrbeck et al. (2015) at Deutsche Telecomm.

The results of this study suggest that detection of weak signals or shifts in the periphery of the horizon during environmental scanning is difficult. BI foresight activities in many companies are not well managed or simply do not exist. In particular, the topic of BI foresight in SMEs is under-researched. Yet it is precisely these activities that companies must embrace in order to achieve competitive advantage in the global marketplace.

The limitations of this study are based on the search methods and defining the scope to BI foresight activities in the firm to discover how these activities may be embedded into the daily work roles of the human actors. The BIS is positioned as an ordinary tool to facilitate BI foresight activities, which means it has neither special status nor poses a burden to the people who use it. The authors did not include published books in this study, although a handful are now being used in academic courses and serve as guidelines for interested practitioners.

In sorting the wheat from the chaff, the authors found that BI foresight in commercial enterprises warrants recognition as a subject for research because the motivation and goals of these organizations are considerably different than the public sector. Furthermore, several studies suggest that BI foresight in the firm may be viewed in the context of CI, which requires an interdisciplinary approach, drawing from fields which include marketing, strategic and innovation management, futures studies, enterprise architecture, and IT governance, advanced resource planning, and knowledge work informatics. The idea of embedding BI foresight throughout an organization using IT tools suggests incorporating *IT-reliant work systems* theory (Alter, 2010), along with frameworks by Markku Nurminen (1997) and other scholars who have investigated embedding knowledge management systems in the workplace. With these thoughts in mind, the authors suggest that BI foresight and IT tools form the basis of successful long-term planning in the firm and invite many opportunities for future research.

References

Alter, S. (2010). Work systems as the core of the design space for organisational design and engineering. *International Journal of Organisational Design and Engineering*, 1(1–2), 5–28.

Ansoff, H. I. (1975). Managing strategic surprise by response to weak signals. *California Management Review*, 18(2), 21–33.

Calof, J. L. and Wright, S. (2008). Competitive intelligence: A practitioner, academic and inter-disciplinary perspective. *European Journal of Marketing*, 42(7/8), 717–730.

Cohen, J. B., Zinbarg, E. D., and Zeikel, A. (1967). *Investment Analysis and Portfolio Management*. Homewood, IL: Richard D. Irwin.

Colakoglu, T. (2011). The problematic of competitive intelligence: How to evaluate and develop competitive intelligence? *Procedia-Social and Behavioral Sciences*, 24, 1615–1623.

Cunha, M. P., Clegg, S. R., and Kamoche, K. (2012). Improvisation as "real time foresight." *Futures*, 44(3), 265–272.

Davies, J., Studer, R., Sure, Y., and Warren, P. W. (2005). Next generation knowledge management. *BT Technology Journal*, 23(3), 175–190.

Du Preez, G. T. and Pistorius, C. W. (1999). Technological threat and opportunity assessment. *Technological Forecasting and Social Change*, 61(3), 215–234.

Eastburn, R. W. and Boland, R. J. (2015). Inside banks' information and control systems: Post-decision surprise and corporate disruption. *Information and Organization*, 25(3), 160–190.

Fleisher, C. S. and Wright, S. (2010). Competitive intelligence analysis failure: Diagnosing individual level causes and implementing organisational level remedies. *Journal of Strategic Marketing*, 18(7), 553–572.

Fowler, F. P., Jr. (1979). The executive intelligence system as a design strategy. MIS Quarterly, 3(4), 21–29.

Graefe, A., Luckner, S., and Weinhardt, C. (2010). Prediction markets for foresight. *Futures*, 42(4), 394–404.

Grublješič, T. and Jaklič, J. (2015). Conceptualization of the business intelligence extended use model. *Journal of Computer Information Systems*, 55(3), 72–82.

Hammoud, M. S. and Nash, D. P. (2014). What corporations do with foresight. *European Journal of Futures Research*, 2(1), 1–20.

Harvey, C. and Jones, G. (1992). Organisational capability and competitive advantage. *Business History*, 34(1), 1–10.

Isik, O., Jones, M. C., and Sidorova, A. (2011). Business Intelligence (BI) success and the role of BI capabilities. *Intelligent Systems in Accounting, Finance and Management*, 18(4), 161–176.

Köseoglu, M. A., Ross, G., and Okumus, F. (2016). Competitive intelligence practices in hotels. *International Journal of Hospitality Management*, 53, 161–172.

Kuilboer, J. P., Ashrafi, N., and Lee, O.K.D. (2016). Business intelligence capabilities as facilitators to achieve organizational agility. In *Twenty-Second Americas Conference on Information Systems*, San Diego.

Lyytinen,K., Hirschheim,R. (1987). Information Systems Failures: A Survey and Classification of the Empirical Literature, *Oxford Surveys in InformationTechnology*, 257–309.

Mayer, J. H., Steinecke, N., Quick, R., and Weitzel, T. (2013). More applicable environmental scanning systems leveraging "modern" information systems. *Information Systems and e-Business Management*, 11(4), 507–540.

Muntean, M., Cabău, L. G., and Rînciog, V. (2014). Social business intelligence: A new perspective for decision makers. *Procedia-Social and Behavioral Sciences*, 124, 562–567.

Nurminen, M. I. (1997). Paradigms for sale: Information systems in the process of radical change. *Scandinavian Journal of Information Systems*, 9(1), 9.

Palomino, M. A., Taylor, T., and Owen, R. (2013). Evaluating business intelligence gathering techniques for horizon scanning applications. In *Mexican International Conference on Artificial Intelligence* (pp. 350–361). Berlin Heidelberg: Springer.

Patton, K. M. (2005). The role of scanning in open intelligence systems. *Technological Forecasting and Social Change*, 72(9), 1082–1093.

Petrişor, I. and Străin, N. A. (2013). Approaches on the competitive intelligence. *USV Annals of Economics and Public Administration*, 13(1), 100–109.

Prescott, J. E. and Miree, C. E. (2015). Small business solutions: Building and leveraging a competitive intelligence capability without going broke. *Journal of Small Business Strategy*, 9(2), 57–76.

Rohrbeck, R., Battistella, C., and Huizingh, E. (2015). Corporate foresight: An emerging field with a rich tradition. *Technological Forecasting and Social Change*, 101, 1–9.

Rohrbeck, R. and Schwarz, J. O. (2013). The value contribution of strategic foresight: Insights from an empirical study of large European companies. *Technological Forecasting and Social Change*, 80(8), 1593–1606.

Rohrbeck, R., Thom, N., and Arnold, H. (2015). IT tools for foresight: The integrated insight and response system of Deutsche Telekom Innovation Laboratories. *Technological Forecasting and Social Change*, 97, 115–126.

Ruff, F. (2006). Corporate foresight: Integrating the future business environment into innovation and strategy. *International Journal of Technology Management*, 34(3–4), 278–295.

Shanks, G., Bekmamedova, N., Adam, F., and Daly, M. (2012). Embedding business intelligence systems within organisations. In A. Respício and F. Burstein (Eds.), *Fusing Decision Support Systems into the Fabric of the Context* (Vol. 238, pp. 113–124). IOS Press.

Urbany, J., & Montgomery, D. (1998). Rational strategic reasoning: an unnatural act?. *Marketing Letters*, 9(3), 285–299.

von der Gracht, A., Bañuls, V. A., Turoff, M., Skulimowski, A. M., and Gordon, T. J. (2015). Foresight support systems: The future role of ICT for foresight. *Technological Forecasting and Social Change*, 97, 1–6.

8 Inventing Consciousness
Beyond Business Intelligence

Al Naqvi

In the business world, executives often spend year after year mentally and intellectually locked into a narrow structure of daily chores. At times, they intentionally ignore the changes taking place around them. At other times, their situational dynamics (e.g. location, industry, business focus) obscure their view to see what is transpiring. New knowledge stays buried in the academic journals, inaccessible and hidden from businesspeople. Then suddenly, from the left field, they are hit by a dramatic change and find themselves unprepared; and in the aftermath, ask questions such as *why did Blockbuster not see Netflix coming?* or *why did Borders fail to become Amazon?* To develop strategic foresight, it is important for business leaders to sometimes take a moment away from what seems real and pragmatic and explore the new developments. This article will walk businesspeople through the interdisciplinary scientific developments taking place in one manifestation of the amazing world of artificial intelligence: inventing consciousness. For businesspeople, (borrowing the term from Pink-Floyd's album) this *Momentary Lapse of Reason* can provide a break from the comfortable and monotonous known. Moreover, businesspeople may discover that these developments are temporally closer than they had anticipated and their strategic plans need to incorporate such innovative scenarios.

The Alluring Trap of Consciousness

Defining consciousness is an age-old philosophical problem. Designing it, a modern scientific challenge. For centuries, the topic of consciousness fluctuated between spiritual and material manifestations—including all shades in between—and at times even faced complete denial that it even exists. In the 20th century, the rise of behavioral psychology nearly shoved the study of consciousness off the scientific stage. Behaviorism had no place to ask the tough question of *what is*, or even *if there is*, consciousness. It could get a lot of mileage by observing how people behave and hence found questions related to consciousness unnecessary. As neuroscience developed and scientists could study the brain via neuroimaging (e.g. fMRI and PET scanners), tremendous progress was made to gain new insights. The rise of modern technology in the 21st century has brought consciousness back into our scientific cognizance and placed it at the center of human quest for enlightenment. Psychologists, biologists, cognitive scientists, neuroscientists, philosophers, mathematicians, computer scientists, and experts from several other fields have launched an interdisciplinary effort to not only understand consciousness but also to build it.

Building consciousness obviously implies a need to define consciousness. This is where things get a little messy. Consciousness, after all, includes the subjective and highly personalized experiences humans feel. For example, the smell of a beautiful spring morning, the blueness of sky, the feeling of wind blowing, the calming sound of waves at a beach—these subjective experiences (sometimes referred to as qualia) are internal to humans. When including these experiences, it is almost as if human consciousness exists independent of the matter that surrounds humans. In fact, in the 17th century Descartes gave an interesting theory of consciousness that separated mind and brain by attributing that brain is composed of matter while mind is nonphysical—a dualist model. Descartes declared that mind and brain interact in the pineal gland and that is where the amalgamation of the nonphysical and physical gives rise to consciousness (Lokhorst, 2016). Of course, one does not need modern scanning machines to notice that Descartes's theory does not explain exactly how the merger process happens. For that matter, he could have chosen knees, or heart, or elbow, as the setting of magical synthesis and that would have made no difference.

The point is that humans do know that humans have personalized, subjective, and internal experiences—but just cannot explain how these experiences happen. Chalmers calls it the "hard problem" of consciousness—as opposed to what he refers as the easy problems like focus of attention, information integration, the ability to discriminate, deliberate control of behavior, difference between wakefulness and sleep, and reaction to environmental stimuli (Chalmers, 2010). The easy problems, Chalmers says, are "straightforwardly vulnerable to explanation in terms of computational or neural mechanisms." Most religions and some philosophers propose the dualist model of consciousness—that is consciousness—arises out of a combination of matter and spiritual components. Others lean towards the materialism model that tries to explain consciousness in terms of matter and energy.

Debates rage in a wide spectrum of cross-disciplinary scientific communities about consciousness; however, the matters are far from resolved. Does clustering of neurons in unique patterns give rise to consciousness? Is it nothing more than chemicals and electrical energy exchanges that propagate neuronal activities and in a blink of a second give rise to conscious thought? Can quantum physics explain the rise of human consciousness? Is it something more than what can be captured in science lab apparatuses? Is it simply a natural and evolutionary response to the adventures and obstacles through which humans hopped and climbed the evolutionary ladder?

Is human concept of self, and hence consciousness, an illusion? The alluring intellectual trap of consciousness continues to fascinate humans as the irony is noticed that studying consciousness is itself a gift of consciousness. The magic continues.

Defined "Not Yet," But It Can Be Modeled

Even though there is little agreement among scientists on what consciousness is, it has not stopped some scientists to work towards designing working models of consciousness. After all, if high-level properties of consciousness can be understood, a machine can be designed that can at least display some of those properties.

One such model is based upon the work done by Bernard Baars, a psychologist. Baars's model is known as Global Workspace Theory. He defines and explains global workspace (GW) as "a functional hub of binding and propagation in a population of loosely coupled signaling elements" and "In computational applications, GW architectures recruit many distributed, specialized agents to cooperate in resolving focal ambiguities. In the brain, conscious experiences may reflect a GW function" (Baars et al., 2013).

Baars clarifies that anatomical studies of the brain show that there are many parts or "hubs" however conscious percepts are "unitary and consistent," implying that brain-based GW capacity must be a functional hub and not localized in any given anatomical hub—and therefore GW capacity is "a dynamic capacity for binding and propagation of neural signals over multiple task-related networks, a kind of neuronal cloud computing" Baars infers. Thus, multiple input streams of conscious contents are propagated and broadcasted in different areas of the brain and a winner-takes-all equilibrium establishes who wins in the battle of consciousness. Baars and Franklin explained that in fleeting memory one consistent content can dominate at any given moment however dominant information is widely distributed in the brain (Baars and Franklin, 2009). This, they argue, can only happen in a nervous system viewed as a massive distributed set of specialized networks and that in such a system a central information exchange can coordinate, control, and solve problems enabling some regions, for example sensory cortex, to distribute information to the whole.

Baars's model became the basis for designing a computer system known as LIDA (Mello and Franklin, 2007). Stan Franklin and other team members led the project to develop a system that is attempting to model consciousness. In an introduction to the system architecture (Franklin et al., 2016), Franklin acknowledged that at the heart of the LIDA model is a technical definition of mind as a control structure for an autonomous agent whose primary function is to continually and iteratively answer the question, "What do I do next?" In his previous work, (Franklin and Graesser, 1997) he had explained that the autonomous agent functions in a changing environment that the agent must understand and interact with to pursue "its own agenda" so as to impact "what is senses in the future." Thus cognition is not just about *now*, as it requires gliding over the time dimensions and encapsulating the future considerations to guide our current actions.

Like Franklin's model, many other such cognitive architectures are being designed and developed. They are based upon different theoretical foundations (Vernon et al., 2007; Doell and Siebert, 2016).

The Building Elements

Scanning the ontological structures of the architectures of consciousness-based systems (biological or otherwise), one can identify the presence of the following four capabilities as the critical building blocks:

1. **Connectivity:** This means the capability to network or communicate with other distributed components of various autonomous parts through which the parts acquire functional coherence in a decentralized structure (for example in brain). Recent neuroimaging studies have shown the presence of various parts that connect with each other to form behaviors and give rise to consciousness. The brain, Baars describes "seems to be a massive collection of neural nets, layers and connections, each specialized in some specific task" and that the "great bulk of these specialized nets operate all at once, in parallel with each other, as one great society" (Baars, 2016).

2. **Information structures:** Dynamic development of neural structures that could be reinforced from previous structures implies that a certain level of organized information architecture exists in the brain. In the absence of such organization, signal conflicts will take a long time to get resolved and hence make communication between various parts of the brain ineffective and inefficient. Evidence is emerging from various imaging studies that indicate this complex network of information (Braver et al., 2003; Sheu and Courtney, 2016; Waskom et al., 2014; Schroeder, 2011; Lindquist and Barrett, 2012; Courtney, 2004). One theory of consciousness proposed by Tononi and known as *Integrated Information Theory* focuses on information and argues that the human brain processes and integrates information resulting in a singular and unified experience (Tononi, 2008). So, if an observer is sitting near a performer who is dressed in blue—the entire information (blueness of her dress, her voice, lyrics, perfume she's wearing, and her face) form a single integrated experience. In some ways when a person focuses on something, he or she is eliminating the possibilities of what that thing is not, and hence this process of elimination results in narrowing down on what that thing *is* and in doing so he or she processes massive amounts of information. Furthermore, as experiences accumulate, they help build new experiences or make sense out of new information. This suggests that brain processes multiple types

of information and then brings it together to form an integrated whole experience.

3. **Efficient algorithms:** This implies that there exist rules or basic biological algorithms that enable efficient processing and that they reduce the cost of processing such that the entity in which consciousness arises does not collapse or gets paralyzed by the emerging structure. Baars and Franklin explain that "the conscious as well as the non-conscious aspects of human thinking, planning, and perception are produced by adaptive, biological algorithms" (Baars and Franklin, 2009). Performing computations, resolving the computational complexity, and doing so efficiently, are important aspects of brain functions.

4. **Processing:** Finally, the massive information processing in a biological or non-biological system (e.g. working memory, conscious, and subconscious) is an amazing feature of the brain. The human brain contains average 80 billion plus neurons (Azevedo et al., 2009). Human ability to recollect memories, recognize situations, and recall past events, is made possible due to the access humans have to massive amounts of information. Approximating the processing capacity, Tuszynski and Woolf elucidate that there are "on the order of 10^4 synapses per large neuron, which switch their states at a rate of some 10^3 switches per second, so that we arrive at a number of 10^{18} operations per second in the brain on average" (Tuszynski and Woolf, 2006).

As shown in the next section, these fundamental building blocks of smart systems are now emerging in the form of global dynamics that are enabling the powerful emergence of artificial intelligence. A self-reinforcing loop is also surfacing that will accelerate the development of conscious agents.

The Rise of Artificial Intelligence

More than three decades ago Nathan Rosenberg, an economic historian, skillfully pierced the black box of technological progress. In his seminal work *Inside the Black Box: Technology and Economics* Rosenberg assembled the disparate elements of what integrates technological growth with economic progress. Rosenberg argued that major innovation is one that becomes the basis for, or provides, the framework for several subsequent innovations "each of which is dependent upon, or complementary to, the original one" (Rosenberg, 1982). To build his case, Rosenberg identified technological change, and in particular *diffusion*, as composed of many different factors: including improvements in performance characteristics of an invention, modifications, adaptations in response to requirements of various submarkets, and complementary products and services that make the original product more useful.

Artificial Intelligence is not a new technology. The field of Artificial Intelligence research was born during the 1950s. The technology made several unsuccessful attempts to become mainstream and break the commercialization barrier. Marred by "overpromising and under-delivering" the field failed to sustain unremitting commercial success despite making powerful strides in research, inventions, and innovations. Expectations were set too high, and failure to match the promised ascent led to disappointed investors and heartbroken researchers. In the brief history of artificial intelligence, three waves of optimism came and left, and were followed by periods of investment stagnation. Waiting for their time to come, researchers quietly withdrew to their labs and continued to innovate.

An important lesson that history of economics teaches is that inventions devoid of right support conditions often fail to achieve their true transformational potential. These right support conditions can manifest in the form of the supporting infrastructure, interdependent technologies, legal structures, institutions, and social conditions. Technological progress, Rosenberg cautioned, is related to economic progress but the relationship is complex and not that straightforward (Rosenberg, 1994). Thus, while the underlying economic variables and microeconomic theory can provide some basis for analysis, the direction taken by scientific knowledge and technological change are not necessarily driven in accordance with the textbook theoretical frameworks. Path dependence can dictate the growth of technological knowledge.

Path dependence is an interesting concept. David defines it as "A dynamical process whose evolution is governed by its own history" is "path dependent"(David, 2007). Innovation and diffusion do not follow a predictable path of development. There are no hard and fast rules that can show how technologies will grow and what path they will take. In a path-dependent sequence of economic changes, eventual outcomes are influenced by temporally remote events, including events impacted by chance elements (David, 1985). David further explained that stochastic processes do not converge automatically to fixed point distributions of outcomes and hence are termed non-ergodic—and therefore "historical accidents" must be included in economic analysis as the dynamic process itself takes on the historic character.

Such historical accidents can compel us to accept and live with a substandard technology (for example, VHS vs. Beta) and they can create new and unexpected opportunities. But some accidents turn out to be "happy accidents." Enter the world of *serendipity*.

While serendipity or "the happy accident" is often viewed as a gift of luck, randomness, or chance, de Rond explained that instead of "being tantamount to chance events, serendipity results from the ability to identify 'matching pairs' of events, or events that are meaningfully, even if not necessarily causally, related" (de Rond, 2014).

One of the happy accidents of our times is the simultaneous development of four capabilities that supported the revival of artificial intelligence. As time moved ahead and artificial intelligence retreated to the trenches, far away from the research labs of artificial intelligence researchers, complementary capability areas developed in parallel. Three of the four capability areas benefited from each other via symbiotic interdependence and the fourth developed independent of the three. "Capability area" implies a classification scheme in which technology/scientific innovations are classified in broad and general areas of innovations that: bring people together (network), help process and analyze information (processing and analysis), improve the efficiency of algorithms (mathematical/computational), and help in managing data (data management):

> **Connectivity and network capabilities:** Network capability class includes technologies that facilitate human or machine connectivity; it brings humans, machines, or both together to form and develop a wide spectrum of relationships. Social media platforms, cloud, mobile technologies, web, and all the software and hardware that supports such nexus of global connectivity falls in this class. For our purposes, one of the key elements of such connectivity is that it connects various disparate, distributed, functionally separate systems and forms a nexus of decentralized structure. The second key element is that it brings people and machines (for example Internet of Things [IoT]) together—that is making machines a stakeholder in this enormous conglomerate of connectivity. In this world machines are not just processors but also providers, evaluators, decision makers, and even thoughtful creators of data and information. This system allows the rise of various networks and associations and structures.

> **Processing and analytical capabilities:** While network capabilities can be implemented to connect people and machines, a separate set of capabilities are needed to increase the efficiency of such connectivity. Having a connected network and sharing of information are no guarantee that such an interaction is efficient or that the system will be able to provide deep insights into how and why connectivity happens. In fact, when Internet was born and global connectivity was established, there was no advanced analytics or processing power that is now available. As such the capability class needed to increase the efficiency of the interactions, quality of relationships, and the analytical rigor to gain deep insights must be different than simple connectivity. The difference comes from technologies such as business analytics software, various analytical tools, and big-data architectures such as Hadoop. Beyond the ability to store and analyze structured data, this capability area enabled the analysis of unstructured data (including image, sound, videos, etc.) and hence has added a new dimension of machine cognition.

> **Data management:** The third capability is also distinct from the first two in the sense that the other two can exist without this capability; however the complementary nature of this capability makes the

other two smoother and more efficient. Data management capability includes processes such as data governance, data quality management, metadata management, and master data management. These capabilities form the ontological structures of information that enable faster processing and efficient connectivity. Prior to data management as a specialty, data was organized with the limited scope of search efficiency. As it is apparent now, governed data is better—simply because it reduces the cost to the system to find, use, and create meaning from data (Fryman et al., 2016). Data management can also help organize the unstructured data.

Mathematical algorithms: In the math departments, researchers and experts developed algorithms to support the applications of artificial intelligence. These algorithms are necessary for training machines (machine learning). Mathematics also developed to analyze vast sets of complicated data. (For example see Zhang and Suganthan, 2016; Zhang et al., 2016; Qiu et al., 2016; Franke et al., 2016; Candes et al., 2016). Machines, like humans, need to be taught. Teaching, as teachers know, is often an iterative process where students progress towards learning, and with time and dedication master the field. In doing so, students patiently inch towards acquiring proficiency and along the way realize what is relevant to learning and reject what is not. As teachers help them correct their mistakes, students learn what is right, as they simultaneously learn what is not right. If every student learned precisely without making any mistakes, there would be a perfect system. Thus, mistake can be considered as the necessary cost of learning and its reduction gets closer to the ultimate learning experience. In mathematical algorithms used in machine learning, the key concept is to efficiently reduce the cost in order to teach a machine. Not that different from teaching students, machines acquire mastery by minimizing this cost function.

As the four capabilities developed, they created an environment ripe for the return of artificial intelligence. Acting as support pillars, the four capability areas provided the foundational platform to build the artificial intelligence revolution (See Figure 8.1). The artificial intelligence field emerged from its final winter and made a dramatic and decisive comeback. In the last few years, this has unleashed an investment storm.

An interesting observation though is that these four capability areas parallel and mimic the core building blocks of the consciousness-inspired systems. It is as if machine learning has acquired transformational energy from these four capability areas and is transcending fast to incorporate consciousness to design and produce autonomous systems and to formulate the foundational map for a connected, decentralized, distributed system that can display the properties of human consciousness.

What is also important to realize is that the future development of the artificial intelligence technology will not be linear. It is reasonably well

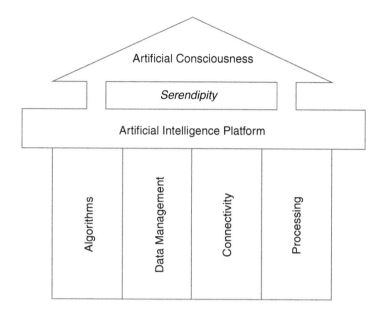

Figure 8.1 The Building Blocks of the AI Revolution

understood that human-to-human connectivity leads to rapid innovation and such networks accelerate innovation. Muthukrishna et al. explain that despite the tendency to think that innovations happen through individual effort (persistence and perspiration of some legendary, superhuman, person), they are "instead an emergent property of our species' cultural learning abilities, applied within our societies and social networks. Our societies and social networks act as collective brains" (Muthukrishna et al., 2016).

When human intelligence and creativity are augmented by machine intelligence and creativity, conditions are created with a self-reinforcing cycle that can propel creativity and intelligence beyond what human connectivity can do alone. Machines are now part of the equation and their role cannot be ignored in advancing innovation. The four capabilities and the integrated platform of artificial intelligence can unleash immense creative power. In a knowledge production ecosystem composed of high interaction, massive information availability, constant idea generation, self-learning machines, and enhanced ability to discover previously unknown patterns, some very interesting things can transpire.

The Global Brain

Observing the massive data managed by companies such as Google, Yahoo, Facebook, and Amazon, Goertzel proposed the emergence of a Global Brain (GB) that can display the characteristics of human consciousness

(Goertzel, 2014). Heylighen had proposed the concept of "global super-organism" (Heylighen, 2007) and then expanded on it in his 2016 article arguing that the rise of information and communication technologies ICT can create a globally connected consciousness (Heylighen and Lenartowicz, 2016). Similar to neural networks in human brain, billions of humans across the globe can function in a parallel processing and distributed manner which can lead to unified and collective actions and decisions (Heylighen and Lenartowicz, 2016; Rosenblum, 2015).

And Then Comes Quantum

Developments from the quantum physics are shedding new light on consciousness. In a seminal collection of articles, Tuszynski and Woolf (2006) explain that the current theory supports that consciousness emerges from complex computations of binary (on and off) interactions and assemblies of neurons (synapses) and hence can be explained with classical physics. However, they argue, that does not preclude the possible role played by quantum physics particularly when electrical impulses and chemical neurotransmitter transmission are involved. In this context, by *quantum* they mean "the smallest unit of a physical quantity the system is able to possess." They explain that the quantum world is the microworld of elementary particles—the fundamental building blocks of matter and since the brain is made up of physical matter like all other living and nonliving systems, ultimately brain science must explain how matter, the physical structure of the brain, gives rise to its functions like higher cognition and consciousness (Tuszynski and Woolf, 2006).

If viewed from this perspective, quantum physics cannot only provide a better explanation of consciousness but also help build the most powerful artificial consciousness. This is where serendipity takes control of the progress path and leads to creative zones that could not have been envisioned under normal conditions.

Discussion

The existing cross-functional and multidisciplinary research, along with a globally coordinated effort and a connected Global Brain, can create the conditions for Singularity. Singularity, the point in time when computers acquire or even exceed human intelligence, is closer than many think. Ray Kurzweil argues in his book *The Singularity Is Near* that conditions now exist that can lead to Singularity by 2029 (Kurzweil, 2005). Goertzel conceptually agrees with the possibility of what he calls Human-Level AI (also known as Artificial General Intelligence) (Goertzel, 2007).

There is a clear distinction between heteronomous and autonomous technologies. In this context, heteronomous technology implies a technology whose response to a given input stimulus is predetermined, predictable, and planned by an external authority (humans). The output responses are composed of a discrete set such that the set cannot grow or improve without external human intervention. All machines ever created by humans (other than the autonomous machines) meet this condition. Machines forming the industrial revolution to modern computers are all examples of such heteronomous machines.

Autonomous technology on the other hand implies a technology whose response to a given stimulus can vary. This machine can improve, adapt, and learn. It can study its environment and observe changes in its environment. Its destiny is not preordained. At some stage, and under some conditions, the technology can formulate its own goals, potentially develop awareness, and even, as seen in this article, consciousness. This technology can learn through experience. It can accumulate experience. Its response patterns to a given stimulus therefore can become situational, continuous, and infinite. The experience or learning can produce different, sometimes unpredictable, outcomes.

It is important to realize that humans have no experience in dealing with intelligent non-human species (except Neanderthals, perhaps). When it comes to machines and the impact machines have on society, culture, economy, politics, and other aspects of human lives, all our theories emanate from the industrial era. But if the underlying definition of machine changes, it could alter a lot of things.

The great transformation of moving into the Narrow AI (problem-solution-centric artificial intelligence without self-awareness e.g. finance or healthcare applications) has already happened. Tens of billions of dollars are being invested to accelerate and increase the pace of innovation in artificial intelligence. As the definition of machine changes, all the existing models of business, strategy, organization, management—and almost all social sciences—would need to be readjusted and even altered. Even the advent of narrow artificial intelligence demands that competitive intelligence and strategic analysis be approached from a different perspective. To stay competitive, a businessperson must stay informed about these developments. After all, once a challenger to the exquisite marvel of human consciousness is invented, everything changes.

References

Azevedo, F.A.C. et al. (2009). Equal numbers of neuronal and nonneuronal cells make the human brain an isometrically scaled-up primate brain. *Journal of Comparative Neurology*, 513(5), 532–541.

Baars, B. J. (2016). *On Consciousness*. Kindle Edition.

Baars, B. J. et al. (2013). Global workspace dynamics: Cortical 'binding and propagation' enables conscious contents. *Frontiers in Psychology*, 4(May), 1

Baars, B.J., and Franklin, S. (2009). Consciousness is computational: The LIDA model of global workspace theory. *International Journal of Machine Consciousness*, 1(1). Available from: www.researchgate.net/profile/Stan_Franklin/

publication/238423831_Consciousness_is_computational_The_LIDA_model_of_global_workspace_theory/links/0f317530ba440c8791000000/Consciousness-is-computational-The-LIDA-model-of-global-workspace-theory.pdf.

Braver, T.S. et al. (2003). Neural mechanisms of transient and sustained cognitive control during task switching. *Neuron*, 39(4), 713–726.

Candes, E. et al. (2016). *Applied Harmonic Analysis, Massive Data Sets, Machine Learning, and Signal Processing*. Available from: www.birs.ca/cmo-workshops/2016/16w5136/report16w5136.pdf

Chalmers, D.J. (2010). *The Character of Consciousness*. Oxford: Oxford University Press., 4

Courtney, S.M. (2004). Emergent properties of information representation. *Cognitive, Affective & Behavioral Neuroscience*, 4(4), 501–516.

David, P.A. (1985). Clio and the economics of QWERTY. *The American Economic Review*, 75(2), 332–337.

David, P.A. (2007). Path dependence: A foundational concept for historical social science. *Cliometrica*, 1, 191–114.

Doell, C. and Siebert, S. (2016). Evaluation of cognitive architectures inspired by cognitive biases. *Procedia—Procedia Computer Science*, 88, 155–162. Available from: http://dx.doi.org/10.1016/j.procs.2016.07.419.

Franke, B. et al. (2016). Statistical inference, learning and models in big data. *International Statistical Review*. [Online] 84(3), 371–389.

Franklin, S. et al. (2016). A LIDA cognitive model tutorial. *Biologically Inspired Cognitive Architectures*, 16, 105–130. Available from: http://dx.doi.org/10.1016/j.bica.2016.04.003.

Franklin, S. and Graesser, A. (1997). *Is It an Agent, or Just a Program?*: A Taxonomy for Autonomous Agents in Proceedings of the Third International Workshop on Agent Theories, Architectures, and Languages Berlin: Springer Verlag., 25

Fryman, L. et al. (2016). *The Data and Analytics Playbook: Proven Methods For Governed Data and Analytic Quality*. Cambridge, MA: Morgan Kaufmann.

Goertzel, B. (2007). Human-level artificial general intelligence and the possibility of a technological singularity. A reaction to Ray Kurzweil's The Singularity Is Near, and McDermott's critique of Kurzweil. *Artificial Intelligence*, 171(18), 1161–1173.

Goertzel, B. (2014). Characterizing human-like consciousness: An integrative approach. *Procedia Computer Science*, 42, 1–25.

Heylighen, F. (2007). The Global Superorganism: An evolutionary-cybernetic model of the emerging network society. *Journal of Social and Evolutionary Systems*, 6(1), 1–37.

Heylighen, F. and Lenartowicz, M. (2016). The Global Brain as a model of the future information society: An introduction to the special issue. *Technological Forecasting and Social Change*, 114. Available from: www.sciencedirect.com/science/article/pii/S004016251630539X.

Kurzweil, R. (2005). *The Singularity Is Near*. London: Duckworth.

Lindquist, K.A. and Barrett, L.F. (2012). A functional architecture of the human brain: Emerging insights from the science of emotion. *Trends in Cognitive Sciences*, 16(11), 533–540. Available from: http://dx.doi.org/10.1016/j.tics.2012.09.005.

Lokhorst, G.-J. (2016). Descartes and the pineal gland. *The Stanford Encyclopedia of Philosophy*. Available from: https://plato.stanford.edu/archives/sum2016/entries/pineal-gland/.

Mello, S.K.D. and Franklin, S. (2007). *Exploring the Complex Interplay Between AI and Consciousness* (pp. 49–54). Available from: www.aaai.org/Papers/Symposia/Fall/2007/FS-07-01/FS07-01-009.pdf

Muthukrishna, M. et al. (2016). Innovation in the collective brain. *Philosophical Transactions of the Royal Society of London. Series B, Biological Sciences*, 371: 20150192. http://dx.doi.org/10.1098/rstb.2015.0192. Available from: rstb.royalsocietypublishing.org.

Qiu, J. et al. (2016). A survey of machine learning for big data processing. *EURASIP Journal on Advances in Signal Processing*. Available from: http://dx.doi.org/10.1186/s13634-016-0355-x.

Rond, M. de (2014). The structure of serendipity. *Culture and Organization*, 20(5), 342–358.

Rosenberg, N. (1982). *Inside the Black Box: Technology and Economics*. Cambridge, MA: Cambridge University Press.

Rosenberg, N. (1994). *Exploring the Black Box: Technology, Economics, and History*. Cambridge, MA: Cambridge University Press.

Rosenblum, F. (2015). Power and politics: A threat to the Global Brain. *Technological Forecasting and Social Change*, 114, 43–47. Available from: http://dx.doi.org/10.1016/j.techfore.2016.06.035.

Schroeder, M. J. (2011). Concept of information as a bridge between mind and brain. *Information*, 2(3), 478–509.

Sheu, Y. S. and Courtney, S. M. (2016). A neural mechanism of cognitive control for resolving conflict between abstract task rules. *Cortex*, 85, 13–24. Available from: http://dx.doi.org/10.1016/j.cortex.2016.09.018.

Tononi, G. (2008). Consciousness as integrated information: A provisional manifesto. *Biological Bulletin*, 215(3), 216–242.

Tuszynski, J., and Woolf, N. (2006). *The Emerging Physics of Consciousness*. J. Tuszynski (Ed.). Berlin, Germany: Springer. Chapter 1, 4

Vernon, D. et al. (2007). A survey of artificial cognitive systems: Implications for the autonomous development of mental capabilities in computational agents. *IEEE Transactions on Evolutionary Computation*, 11(2), 151–180.

Waskom, M. L. et al. (2014). Frontoparietal representations of task context support the flexible control of goal-directed cognition. *Journal of Neuroscience*, 34(32), 10743–10755. Available from: www.jneurosci.org/cgi/doi/10.1523/JNEUROSCI.5282-13.2014.

Zhang, C. et al. (2016). Neurocomputing MapReduce based distributed learning algorithm for restricted Boltzmann machine. *Neurocomputing*, 198, 4–11. Available from: http://dx.doi.org/10.1016/j.neucom.2015.09.129.

Zhang, L. and Suganthan, P. N. (2016). A survey of randomized algorithms for training neural networks. *Information Sciences*, 364–365, 146–155. Available from: http://dx.doi.org/10.1016/j.ins.2016.01.039.

9 Corruption Intelligence and Analysis

Duane Windsor

Introduction

Corruption remains pervasive in various countries. Anti-corruption control involves transparency, intelligence, preparation, and prevention. Global businesses—multinational enterprises operating across countries—locate at the interface between international anti-corruption accords and national anti-corruption laws on the one hand and bribery and facilitation demands in host countries on the other hand (Cuervo-Cazurra, 2016). Increased anti-corruption enforcement and increased public attention to corruption scandals make intelligence and analysis vitally important. In reaction to corruption conditions and scandals, governments have been replaced in elections as in the Ukraine or through impeachment of chief executives as in Brazil and South Korea. China and India have embraced major anti-corruption campaigns.

Businesses operating abroad must prepare for actual conditions in each host country—and conditions do vary considerably. Global businesses are expected not only to obey anti-corruption laws in both home and host countries but further to commit voluntarily to combating corruption as reflected in the tenth anti-corruption principle of the UN Global Compact (Healy and Serafeim, 2016; Hess, 2009).

This chapter assembles information about corruption intelligence and analysis and anti-corruption planning by global businesses. Intelligence, analysis, and planning can better prepare companies and executives for actual conditions in the field (Esslinger, 2016; Fleisher and Hursky, 2016). Businesses must study international standards, home country and host country laws, and ISO 37001 (2016) anti-corruption systems. Businesses must keep track of prosecution cases and investigations by authorities (ETHIC Intelligence, 2016; FCPA Blog, 2017).

This chapter has four objectives. First, this introduction points out four key considerations for global businesses. The second section explains some basic considerations about corruption that a business should understand. The third section explains where to locate more detailed information about specific countries and the regions in which those countries are located. A fourth objective—captured in the citations linked to the reference section—is to point businesses to important literature about corruption conditions and anti-corruption reforms. The concluding section summarizes the chapter's contributions.

Business executives should appreciate four key considerations when operating abroad: (a) host country operations require different non-market capabilities: (b) anti-corruption enforcement raises business costs; (c) some other firms may well be corrupt; and (d) a business is not fully insulated against responsibility by agents or compliance programs.

First, drawing on a study by Hong (2016), global businesses may tend to assume that home country non-market capabilities (such as lobbying or even domestic bribery skills) may transfer readily to host countries. On the contrary, each host country may involve additional institutional costs that are not readily apparent. Additional costs work in both directions: to a host country with higher corruption, and to a host country with lower corruption. A business must adapt in both directions, by higher investments in non-market capabilities.

Second, drawing on a study by Graham and Stroup (2016), anti-bribery enforcement tends to raise the cost of doing business. The authors studied Foreign Corrupt Practices Act (FCPA) enforcement actions by the US Department of Justice. When a country has been previously targeted in such enforcement, on average there follows a 40% reduction in fixed capital investments by US businesses, which become less likely to acquire foreign firms in that country.

Third, there is corruption competition from other firms (Pinto, Leana, and Pil, 2008). This competition stems from corruption within businesses (Campbell and Göritz, 2014). Demand for corruption can arise from both business and government sides (Gorsira, Denkers, and Huisman, 2016; Navot, Reingewertz, and Cohen, 2016). Transparency International's Bribe Payers' Index 2011 reports comparative information on perceived propensity to bribery by the multinationals of 28 countries (Transparency International, 2011). Indonesia, Mexico, China, and Russia are at the bottom. There are four basic sources of business corruption.

- Corruption can reflect orchestration within top management ranks. Until uncovered by German and US prosecutors, Siemens (of Germany) for years operated a massive corruption scheme in certain lines of businesses across multiple countries. Siemens has borne several billions of dollars in liabilities and reform costs.
- Corruption often involves misconduct by employees in violation of formal company policies supporting compliance with anti-corruption laws and international standards. There may be a belief among employees that bribery is a necessary—and thus not unethical—instrument for business in various countries.
- Corruption can involve misconduct of agents or consultants in violation of formal company policies. Such corruption may be intended by

corporate management or employees. Siemens reportedly used some 2,700 consultants in operating outside Germany.
* Firms may be tainted by corruption misconduct of business partners. In March 2017, information suggested a Dutch criminal investigation of the largest Dutch bank ING concerning corruption and money laundering (Netherlands, 2017). Allegedly, the bank may have been involved in payments by a business made to a company owned by an Uzbek government official.

Fourth, a business does not fully shield itself against responsibility through the use of agents or anti-corruption compliance codes and programs. Under the FCPA, at trial in a US federal court, the judicial doctrine of *respondeat superior* "automatically imposes criminal responsibility on corporate defendants, even if there was a compliance program" (Cassin, 2017). That is, paraphrasing the US Sentencing Guidelines (May 2004), this criminal responsibility attaches when an employee is acting within "the apparent scope of . . . employment, even if the employee acted directly contrary to company policy and instructions" (Cassin, 2017). *Respondeat superior* is the common law doctrine that an employer is responsible for the employment-related actions of an employee. This doctrine extends to actions of an agent, paraphrasing from a judge's jury instructions in the 2011 trial of Lindsey Manufacturing (Cassin, 2017). Lindsey Manufacturing was the first privately held firm to go to a jury trial for alleged violation of the FCPA; the firm lost at trial, but the case was then dismissed due to prosecutorial misconduct (Cassin, 2017).

Understanding Corruption

World Bank President Dr. Jim Yong Kim characterized corruption as "public enemy No. 1" in the developing world (Reuters, 2013, Paragraph 4): "Every dollar that a corrupt official or a corrupt business person puts in their pocket is a dollar stolen from a pregnant woman who needs healthcare. . . . In the developing world, corruption is public enemy No. 1." There is thus a strong moral indictment of corruption. There are also political and economic indictments of corruption, as undermining constitutional democracy and distorting markets. The World Bank Group (2016) estimates global bribery at about $1 trillion, resulting in considerably greater economic losses. Any multinational—like any domestic business—has a very difficult problem in defending any participation in corruption as a business necessity.

Formal Global Consensus Against Corruption

Supporting moral, political, and economic objections to corruption, domestic laws in virtually every country prohibit various forms of corruption, especially bribery of public officials by businesses or individuals. This prohibition often extends to private-to-private corruption among businesses, in various forms (Argandoña, 2003; Goel, Budak, and Rajh, 2015). Evidence suggests private corruption in both Denmark and Estonia, countries featuring small and medium-sized enterprises (SMEs) (Johannsen, Pedersen, Vadi, Reino, and Sööt, 2016).

The UN Convention Against Corruption (UNCAC) formalizes an international consensus against corruption. This consensus is reinforced by several multilateral regional anti-corruption agreements and the anti-corruption principle of the voluntary UN Global Compact.

The UNCAC is a legally binding and universal anti-corruption convention, signed by most members of the United Nations. At December 12, 2016, there were 140 signatories and in total 181 parties—including the European Union. The agreement (adopted by the UN General Assembly on October 31, 2003) entered into force on December 14, 2005. Only a very few countries have not signed or ratified, for example: in Africa—Chad, Equatorial Guinea, Eritrea, and Somalia; in South America—Suriname; and North Korea (UNODC, 2016).

> The Convention requires countries to establish criminal and other offences to cover a wide range of acts of corruption, if these are not already crimes under domestic law. In some cases, States are legally obliged to establish offences; in other cases, in order to take into account differences in domestic law, they are required to consider doing so.
>
> (UNODC, 2017b, Paragraph 2)

The World Bank Group and various regional multilateral development banks (African Development Bank, Asian Development Bank, European Bank for Reconstruction and Development, and Inter-American Development Bank) are members of the Agreement for the Mutual Enforcement of Debarment Decisions (AMEDD). The African Infrastructure Investment Bank has announced intention to join AMEDD (Sharif, 2017). "The ultimate sanction is that a firm may be debarred from doing business with these banks" (Sharif, 2017, Paragraph 2).

Defining and Recognizing Corruption

Corruption is a broad term for a variety of forms: "The [UNCAC] Convention covers many different forms of corruption, such as bribery, trading in influence, abuse of functions, and various acts of corruption in the private sector" (UNODC, 2017a, Paragraph 3). The UNCAC addresses both government and private sector corruption. Government corruption involves a public official and either an employee of a business or an individual. This corruption may occur through an act of extortion (by the public official) resulting in a forced bribe or facilitation payment by the business employee or the individual; or through an act of unsolicited bribery (by the business employee or the individual) offered to a receptive public official. Private sector corruption involves two businesses or an individual and a nongovernmental organization (as in education or healthcare).

In December 2009, the Organisation for Economic Co-operation and Development (OECD) recommended that its members act to prohibit exceptions for facilitation ("grease") payments, such as permitted in the FCPA. The UK Bribery Act 2010 prohibits such payments.

A critical problem is how little detail is known about causes and functioning of corruption—government and private—and about effectiveness of anti-corruption reform efforts (Chen, Yasar, and Rejesus, 2008; Lee and Guven, 2013; Martin, Cullen, Johnson, and Parboteeah, 2007; O'Hara, 2014). In providing a detailed list of questions that for this chapter a business can ask about corruption in each country, Chayes (2014b, Paragraph 2) states: "despite the significance of the problem, little is known about how corrupt systems function." What is commonly understood is that systemic corruption in various countries may be essentially a form of "disguised crime syndicates" operating as governments:

> But in a range of countries around the world, corruption is the system— and a remarkably effective one. Governments are restructured to serve a purpose that has nothing to do with public administration. The aim is amassing personal wealth for the benefit of ruling networks—an objective they achieve with intent, skill, and efficiency. Capacity deficits and other weakness may in fact be part of the way the system functions, rather than evidence of a breakdown.
>
> (Chayes, 2014b, Paragraph 3)

> An even more daunting task is to find a cure for corruption, since historical experience does not provide many obvious examples of countries that have been successful in eradicating it. Corruption may be endemic and linked to deep-rooted cultural or "institutional" features of a society, which are not easily overturned by specific policy measures.
>
> (De Rosa, Gooroochurn, and Görg, 2010, p. 2)

There are simple basics to which businesses should pay attention (Treisman, 2007). First, drawing on Transparency International's Corruption Perceptions Index (CPI) information, it appears that, as a correlation, corruption rises with increasing state failure (Chayes, 2014a). Second, drawing on World Bank and World Governance Indicators, it appears that, again as a correlation, corruption falls with political stability and absence of violence or terrorism (Chayes, 2014a). Third, in relationship to violence, onshore oil discoveries (or windfalls) tend to increase the probability of internal conflict (for control or looting to finance rebellions), whereas offshore oil discoveries tend to decrease that probability (because the government can fund its fighting capacity). Andersen, Nordvik, and Tesei (2017) base these findings on a study of a panel of 132 countries over the years 1962 to 2009.

Sources of Information on Corruption

Some Publicly Available Sources

In general terms, there are periodic (a) country corruption reports, (b) surveys of firms, and (c) surveys of citizens—all of which can provide for global businesses insights into country conditions.

A principal source of country corruption reports is Transparency International's annual CPI database, now available for 2016 (Transparency International, 2016). The nongovernmental organization, with national chapters in many countries, draws on various surveys to estimate perceived corruption by country. (Not all countries or other political entities are included.) National embassies, country experts, and national chapters of Transparency International (TI) may have more detailed local information than is readily available in public data sets or academic publications. There appears to be considerable variation by industry. There are also valuable reports concerning specific business experiences (in Russia, Graham, 2012; in Saudi Arabia, Smith, 2014).

One online source, drawing on CPI information for 174 countries (or entities), organizes the information by region (FindTheData, 2017). One must cross-check accuracy of the information against the CPI original source. For Africa of 52 included entities, basically Cape Verde is the cleanest country, while Equatorial Guinea, Chad, Sudan, and Somalia are the most corrupt countries. For Asia, of 45 included entities, while Singapore, Hong Kong, and Japan are relatively clean, North Korea, Afghanistan, and Myanmar at the bottom are worse than many countries in Africa. Europe, covering 43 included entities, has Belarus, Azerbaijan, and Ukraine at the bottom although a little cleaner than the worst countries in Africa or Asia. In South America, of 12 included entities, Paraguay and Venezuela feature at the bottom. North America encompasses the Caribbean and Central America: Haiti is by far the most corrupt country.

The World Bank Group (2016, 2017a, 2017b) surveys firms in various countries to obtain microdata about corruption and related conditions. The presently available online dataset draws on more than 125,000 firms in 139 countries. This source permits grouping and graphing of available data in various ways. Officially expressed, the surveys help businesses gauge "the prevalence of different types of bribery" across the included countries. There are surveys conducted in Latin America (with the Inter-American Development Bank), the Caribbean (with the Inter-American Development Bank and COMPETE Caribbean), in the Middle East and North Africa (with the European Bank for Reconstruction and Development and the European

Investment Bank), in South Asia and in part of Sub-Saharan Africa (with the UK Department for International Development), and in francophone West Africa (with the Dutch Good Growth Fund). There is also an Enterprise Survey conducted in Eastern Europe and Central Asia transition countries conducted with the European Bank for Reconstruction and Development. This last Enterprise Survey has the special name of the Business Environment and Enterprise Performance Survey (BEEPS). The first BEEPS was a survey in 1999–2000 of more than 4,000 firms in 22 countries. The special focus was on the process of transition from communism (and Soviet domination) to market-oriented, democratic regimes. The survey seeks to obtain information on "corruption, state capture, lobbying, and the quality of the business environment" (World Bank, 2017, Paragraph 1). There have been additional rounds of BEEPS, with the 2008–2009 survey covering over 11,000 firms in 28 countries. (The disintegration of Yugoslavia resulted in more countries in Eastern Europe, for instance.) The survey expanded to 29 countries in 2014. There are reports of significant traffic police corruption in some transition countries.

Transparency International also conducts periodic "global barometer" surveys of citizens across countries in regions such as Africa or Asia. These surveys are discussed in the next subsection on country and regional differences.

There are a number of other sources of information about countries publicly available from various organizations. A great deal of data is available through the World Bank Open Data (2017) source. The US Central Intelligence Agency (CIA) (2017) provides online basic information for some 267 world entities. This information includes "history, people, government, economy, geography, communications, transportation, military, and transnational issues." World Bank Doing Business (2017) provides annually, since 2003, a report that attempts to measure costs of firms of business regulations. The most recent ranking report for 190 economies and some selected cities is for 2017. The United Nations Office on Drugs and Crime (UNODC) provides online country information about corruption, money laundering, and organized crime. The World Bank's Worldwide Governance Indicators (WGI) project provides various governance indicators for over 200 entities (countries and territories) over presently the period 1996 to 2015. The indicators emphasize six governance dimensions: voice and accountability, political stability and absence of violence, governmental effectiveness, regulatory quality, and rule of law—in addition to, for purposes of this chapter, control of corruption (World Bank Worldwide Governance Indicators, 2017). The Heritage Foundation (2017) provides information concerning 12 dimensions of economic freedoms (such as property rights and financial freedom) in 186 countries. The Heritage Foundation groups the 12 dimensions into four broad categories ("pillars" of economic freedom): rule of law, government size, regulatory efficiency, and market openness. The World Economic Forum (2016, 2017) publishes reports on global competitiveness and global risks. Law firms specializing in international business issue various guides that may be valuable (see STEELE, 2016). Researchers publish detailed studies of countries: see Batory (2012) and Hanousek and Kochanova (2016), on Central Eastern Europe; Johannsen and Pedersen (2011), on the Baltic republics; Xu (2014), on India.

Understanding Country and Regional Differences

While available information affords a general overview of country conditions, one must emphasize how much variation there is within any comparison across countries. Zaum (2013, p. 1) points out that:

> Afghanistan and Burma (Myanmar) might have the same score on Transparency International's Corruption Perceptions Index, but how corruption affects governance, economic development, and security, what its implications are, and how it is best addressed will be different for each of these countries.

Variations in host country institutions' arrangements and relationships require detailed microdata and local knowledge. For example, in Brazil there are government-owned enterprises and other entities (such as hospitals and public utilities) for whom key individuals might be regarded as government officials under anti-corruption laws such as FCPA or the Clean Companies Act (CCA) of Brazil, in effect 2014 (Jones, Medina, and Sheahen, 2017).

Chayes (2014a) suggests that there are two broad categories of pervasively corrupt governments. These variations have significance for global businesses. One category is what Chayes analyzes as structured kleptocracy with vertical integration of corruption networks: corruption pyramids toward the top. Instances, today or in the recent past until changes in government, include (per Chayes): Algeria, Angola, Azerbaijan, Cameroon, Egypt, Nigeria, Peru, Russia, Tunisia, Ukraine, Uzbekistan, and Venezuela. The second category is what Chayes characterizes as pervasive corruption without such consolidation at the top of a pyramid. Instances today or in the recent past include: Colombia, Guatemala, Honduras, India, Ivory Coast, Mexico, Somalia, and South Sudan.

Cybercrime, like money laundering, may be an increasing aspect of corruption. A US investigation appears in March 2017 to identify North Korea, perhaps acting through Chinese middlemen, as the source of the electronic cybercrime heist of some $101 million ($81 million remaining lost) of Bangladesh central bank funds held in deposit at the New York Federal Reserve Bank in February 2016 (Viswanatha and Hong, 2017). The hackers had requested transfer of $951 million, and the Federal Reserve Bank became suspicious during the hacking process. The funds went to accounts in Sri Lanka and the Philippines.

European Union (Western and Central Eastern Europe)

Even the European Union, expanding to include Central Eastern Europe and facing BREXIT, is not strictly free of corruption. CPA data make clear that some countries—France, Italy, Portugal, and Spain for instance—are not as clean as Scandinavia is reputed to be. Central Eastern Europe into the Baltic States and the Balkans remains in transition from Soviet-dominated communist regimes in the recent past.

In February–March 2013, the European Commission (2014, p. 3) surveyed 27,786 respondents across 27 member states and also Croatia (then in process of accession). The report indicates that 76% of respondents thought corruption to be widespread in their own country (2014, p. 6). Above 90% of respondents thought so in (in order of proportion from highest to lowest): Greece (99%); Italy (97%); Lithuania, Spain, and Czech Republic (95%); Croatia (94%); Romania (93%); Slovenia (91%); Portugal and Slovakia (90%) (2014, p. 6). Only in Nordic countries did a majority of respondents think corruption rare: declining from 75% in Denmark to 64% in Finland to a bare majority (54%) in Sweden (2014, p. 6). Across the respondents, 38% thought there was corruption among private companies (2014, p. 6).

Sub-Saharan Africa

Between March 2014 and September 2015, TI and Afrobarometer surveyed 43,143 respondents across 28 countries of Sub-Saharan Africa (not including North Africa) (Transparency International, 2015). TI estimates from the responses that nearly 75 million people likely paid a bribe in some form during a one-year period. These bribe payments included avoiding punishment by police or courts, and also access to basic services. A majority of respondents felt corruption is increasing and anti-corruption efforts are failing. The most negative information came from Ghana, Liberia, Nigeria, and Sierra Leone. The 2010 annual Africa Development Indicators report of the World Bank concluded that what it termed "quiet corruption" is widespread—with effects on agriculture, education, and health sectors (Voa News, 2010).

Asia and Pacific

Between July 2015 and January 2017, TI surveyed 21,861 respondents across 16 countries and territories of Asia and the adjacent Pacific Ocean region (Transparency International, 2017a, 2017b). Relative to population (the region includes several large countries), the survey proportion seems smaller relative to Africa. The countries surveyed include from west to east and south (ending at Papua-New Guinea and Australia): Pakistan, India, Ceylon, China, Hong Kong, Taiwan, Mongolia, South Korea, Japan, Myanmar (Burma), Thailand, Cambodia, Vietnam, Malaysia, Indonesia, and Australia. Thus Bangladesh and the Philippines, as well as a number of other countries, were excluded. TI estimates from the responses that some 900 million persons (over 25% of the 16-entity region's population) paid a bribe in some form during a one-year period. Reported rates were highest (nearly 67%) in India and Vietnam. Reported rates were lowest (in alphabetical order) in Australia, Hong Kong, Japan, and South Korea. Across Asia, police were the most frequent source of kickback demands, as reported by just under one-third of respondents.

Conclusion

A critical problem is the limited effective information about causes and functioning of corruption—government and private—and about effectiveness of anti-corruption reform efforts in general. The practical details of corruption vary considerably across countries. This chapter assembles public sources of information about corruption that companies can access in order to begin assembling corruption intelligence for analysis and planning purposes. Preparation to confront corruption is important for global businesses. Corruption—in various forms—is pervasive in some countries and found in many countries. Even countries relatively clean from government corruption may feature private-to-private corruption among businesses and individuals, as has been reported in recent literature. Businesses should collect intelligence on various conditions in host countries, analyze that intelligence, and prepare for dealing with those conditions—including preparing employees, agents, and business partners (domestic and global). There are multiple sources of information available: Transparency International and its country chapters, World Bank, national embassies, country experts, international law firms, academic studies, and reports of specific business experiences. This chapter provides a starting point for intelligence gathering rather than a comprehensive listing.

References

Andersen, J. J., Nordvik, F. M., and Tesei, A. (2017, March 16). *Oil and Civil Conflict: On and Off (Shore)*. Available from: https://ssrn.com/abstract=2933428

Argandoña, A. (2003). Private-to-private corruption. *Journal of Business Ethics*, 47(3), 253–267.

Batory, A. (2012). Why do anti-corruption laws fail in Central Eastern Europe? A target compliance perspective. *Regulation & Governance*, 6(1), 66–82.

Campbell, J. L. and Göritz, A. S. (2014). Culture corrupts! A qualitative study of organizational culture in corrupt organizations. *Journal of Business Ethics*, 120(3), 291–311.

Cassin, R. L. (2017, March 17). *Practice Note: A Jury Instruction on FCPA Corporate Responsibility*. Available from: http://fcpablog.squarespace.com/blog/2017/3/17/practice-note-a-jury-instruction-on-fcpa-corporate-responsib.html

Chayes, S. (2014a, June 6). *Corruption: The Unrecognized Threat to International Security—Acute, Structured Government Corruption Impacts Many of the West's*

Security Priorities. But the Role It plays in Exacerbating International Insecurity Is Often Overlooked. Available from: http://carnegieendowment.org/2014/06/06/corruption-unrecognized-threat-to-international-security/hcts

Chayes, S. (2014b, September 9). *Corruption: The Priority Intelligence Requirements— The Questions Decision Makers Need to Ask to Truly Understand Countries Where Corruption Pervades the Political System*. Available from: http://carnegieendowment.org/2014/09/09/corruption-priority-intelligence-requirements-pub-56572

Chen, Y., Yasar, M., and Rejesus, R. M. (2008). Factors influencing the incidence of bribery payouts by firms: A cross-country analysis. *Journal of Business Ethics*, 77(2), 231–244.

Cuervo-Cazurra, A. (2016). Corruption in international business. *Journal of World Business*, 51(1), 35–49.

De Rosa, D., Gooroochurn, N., and Görg, H. (2010, August). Corruption and productivity. Firm-level evidence from the BEEPS survey. *World Bank Policy Research Working Paper*, No. 5348. http://dx.doi.org/10.1596/1813-9450-5348. Available from: https://core.ac.uk/download/pdf/6293376.pdf

Esslinger, G. (2016, April 1). *Political Risk Analysis Can Save Your Compliance Program*. Available from: www.fcpablog.com/blog/2016/4/1/greg-esslinger-political-risk-analysis-can-save-your-complia.html

ETHIC Intelligence. (2016). Available from: www.ethic-intelligence.com/compliance-tools/102-anti-corruption-case-law/

European Commission. (2014, February). *Special Eurobarometer 397: Corruption*. Available from: http://ec.europa.eu/public_opinion/archives/ebs/ebs_397_en.pdf

FCPA Blog, The. (2017, March 26). Available from: www.fcpablog.com/

FindTheData by Graphiq. (2017). *Compare Corruption By Country*. Retrieved from http://country-corruption.findthedata.com/

Fleisher, C. and Hursky, R. (2016). Empowering insight: The role of collaboration in the evolution of intelligence practice. *South African Journal of Information Management*, 18(2), 1–10.

Goel, R. K., Budak, J., and Rajh, E. (2015). Private sector bribery and effectiveness of anti-corruption policies. *Applied Economics Letters*, 22(10), 759–766.

Gorsira, M., Denkers, A., and Huisman, W. (2016). Both sides of the coin: Motives for corruption among public officials and business employees. *Journal of Business Ethics*. Available from: https://link.springer.com/article/10.1007%2Fs10551-016-3219-2

Graham, A. (2012, November 27). *The Thought Leader Interview: William J. O'Rourke: The Former Head of Alcoa Russia Teaches Executives That in International Business Practice, Ethics and Competitive Advantage Go Hand in Hand*. Available from: www.strategy-business.com/article/00149?gko=924a7

Graham, B. and Stroup, C. (2016). Does anti-bribery enforcement deter foreign investment? *Applied Economics Letters*, 23(1), 63–67.

Hanousek, J. and Kochanova, A. (2016). Bribery environments and firm performance: Evidence from CEE countries. *European Journal of Political Economy*, 43(1), 14–28.

Healy, P. M. and Serafeim, G. (2016). An analysis of firms' self-reported anticorruption efforts. *The Accounting Review*, 91(2), 489–511.

Heritage Foundation, The. (2017). *2017 Index of Economic Freedom*. Washington, DC: The Heritage Foundation in partnership with *The Wall Street Journal*. Retrieved from www.heritage.org/index/about

Hess, D. (2009). Catalyzing corporate commitment to combating corruption. *Journal of Business Ethics*, 88(4), 781–790.

Hong, S. J. (2016). Experiential learning about host country non-market environment. *Journal of Multinational Corporation Strategy*, 1(3/4), 204–216.

International Standards Organisation (ISO) 37001. (2016). *Anti-Bribery Management Systems*. Accessed December 20, 2016. Available from: www.iso.org/iso/iso_37001_anti_bribery_mss.pdf

Johannsen, L. and Pedersen, K.H. (2011). The institutional roots of anticorruption policies: Comparing the three Baltic states. *Journal of Baltic Studies*, 42(3), 329–346.

Johannsen, L., Pedersen, K.H., Vadi, M., Reino, A., and Sööt, M.-L. (2016, February 4). *Private-to-Private Corruption: A Survey on Danish and Estonian Business Environment*. Aarhus University, Tartu University, and the Estonian Ministry of Justice. Available from: www.korruptsioon.ee/sites/www.korruptsioon.ee/files/elfinder/dokumendid/private-to-private_corruption_final_report_2.pdf through www.korruptsioon.ee/en/node/28540

Jones, J., Medina, A., and Sheahen, K. (2017, March 23). *After Odebrecht: Coordinated International Enforcement Is the New Reality*. Available from: www.fcpablog.com/blog/2017/3/23/after-odebrecht-coordinated-international-enforcement-is-the.html

Lee, W.S. and Guven, C. (2013). Engaging in corruption: The influence of cultural values and contagion effects at the microlevel. *Journal of Economic Psychology*, 39, 287–300.

Martin, K.D., Cullen, J.B., Johnson, J.L., and Parboteeah, P. (2007). Deciding to bribe: A cross-level analysis of firm and home country influences on bribery activity. *Academy of Management Journal*, 50(6), 1401–1422.

Navot, D., Reingewertz, Y., and Cohen, N. (2016). Speed or greed? High wages and corruption among public servants. *Administration & Society*, 48(5), 580–601.

Netherlands: ING Drops After Saying Probe May Lead to Significant Fines. (2017, March 23). Available from: http://ethixbase.com/eanews/netherlands-ing-drops-saying-probe-may-lead-significant-fines/

O'Hara, P.A. (2014). Political economy of systemic and micro-corruption throughout the world. *Journal of Economic Issues*, 67, 279–307.

Pinto, J., Leana, C.R., and Pil, F.K. (2008). Corrupt organizations or organizations of corrupt individuals? Two types of organization-level corruption. *Academy of Management Review*, 33(3), 685–709.

Reuters. (2013, December 19). *World Bank President Calls Corruption 'Public Enemy No. 1'*. Available from: www.reuters.com/article/us-worldbank-corruption-idUSBRE9BI11P20131219

Sharif, H. (2017, March 22). *Hamid Sharif: Asian Infrastructure Investment Bank Takes Strong Stance Against Corruption*. Available from: www.fcpablog.com/blog/2017/3/22/hamid-sharif-asian-infrastructure-investment-bank-takes-stro.html

Smith, C. (2014, December 8). *Corruption: Can You Ignore It?* Available from: http://knowledge.insead.edu/ethics/corruption-can-you-ignore-it-3736

STEELE Compliance & Investigation Services. (2016). *E-Book: Legally Obtainable Data in BRIC Countries*. San Francisco: CIS-1006161. Available from: http://confidence.steelecis.com/legally-obtainable-data-ebook-dwnld-fcpab?submissionGuid=cc3e8ef4-be56-44ac-8253-92c9c0010eeb

Transparency International. (2011). *2011 Bribe Payers Index*. Available from: www.transparency.org/bpi2011

Transparency International. (2015, December 1). *People and Corruption: Africa Survey 2015—Global Corruption Barometer*. Available from: www.transparency.org/whatwedo/publication/people_and_corruption_africa_survey_2015

Transparency International. (2016). *Corruption Perceptions Index 2016*. Available from: www.transparency.org/news/feature/corruption_perceptions_index_2016

Transparency International. (2017a, March 7). *Corruption in Asia Pacific: What 20,000+ People Told Us.* Available from: www.transparency.org/news/feature/corruption_in_asia_pacific_what_20000_people_told_us

Transparency International. (2017b, March 7). *People and Corruption: Asia Pacific—Global Corruption Barometer.* Available from: www.transparency.org/whatwedo/publication/people_and_corruption_asia_pacific_global_corruption_barometer

Treisman, D. (2007). What have we learned about the causes of corruption from ten years of cross-national empirical research? *Annual Review of Political Science,* 10(1), 211–244.

United Nations Office on Drugs and Crime (UNODC). (2016, December 12). *Signature and Ratification Status.* Available from: www.unodc.org/unodc/en/corruption/ratification-status.html

United Nations Office on Drugs and Crime (UNODC). (2017a). *Corruption.* Accessed September 30, 2017. Available from: http://www.unodc.org/unodc/en/corruption/uncac.html

United Nations Office on Drugs and Crime (UNODC). (2017b). *United Nations Convention Against Corruption.* Accessed March 27, 2017. Available from: www.unodc.org/unodc/en/treaties/CAC/convention-highlights.html

US Central Intelligence Agency (CIA). (2017). *The World Factbook.* Accessed September 10, 2017. Available from: https://www.cia.gov/library/publications/resources/the-world-factbook/index.html

Viswanatha, A. and Hong, N. (2017, March 23). Feds tie North Korea to bank heist. *The Wall Street Journal* (Eastern Edition) CLLXIX(67), A1, A12.

Voa News. (2010, March 15). *World Bank Report Claims 'Quiet Corruption' in Africa.* Available from: www.voanews.com/a/world-bank-report-claims-quiet-corruption-in-africa-87800482/114188.html

World Bank. (2017). *Business Environment and Enterprise Performance Survey* (BEEPS) Datasets. Accessed September 10, 2017. Available from: http://go.worldbank.org/ET22JRDBU0

World Bank Doing Business. (2017). Doing Business. Accessed March 26, 2017. Available from: www.doingbusiness.org/

World Bank Group. (2016, November 28). *Anti-corruption.* Available from: www.worldbank.org/en/topic/governance/brief/anti-corruption

World Bank Group. (2017a). *Corruption.* Enterprise Surveys: What Businesses Experience. Accessed March 26, 2017. Available from: www.enterprisesurveys.org/data/exploreTopics/Corruption

World Bank Group. (2017b). *Enterprise Surveys: What Businesses Experience.* Accessed March 26, 2017. Available from: www.enterprisesurveys.org/

World Bank Worldwide Governance Indicators. (2017). Worldwide Governance Indicators. Accessed March 26, 2017. Available from: http://info.worldbank.org/governance/wgi/index.aspx#home

World Economic Forum. (2016). *The Global Competitiveness Report 2016–2017.* Available from: www3.weforum.org/docs/GCR2016-2017/05FullReport/The-GlobalCompetitivenessReport2016-2017_FINAL.pdf

World Economic Forum. (2017). *The Global Risks Report 2017.* Available from: www.weforum.org/reports/the-global-risks-report-2017

Xu, B. (2014, September 4). *Governance in India: Corruption.* New York City and Washington, DC: Council on Foreign Relations. Available from: www.cfr.org/corruption-and-bribery/governance-india-corruption/p31823

Zaum, D. (2013, September). *Political Economies of Corruption in Fragile and Conflict-Affected States: Nuancing the Picture.* U4 Anti-Corruption Resource Center, U4 Brief No. 4. Available from: www.u4.no/publications/political-economies-of-corruption-in-fragile-and-conflict-affected-states-nuancing-the-picture/

10 Enterprise Performance Management and Best Practices in Business Planning and Advanced Analytics

Jason Balogh and Sholape Kolawole

Much has been written over the years about performance management as a management theory, but with the advent of advanced technologies and the explosion of business complexity and new business models, the concept has re-emerged as a critical differentiator in organizational performance. Performance management is, at its core, a fundamental underpinning of the business. It is essentially how companies operate: work is planned, resources are allocated, business is conducted either in line with or outside of expectations, the business reacts, and people are compensated for their contribution.

While every business "does" some form of performance management, many do not optimize their execution of the cycle, resulting in less-than-ideal levels of efficiency and effectiveness.

The Hackett Group, through its empirical methodology and experience in the field, has identified the factors separating top performers from other, more typical companies, which the authors deem as the "peer group," or "peers." Differences occur both in external financial performance and in the internal business process performance measures used. Beginning with the external view, this research has proved that companies with high-performing enterprise performance management (EPM) capabilities are 50% more likely to outperform their industry peers in financial net margin performance. This is a dramatic level of differentiation in today's highly competitive market climate. From a business process perspective, the gap between peers and top performers is significant as well. Further The Hackett Group's data reveals that top performers execute EPM-related processes at 30% less cost than peers, are three times more accurate in their forecasts, issue 58% fewer reports across the enterprise, and spend one-third less time manually collecting and compiling data for analysis. This data makes clear that the superior financial outcomes of EPM top performers are due to their stronger ability to predict, react, and respond efficiently and effectively to changes in the business climate.

The vastly increased complexity of business models today explains the disparity in EPM capability levels and amplifies the financial performance advantage that can be derived from EPM outperformance. Expansion of

> **Global Life Sciences Conglomerate Addresses EPM/BI Complexity**
>
> **Challenge**
> The company had grown for decades through acquisition in a multi-business unit model with decentralized decision authority, resulting in over 500,000 performance reports and over 150 ERP / reporting systems across the footprint. This resulted in below-peer-group efficiency and effectiveness levels in finance and IT functions.
>
> **Solution / Benefits**
> The organization launched a two-year transformation to address these complexities through process and system redesign and standardization.
> - Targeted report rationalization efforts to remove over 60% of the reporting volumes across the enterprise.
> - Developed a roadmap to migrate to less than 20 ERPs and reporting systems.

Figure 10.1 Sample Client Challenge and Solution

product lines, service offerings, management structure, geographic diversity, mergers, acquisitions, and regulatory dynamics has made it extraordinarily complicated to answer the question, "How do I know if we had a good day today?" Fragmented information technology and a rapidly changing digital technology landscape only add fuel to the fire (see Figure 10.1).

Top performers studied by The Hackett Group focus on the aggressive reduction of EPM complexity within the above context, along with the simultaneous embrace of new waves of digital capability that can yield greater insights to the business. However, a set of common definitions of terms is a fundamental starting requirement.

EPM Defined: A Cycle to Run the Business

The authors submit that performance management is truly a cycle; indeed, it is the core cycle by which a business is run. Figure 10.4 illustrates this cycle, beginning with strategic planning and moving through the various steps of business operation, ultimately reaching the phases of reward, coach, and incentive compensation.

Strategic Planning and Target Setting

This is usually an annual event in which the executive leadership team (at the corporate, business-unit, and functional levels) comes together to look ahead and set long-term performance objectives based on expectations about the future business climate. One critical input to this process is the single set of internal and external assumptions that are used to substantiate the estimates. Another critical factor is the healthy relationship of the corporate body with the business-unit body of management. In high-performance environments, corporate takes the role of challenging a part of the portfolio to achieve a certain performance level, while that business unit builds the estimate for what can be achieved. The result often involves decisions about the deployment of future capital and resources to meet the desired outcome. Thus, the business is anchored not on a corporate number or a business-unit number, but a single, shared target. It is also critical that the targets for the next year are a natural cascade back from the three- or five-year strategic plan result, thereby making the strategic plan more real and eliminating "hockey stick" upticks in performance that are unrealistic in the out-years of the plan.

Annual Planning

The annual plan is the primary planning event of the organization's fiscal year and is often the leading cause of late nights and weekends for professionals in multiple functions. It does serve an important purpose, however, as the core to accountability at the enterprise, business-unit, and even individual level. For this reason, annual planning remains a critical component in the EPM cycle. But it should be stripped of needless complexity through automation, use of business drivers, and reduction in iterations.

Periodic Forecasting

This activity, involving the recasting of expectations based on the latest actual performance of the business, is often both time-consuming and error-prone. Whether at monthly or quarterly increments, top performers tend to rigorously proceduralize this event, similar to a financial close process, and "rise up" the level of detail and use of operational drivers to minimize the manual work involved. By taking these steps and leveraging planning technology, organizations are working toward de-emphasizing the annual planning event. Instead, they are replacing it with ongoing "fast forecast" capabilities that link forecasts across demand, supply, and financials with integrated workflow automation and transparency to the underlying operational and financial numbers.

Reporting, Business Reviews, and Gap Closure

This step in the EPM cycle involves the reporting of actual performance across the business, often the formalized reviews of (a) each part of the portfolio on a monthly basis, and (b) what mechanisms are used to determine how to close gaps that have arisen between actuals and planned commitments. The reporting activities may well present another opportunity to reduce complexity in execution. The Hackett Group's data indicates that top performers rely on 58% fewer business performance reports than the peer group; further, a far greater portion of these are delivered via automated (as opposed to manual) means. The content of the reports differs, as well: top performers define

	Characteristics	Key Questions
1	Linked to Objectives	Can the measure be aligned with an objective?
2	Controllable / Influenceable	Can the results be controlled or significantly influenced under a span of responsibility?
3	Actionable	Can action be taken to improve the metric's performance?
4	Simple	Can the measure be easily and clearly explained?
5	Credible	Is the measure resistant to manipulation?
6	Integrated	Can the measure be linked both down and across the organization?
7	Measurable	Can the measure be quantified?

Figure 10.2 Reporting and KPI Checklist

their key performance indicators (KPIs) at the enterprise level by tying them to their strategic objectives, not just financial performance. Top performers aim for a balance among KPIs for quality, cost, time, and service levels, and cascade these through the organization. This approach lets teams focus on what matters from an enterprise standpoint; it has the added benefit of helping the business avoid wasting time measuring and managing things that do not ultimately matter. Figure 10.2 offers a simple yet powerful checklist to consider when refining reporting and KPIs.

Additionally, top performers streamline the business review process by spending less time debating about definitions of metrics and what has already occurred, and more on alternative responses, the likely results of each response, and the potential costs and benefits of each. This requires executive pressure to standardize even to the extent of the size, structure, and content of presentation materials; information that is outside the business review standard package may be interesting, but not relevant to the review itself (see Figure 10.3).

Incentive Compensation

The authors' experience has shown that the most effective, least expensive way to influence behavior is to change how an individual or a part of the business is compensated. The power of incentive compensation is great, but therefore must be carefully adjusted and aligned to achieve the desired

---

Global Automotive Company Drives KPIs Through the Enterprise

Challenge

The company required assistance with simplifying, standardizing, and eliminating non-value-added and duplicative work across the organization, as well as wanted to reset the business on the right measures at every level.

Solution / Benefits

The organization launched a six-month project to identify the appropriate KPIs, cascading them throughout the organization and developing scorecards and reports to aid in achieving the overall strategy.

- Aligned each KPI to the appropriate level in the organization and associated each KPI with the appropriate strategic objective it supports, which eliminated duplication of effort and data inconsistencies.
- Eliminated approximately 40% of the non-essential reports in the business.
- Addressed value chain issues through shipments of vehicles across the global footprint by aligning incentives more appropriately to maximize enterprise profit.

Figure 10.3 Sample Client Challenge and Solution

(as opposed to unintended) consequences. Without delving too far into the dynamics of best practices in incentives, EPM cycles should employ reward systems that tie directly to the desired outcomes. Often, organizations miss this step, with the result that new metrics and reports fail to change behaviors. The reality is that visibility to information does not in itself change decision modes unless somehow factored into the compensation model itself (see Figure 10.4).

Having documented the performance and value gaps that exist between top performers and the peer group, and having defined the cycle of EPM, the next order of business is to define the specific practices or characteristics that top performers exhibit in the EPM cycle that explain their substantial performance advantage. The Hackett Group has developed a service delivery model outlining the core components of EPM capabilities. In the next section, the model to categorize and explore these differences in performance levels is used.

EPM and the Service Delivery Model

EPM capabilities are contingent on the organization's maturity and capability in several service delivery dimensions, illustrated in the blue sphere below. The center of the model outlines the new, overt focus on the customer and customer-centricity, with the core enterprise capabilities of "Digital," "Agile," and "Data Driven" anchoring the new ways by which organizations are becoming more customer-centric. The outer components define the assets of service delivery that the organization can employ to execute within its business model. Specifically, these are: technology, service design, analytics and information management, organization and governance, service partnering, and human capital. Experiences with clients indicate that top performers do not tend to outperform in any one dimension, but rather

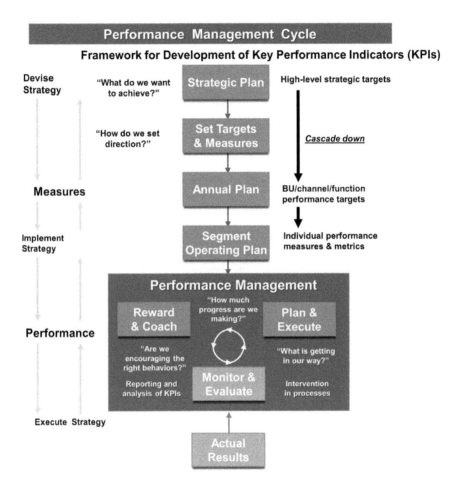

Figure 10.4 Performance Management Linkage

demonstrate a balanced, mature degree of capability across the entire spectrum. Thus, investments in technology alone do not guarantee the benefits of EPM referenced at the start of this chapter.

Another important consideration in service delivery is that it is situational and contingent upon the strategic objectives of the business as well as the core business operating model. For instance, while The Hackett Group's research points to data and technology standardization as being highly correlated with top performance, the actual methods and solutions employed by an organization will differ based on its place on the spectrum of centralization in decision-making and governance. A company consisting of multiple businesses would place greater responsibility on business units to drive standards in these areas, as opposed to an integrated operating model

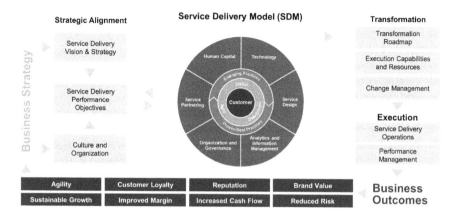

Figure 10.5 Hackett Service Delivery Transformation Lifecycle

that would work toward further enterprise-wide standards. Performance in each dimension will determine value that can be derived in EPM for a given organization. The authors focused on further definition of three with the greatest impact on EPM capability: technology, analytics and information management, and human capital (see Figure 10.5).

Technology

This involves the degree by which the organization's technology landscape contributes to the EPM cycle. Attention has been paid to the design and implementation of a variety of EPM-specific technologies that sit atop legacy and ERP applications as a proven enabler and set of "guardrails" for the EPM cycle. Top performers drive standards in tool selection, design, and adoption. They also reach beyond the EPM layer and focus on the effectiveness of the entire architecture—ERP, data warehousing, data integration tools, and EPM and BI applications, as well as a variety of information delivery tools. With the advent of digital transformation, leaders are able to quickly extend their technology architecture to factor in external data sources, big data and advanced analytic applications, and social and mobile platforms as well. While initially digital technology appears to further complicate the architecture dynamic, top performers are fast realizing that the benefits of increased insight are worth the added complexity.

Analytics and Information Management

This dimension of service delivery is at the core of EPM because it holds the value lever of enhanced insight and predictive capability of the business. It is also essential to organizations because the degree to which they can provide these insights will directly correlate with each function's level of support to the business, in the eyes of the business leader. Analytics are certainly an area in which there are degrees of maturity, as well as a significant dynamic of functional and industry requirements. Given the breadth of the area, we recommend that organizations take some time to inventory their current analytics capabilities across the various functions of the enterprise. They are likely to find pockets of capability that are not being leveraged business-wide, as well as gaps in specific analytics that don't exist anywhere internally. When meshed with business priorities, organizations can develop a tailored "analytics road map" that they can then work toward in terms of defining, piloting, and deploying improved analytics capabilities (see Figure 10.6).

Human Capital

This is an often overlooked but critically important enabler of EPM capability and insights for the business. The reason is that it is easy for organizations to be lured by the prospect of new technologies and emerging analytics tools, without understanding the importance of the hard work necessary to develop professionals with the skills and capabilities required to exploit them. By contrast, top performers continually adjust training priorities to refresh their competency models and augment their professional development plans. Rather than build data scientists, these companies work to deepen the analytics capabilities of professionals more broadly in areas such as scoping/hypothesis development, understanding what analytics techniques are the best fit for different situations, skillful written and verbal communication, and effective delivery mechanisms. These examples, when factored together, begin to

---

Global Aerospace and Defense Company Utilizes Metrics to Manage for Growth, Efficiency, Optimization, and Achievement

Challenge

The organization was unable to link or align accountability to controllable actions between functions, between organizations, or within financial performance reporting. There was undefined ownership of activities and line items at the functional level of the organization, and no linkage between the company's operational metrics and their impact on the financial statements.

Solution / Benefits

In the words of an Executive Committee leader of the company, the solution "is fundamentally changing the way [the company] is managing its business." A project team worked with the organization and functional areas – from corporate down through six operational levels – and identified information gaps between functional and operational areas and finance using an end-to-end process approach. The company utilized a range of The Hackett Group's tools, content and best practices to recommend the "Measures That Matter" as leading KPIs (along with standard metrics) for managing each functional area and linking operational performance between functional areas, and relating how such performance contributed to the financial performance of programs and overall financial performance.

Figure 10.6 Sample Client Challenge and Solution

reshape the picture of an analytics-driven enterprise and the analytics professionals within.

With the articulation of the value EPM presents, the core components of the EPM cycle, and how a company's service delivery model ultimately defines its degree of maturity and capability, deeper exploration of the business planning events is merited. For many Fortune 500 organizations, planning is a massive undertaking that consumes thousands of hours throughout the year, yet results in plans that diverge significantly from actuals. Further, there is a lack of connectivity between forecasted financials and the underlying drivers of the business. When done well, planning can free up large portions of the enterprise to add more value through insightful analysis and to deliver greater forecast accuracy.

The authors have found that organizations seeking to transform their business planning processes drive clarity around seven key planning levers. Each of these levers is, by itself, a critical solution component for improved planning. When all of them are harnessed to drive change, the result is a much more efficient and effective way of planning.

Planning Improvement Levers

Establish a Clearly Defined Purpose for Each Planning Event

Planning events left ungoverned have a tendency to devolve into entropy over time, due to a combination of individual management preferences, different business-unit strategic priorities, resource constraints, employee turnover, and inevitable marketplace vagaries. It is therefore a critical first step in improving the planning process to challenge, evaluate, and reaffirm the purpose of each planning event undertaken by the organization. Each event has a different purpose, with therefore differing inputs, process steps, outputs, and audiences. For example, the purpose of a strategic plan could be broadly defined as "an outcome an organization aspires to reach;" in other words, "where would we like to go?" This goal differs from that of an annual plan, which is defined as "a planned means to deliver on a set of targets, including resource allocations and commitments," or, "what do we want to happen?" Both events would in turn be different from a forecast, which is defined as "an expected path and outcome based on current assumptions and past realities," that is, "what do we think will happen?"

This foundational defining exercise is crucial because clarity of purpose for the various planning events enables an informed assessment of the requirements, frequency, and level of effort associated with each event. Consider, for example, a forecast which is further defined or contextualized based on the timing in the year: a first-quarter forecast, which might have the added definition of being "a light review of the organization's expected path or outcome," should require less effort, involvement, and detail than a mid-year forecast; the latter being further defined as "a deeper dive into current assumptions and realities given half the year has elapsed." This event naturally requires more effort and involvement than the first-quarter forecast.

Note that each planning event, while distinct, should integrate with the others to support the overall decision-making model of the organization, and should consider and account for cultural norms, typical business dynamics, and expected marketplace volatility.

Key Considerations for Planning Purpose Definition

- Establish the objectives of each event (accuracy, accountability, inspiration, and so on).
- Challenge the status quo; just because a planning event exists does not mean it needs to remain.
- Determine the level of effort required to achieve the objectives of the planning event and compare the purpose.
- Clarify the audience or customer of the planning event outputs (external versus internal).
- Identify principal stakeholders who need to be involved in each planning event and ensure alignment on the purpose and requirements.

Expected Benefits

- Mitigates natural expansion/evolution of work over time to greater frequency, longer horizons, and greater levels of detail.
- Enables a common understanding of the required work and associated processes.
- Allows requirements to be more effectively defined for each planning event.
- Allows appropriate segregation of work into each planning step/event so that organizational objectives are more effectively addressed by the appropriately defined processes.

Develop an Integrated Calendar With Defined Timing and Cadence of the Planning Process

Although planning calendars typically exist at the corporate and operating-unit levels, these do not always present an integrated view of activities, output dependencies, and related responsibilities. An integrated, cross-functional, year-at-a-glance calendar that sequences major planning activities across functions and operating companies provides key insights about integration points, sequenced and parallel activities, duplicative efforts, and opportunities to streamline overall cycle time.

When integration is enabled via a well-synchronized and sequenced calendar, the planning process is enhanced in terms of information efficiency and elimination of duplicative work. For example, the strategic plan, while primarily aspirational, should include information elements such as new product launches or market-share assumptions for the first year of the strategic plan that can be effectively cascaded and used as a starting baseline for the annual plan if an integrated and harmonized calendar has been developed. Similarly, clear integration points throughout business units, regions, functions, and the like are made visible in an integrated calendar, thus significantly reducing the potential for overlap and redundant work.

The graphic below illustrates a conceptual "current/future" set of planning events. While seemingly simplistic, making adjustments to the duration and timing of various events, tying them together synergistically, and even eliminating some from the model has very real benefits in terms of capacity creation (see Figure 10.7).

Key Considerations for Developing an Integrated Calendar

- Evaluate individual business segment calendars with a view to coordinating and sequencing all planning and forecast events at the operating company level.
- Develop an integrated enterprise calendar, sequencing all planning and forecast events at the regional, franchise, and corporate level.

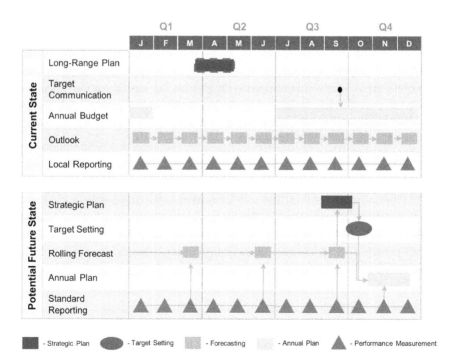

Figure 10.7 Integrated Calendar

- Identify functional integration points, handoffs, and responsibilities within the business segments and operating companies (for example, Sales and Marketing, R&D). Outline interdependencies.
- Identify functional integration points, handoffs, and responsibilities within regions, corporate and across global functions (for example, supply chain). Outline interdependencies.

Expected Benefits

- Increased accountability within operating units, driving action versus rationalization of past performance.
- Defined linkage between strategic plan and lowest-level departmental plan.
- Strong linkage among strategic planning, target setting, planning, budgeting, forecasting, analysis, and reporting.
- Multiyear planning; forecasting time horizon focused beyond year-end.
- Reduced cycle time.
- Lower resource requirements; greater visibility into resource requirements and job demands across the enterprise.

Implement a Structured Target-Setting Process

The target-setting process is often a source of significant pain for planners, who crave better insight into how targets are calculated and want increased participation in the target-setting process. A top-down approach to target setting remains a best practice to ensure alignment with enterprise strategic priorities. However, the opportunity to improve the process lies with the ability of senior leaders to provide early insights about targets prior to finalization. Early insight provides business-unit and region leaders with a window in which to identify key actions and trade-offs required to achieve targets, which they can propose to senior leaders. The insertion of a target-discussion step aimed at understanding key actions and required trade-offs prior to target finalization is important to ensure acceptance and organizational accountability to set targets.

Furthermore, to prevent the risk of rework and churn due to changing targets, detailed planning work should be delayed until targets are finalized. Planners' ability to work with a fixed target, previously identified target assumptions, and agreed-on required trade-offs significantly enhances the effectiveness of the process and the ability of the organization to actually achieve the set target.

Key Considerations for Developing a Structured Target-Setting Process

- Determine the level of detail for targets and period covered (such as net income only versus sales and net income; quarterly versus annual).
- Designate responsibility for setting targets.

- Develop an approach to define how low, organizationally speaking, the targets will be cascaded.
- Develop recommendations for streamlining the target-setting/nego-tiation process for functional areas, such as finance, human resources, information technology, procurement, and so on.
- Standardize the process with regard to timing, target content, linkage to other planning cycles, and levels of organizational participation.

Expected Benefits

- Targets effectively drive linkage between strategic planning and execu-tion of the operating plan.
- Improved sequencing and linkage between forecast updates and strate-gic planning (via targets) provide greater clarity and reduce rework.
- Greater specificity of expectations earlier in the process reduces itera-tion and churn.
- Early alignment to functional targets will minimize organizational fric-tion and negotiations.

Adopt a Driver-Based Process

Experiences have shown that while a detailed, bottom-up approach to plan-ning and analysis is sometimes needed, it is not always the right approach. In fact, it might preferred only due to cultural preference, management phi-losophy, or habit. In circumstances where there is a need to tighten controls on spending, aggressively cut costs, or harness acquisition synergies, a zero-based approach might be more appropriate.

For more effective planning, it is important to perform an assessment of the volatility and materiality of all planning accounts in order to deter-mine which should be planned using drivers to enable rapid planning, quick business insights, and scenario-analysis capabilities. An analysis should be performed across the matrix below to look across each planning view (accounts, products, cost centers, and so on) for opportunities to remove immaterial detail from the plan and forecast (see Figure 10.8).

Key Considerations for Driver-Based Planning Design

- For each operating unit, identify financial statement lines that are either material, variable, or critical (or all three). These lines represent target areas for key driver design and standardization.
- Test and prioritize drivers to identify the critical few that impact the selected financial statement lines, per planning event (unit, price, materials).
- Minimize the relative number of drivers to be utilized by planning event, limiting them to just the major drivers.

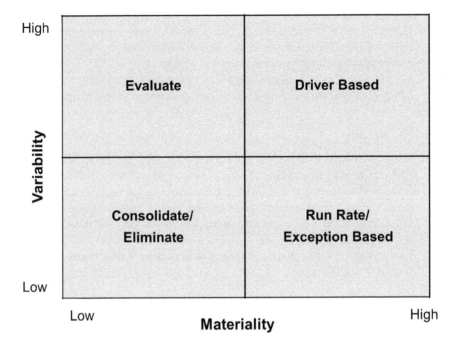

Figure 10.8 A Driver-Based Approach

Expected Benefits

- Improves planning accuracy by eliminating unnecessary detail and focusing attention on the most impactful drivers of business performance.
- Enables enhanced scenario analysis and "what-if" modeling capability.
- Supports faster response time to external changes.
- Reduces time spent on data collection and consolidation and increases capacity for business analytics.
- Reduces planning line-item level of detail by identifying key factors that translate operational activity into financial outcomes.
- Improves cycle time for plan production.
- Promotes the linkage between operations and the finance organization.
- Reduces time spent on data collection and consolidation; increases emphasis on analytics.

Determine the Most Appropriate Level of Planning Detail

The driver-based approach and level of planning detail are strongly linked by factors such as materiality, volatility, and business criticality. Along with a standardized, driver-based approach to planning, it is necessary to determine the appropriate level of detail for various management decision views, such as account, geography, and product, for each planning event. Equally important is the level at which the planning detail will be aligned to actuals reporting. As the planning level of detail is streamlined to focus more on planning what truly matters, consideration must be given to required changes to variance analysis and the analytical retraining that would be required for variance comparisons to be performed at a higher level.

Key Considerations for Level of Detail Design

- Identify material, variable, and critical financial statement lines for each operating unit.
- Determine the appropriate level of detail for other planning views, such as geography, business unit, and SKU.
- Define participating entities for each planning event.
- Determine technology changes required to deliver the revised level of planning detail and support variance comparisons to the detailed actual reporting.
- Identify the stakeholders who need to be involved in each planning event and ensure alignment on the level of detail planning changes and reporting implications.
- Document the implications of planned changes and determine analytical training required.

Expected Benefits

- Reduces time spent on data collection and consolidation while increasing capacity for business analytics.
- Materiality thresholds and streamlined detail eliminate "false precision" and analytical churn, and reduce cycle time.
- Focusing on key planning entities reduces staff effort while ensuring major market coverage.
- Mitigates the natural tendency for work to expand and evolve over time toward greater frequency, longer horizons, and greater detail.
- Provides clear leadership to a critical few business items that, when adjusted, produce material change in key performance measures, like revenue, expenses, and profit.

Maximize Technology Leverage

A key ingredient for a more effective planning process is the availability of the right tools and technical infrastructure to integrate information from disparate sources. It is also important to spur enterprise-wide user adoption of the technology to prevent shadow processes and a fractured approach to business-unit plan development and enterprise plan consolidation. Without the appropriate technology, it is challenging to achieve all the benefits enabled by the other planning levers. For example, it is difficult to effectively implement driver-based forecasting and collect relevant data at the business-unit level for consolidation at the corporate level.

Key Considerations for Technology Leverage

- Ensure integration of all relevant source systems required for planning and reporting; reduce manual inputs as much as possible.
- Aggressively adopt predictive modeling using available technology to link operational drivers to financial outcomes and improve visibility to potential outcomes of future operational assumptions.
- Define requirements from the perspective of end users; involve the right stakeholders to enhance user adoption post-implementation.
- Ensure an adequate amount of training on the new tools to ensure user adoption and discourage shadow processes.
- Ensure process changes are effectively integrated and enabled by the new technology.

Expected Benefits

- Improves access to information, reduces manual collection and reporting, creates transparency and auditability.
- Frees up capacity for value-added analysis by eliminating unproductive time spent manually compiling, cleansing, and integrating data.
- Reduces risk of data errors in manual transition of data between systems.

For example, at one Paper and Plastics Products Provider, a transformational program designed to address pressure on pricing and cost structure led to a comprehensive Sales & Operational Planning transformation that enabled the company to double its EBITDA performance in just 18 months (see Figure 10.9).

Leading Paper and Plastic Products Provider Established Foundational S&OP Process and Enhanced Pricing and Profitability Capability

Challenge

The market was under growing pressure on product pricing and cost structure, with the economic downturn only exacerbating the situation. The company's specific situation was also characterized by its own network overcapacity, poor fill rates and service levels, and challenges in understanding the real underlying profitability of their product/customer portfolio.

Solution / Benefits

In response to this situation, the company launched a transformational program to address these challenges and to reposition itself to enhance economic performance within the challenging market dynamics. The components of the transformation included:

- Sales and operations planning (S&OP) process overhaul with enabling technologies which improved cash flow management, customer service levels, and plant capacity analyses.
- Deep analysis of pricing leakage with remediation tactics identified, resulting in a roughly $10 million annual net sales increase.
- Strategic business, customer, and product profitability reporting and analysis capability.
- Modeling capabilities including deal reviews, product category reviews, price resets, channel and customer segment market share penetration.

This effort resulted in a doubling of EBIDTA performance through enhanced customer and product profit and price decisions over an 18-month period.

Figure 10.9 Sample Client Challenge and Solution

Drive Organizational Leverage

Planning organizations achieve effectiveness by not only implementing best practices but also by ensuring that an optimal service delivery model is employed, one where the right individuals in the organization are correctly aligned to perform the right set of activities. The appropriate service delivery model design and the related degree of process centralization will vary depending on the culture of the organization, readiness for and receptiveness to change, and approach to governance for long-term sustainability. Organizations that want to aggressively pursue global standards and capabilities that would apply in every area of the enterprise are increasingly using FP&A Centers of Excellence (COEs). These organizations are leveraged to champion enterprise-wide standardization of key planning drivers, adherence to defined levels of detail, and optimized use of planning technology.

Key Considerations for Organizational Leverage

- Evaluate the degree of centralization the organization is ready to absorb.
- Ensure clarity in roles and responsibilities; be clear about what the new CoE will do and how those activities will effectively transition.
- Define and clearly document interaction points between all groups.
- Review the reporting-line structure to ensure the CoE is empowered to drive standardization and govern the new processes.
- Position and equip the CoE to lead continuous improvement as the organization naturally evolves.

Expected Benefits

- Provides resource leverage and scale so operational leaders can redirect resources to growing and managing the business.
- Enables the development of a specialized planning and analytics delivery group that will deliver standard improved practices, promote synergies, and improve service quality and effectiveness.
- Establishes clearly defined and balanced accountabilities across all groups; eliminates process redundancy.
- Improves employee empowerment and provides development and career-enhancing opportunities.

These seven levers have proven to help organizations improve the efficiency of their planning events, strengthen forecast accuracy, and create capacity in the various functions to support the business.

What's Next: The New Horizon for EPM, Planning, and Analytics

This chapter has reviewed a series of core components of high-performing EPM and delved into the ways companies are improving their business planning capability. However, today's top performers are not standing still. Rather, they are aggressively seizing new opportunities presented by advances in digital business to set a new bar for how EPM and advanced analytics can optimize business performance.

The following graphic illustrates the evolution from stagnant reporting to more advanced analytics by moving beyond purely internal sources of data to incorporate external, big-data elements as well. Combining the two data types permits entirely new insights can be that can help explain, predict, and therefore influence a financial outcome (see Figure 10.10).

For example, when a traditional product might be off in volume for a period, explanations might center on price pressures, the impact or shift of a large customer order, or perhaps the efficacy of a trade promotion program. As a result of this dialogue, management may decide to take minimal action, as the expectation from the product team is that the product will bounce back toward the end of the year (directly tying to their incentive model). When more advanced analytics is applied, an entirely different and broader set of factors can be explored. Have consumer preferences changed? Are traditional promotion measures no longer effective? Has poor shelf placement depressed demand? Have competitors introduced pricing actions on

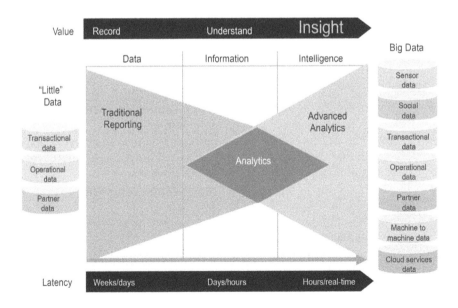

Figure 10.10 Reporting and Analytics Evolution

similar items that discouraged purchases of the product? What have the statistical trends been and is this a normal shift? Is there an issue with retail sentiment that is cascading to the product line? These can be addressed by taking both internal and externally available data sets and running analyses with analytics tools and resources. Some powerful new analytics tools can be relatively quickly deployed and are designed to offer unprecedented levels of flexibility.

For many organizations, a large portion of their business is relatively stable from year to year, based on a backbone of mature, market-accepted products. By applying operational drivers and external data sets to internal and historical performance data using advanced analytics technologies and techniques, it is highly likely that whole portions of the business can be more accurately forecasted with a minimum of human intervention. In fact, interventions tend to degrade, not enhance, the accuracy of estimates. New analytics tools and technologies will afford planners precious time to invest in innovating products, channels, geographies, and acquisitions. And, they will be able to apply their considerable skills to support the business with the types of analytics that are fast becoming a competitive necessity.

Part III

Strategies for Global Business Intelligence Success

11 Agility in Business Intelligence

Richard "RJ" P. Podeschi II

Introduction

Organizations of all sizes are surrounded by data on an ongoing basis, both internally and externally. Individuals at all levels of the organization need access to critical business information and the ability to analyze and share with the appropriate parties. With accurate and timely information, individuals can use it to make informed business decisions rather than "going with the gut" or performing "trial and error" (Mrdalj, 2007). Clive Humby is credited with the following analogy and its use over the past ten years that "data is the new oil." The analogy is appropriate as unrefined crude oil has little market value, but refined oil can be made into plastics, chemicals, and gasoline. A single data element, by itself, is meaningless unless transformed into meaningful information, compared with company or industry trends, and analyzed to make future predictions (ANA Marketing Maestros, 2006; Rotella, 2012; Vanian, 2016). The challenge is to ensure that the right people have the right information in a timely manner. In order for organizations to make effective decisions based on data-driven evidence in a timely manner, an agile approach to managing business intelligence (BI) is essential for competitive advantage in a global environment.

The business value of data has become even more apparent as more devices are internet-enabled and continually gather data. The data an organization encounters varies widely and is not necessarily meaningful unless it is transformed into a usable form and has the appropriate context. The typical BI architecture can be cumbersome as it is responsible for managing data from multiple sources. As a result, these architectures are responsible for integrating, cleansing, and standardizing data for use (Chaudhuri, Dayal, and Narasayya, 2011). Recently, there have been several developments of BI software platforms that support end-user development rather than being tied to traditional centralized information technology (IT) management models. These software titles can be operated in the cloud via a web browser or from a desktop application, thereby reducing the IT infrastructure requirements and placing more powerful analytical tools into the hands of everyday users. Having a BI platform in place that can also be agile to change with the organization as its data needs change is equally important to an agile framework for managing BI.

When searching academic databases such as: ACM *Digital Library*, *IEEE Xplore*, *Business Source Complete*, and *ScienceDirect*, 28 relevant peer-reviewed papers were identified using the search term *Business Intelligence* and *Agility* (or *Agile*) in the abstract and title since 2011. While one paper discussed the use of agile development methodologies within BI, none of the 28 addressed the combination of agile methods in the context of recent BI platforms that focused on end-user-driven development and was recognized as a research gap in 2015 (Krawatzeck, Dinter, and Thi, 2015). Previous research is limited to agile development methodologies from a centralized IT vantage point (Dasgupta and Vankayala, 2007; Krawatzeck et al., 2015; Sprague, 1980).

This chapter will discuss and explore how pursuing an agile approach to managing the leading decentralized BI software solutions enables organizations to be more effective in managing data. A conceptual framework is provided to manage BI platforms in the context of a specific agile methodology, scrum. The framework is geared toward managers, recommenders, and users of BI technology.

Review of Literature

Business Intelligence Systems

Business Intelligence (BI) is defined by Watson as a "broad category of applications, technologies, and processes for gathering, storing, accessing, and analyzing data to help business users make better decisions" (2009). The term has grown from what was previously known as Decision Support Systems (DSS) and encompasses frameworks for moving transaction-based data models into analytical data models (Sprague, 1980). While the term BI is often used by the IT community, Business Analytics (BA) and Big Data are often used interchangeably. BA is more frequently used by the business community while vendors and academics appear to use all three interchangeably (Sircar, 2009). To be consistent with the context of this research, the term "Business Intelligence" (BI) is used throughout.

Largely, DSS, and later BI, grew out of the data needs of an organization. While E. F. Codd's ground-breaking work on relational database design changed the way transactional data was stored, it was tied to the business process of capturing and storing data so that it could be reported at an operational level, not necessarily analyzed at the tactical or strategic level (1979; Sprague, 1980). For higher-level analysis, data warehouses and data marts were necessary to snapshot and aggregate data from relational databases covering multiple functional business areas (e.g. finance, accounting, sales) into reports, online analytical processing (OLAP), and dashboard applications in the form of visualizations (Watson, 2009).

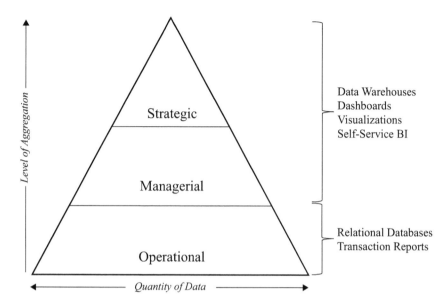

Figure 11.1 Data Pyramid

Typically, executive dashboards (sometimes referred to as scorecards) displayed institutional data compared with industry data and performance metrics known as critical success factors (CSFs) (Watson, 2009; Rockart, 1979). Individuals that operate in managerial or executive positions need data that is highly summarized (less granular). See Figure 11.1. As a result, BI solutions are well-suited for those making tactical or strategic decisions for the organization.

While tried and true methodologies like data warehousing are effective for cleansing, normalizing, and modeling data for reporting across the enterprise, the process for extracting, transforming, and loading data (ETL), in preparation for reporting, can be time-consuming and users may not always have access to the most up-to-date information (Chaudhuri et al., 2011; Inmon, 1992; O'Leary, 2011). In addition, data warehouses can only store data that fits neatly into rows and columns. Therein lies the challenge. Today's organizations are inundated with vast amounts of data, both internal and external, to the firm. In a *Harvard Business Review* study of 442 business executives, less than half felt confident that data was available and easy to access (Deighton, 2013). Furthermore, the data consists of both structured and unstructured data. Structured data refers to traditional data like numbers and text that fit into transactional databases and data warehouses. Unstructured data refers to documents, images, videos, and social media data. Unstructured data refers to the data that is too large and complex, and therefore cannot be addressed by traditional IT methods such as relational databases and data warehouses (Larson, 2009; Zikopoulos, Eaton, deRoos, Deutch, and Lapis, 2012). The term Big Data is grounded in this difference and also refers to the way in which data grows in *volume* (quantity), *variety* (varying attributes), and *velocity* (pace) (Zikopoulos et al., 2012). Some have built upon this definition by adding *value* and *veracity*; however, the original three "Vs" are sufficient to understand the impact large data sets have on organizations' business intelligence strategies (Kimble and Milolidakis, 2015). Traditional BI methods are not effective at handling large scale data problems that include both structured and unstructured data. As a result, the ability for centralized BI systems to develop timely and relevant data for key stakeholders to make business decisions is in jeopardy.

Agile Development Methodologies

The software development lifecycle (SDLC) initially consisted of a "waterfall" or "cascade" model that relied on structured, independent, and linked processes. The waterfall method consisted of the broad categories of requirements planning, designing, development, testing, deployment, and evaluation. Each phase had to be completed before the next phase began. This methodology gave preference to requirements definition prior to design or development to limit changes later in the process (Benington, 1956; Ruparelia, 2010). The waterfall method lacked flexibility, and bottlenecks in any given phase were likely. Later enhancements to the waterfall method were applied by Royce to include a feedback loop for iteration at the end of each stage to reduce its rigidity (1970). However, the waterfall method was tied to the business process cycle and not necessarily end user focused.

Later, other development methodologies were adopted such as rapid application development (RAD) which was more iterative in nature, but risked scope creep and changes to requirements (Ruparelia, 2010). Others such as eXtreme Programming (XP) and Joint Application Development (JAD) were developed to be more user-driven and encourage cooperative development, respectively (Ruparelia, 2010). These methods had the upside of driving down project costs and project times, but continued to risk scope creep and changing requirements.

In 2001, 17 people formed the Agile Software Development Alliance and provided the groundwork for the Manifesto for Agile Software Development. The group's work primarily valued:

- individuals and interactions over processes and tools;
- working software over comprehensive documentation;
- customer collaboration over contract negotiation;
- responding to change over following a plan (Fowler and Highsmith, 2001).

The Agile Manifesto, as it is commonly referred to, put the user and his/her needs first and fostered collaboration between the user and IT rather than barriers.

Ken Schwaber and Jeff Sutherland, both members of the Agile Manifesto team, conceived the scrum process to create high-functioning, cross-functional teams for software development (Scrum Alliance, n.d.). Scrum is a process management framework for incremental product development that includes a structure of roles, meetings, rules, and artifacts. The methodology uses fixed-length iterations, called sprints, to build a product increment through every iteration cycle of designing, building, and testing (Sutherland, 2014). The Daily Scrum Meeting is a key feature of the methodology where the team meets every day to assess progress and make necessary adjustments. This feedback loop enables transparency and adaptability within the team. Scrum projects have defined roles for self-organizing team members including a product owner and scrum master and will include both business and technology experts. A product owner is responsible for the vision and direction of the project, prioritizes work, and decides when (and whether) to release the product. The scrum master resolves project roadblocks and shields the team from interference and distractions. In scrum, the user is always available as part of the development team to validate the work in progress and maintain product backlogs which are used to form requirements. Each sprint ends with a review and reflection to understand what went well and what could be improved in future iterations. The methodology has been widely successful and has found its way into other foray beyond IT, such as business ideation and incubation.

Frameworks for Agile Business Intelligence

The original models of BI through DSS were conceived to be data driven rather than process driven, which allowed the management of such to move from traditional waterfall development methods to more agile methods such as RAD and scrum (Dasgupta and Vankayala, 2007; Krawatzeck et al., 2015). However, as data warehouses and ETL processes were built to cleanse and normalize data from multiple sources, the ability to adapt to changing business needs became increasingly difficult. Based on previous studies, the complexity lies on the back end of BI systems (infrastructure, servers, and data models) not the front-end tools (spreadsheets, dashboards, and drag-and-drop software) (Baars and Hütter, 2015; Cohen, Dolan, Dunlap, Hellerstein, and Welton, 2009). Even when the initial DSS models were first conceived, it was recognized that the waterfall model was inappropriate and an iterative and evolutionary model would allow users to hone in on their needs for decision-making (Sprague, 1980; Watson, 2009). Ruparelia's work provides the basis for understanding which development methods are more effective, given the application, by dividing applications into three broad categories and aligning them with the appropriate development methodology (2010). See Table 11.1 below.

Over time, BI solutions for the enterprise have evolved from large data warehouses with complex batch processes for cleansing and refreshing data to more self-service-oriented BI tools for power users that can be built, accessed, and maintained from a desktop workstation using cloud or in-memory technology. The movement is aligned with the broader trend of decentralizing IT into the various functional business units and fits with the evolution of computing that is taking place. Self-service BI tools have enabled users to use their data more effectively, which has expanded their knowledge through improved understanding of their corporate data (Schlesinger and Rahman, 2015). Companies are amassing data faster than it can be analyzed as it is forecasted that the total amount of data stored will eclipse 35 zettabytes (ZB) (or 1 billion terabytes) by 2020 (Zikopoulos et al., 2012). Traditional BI solutions cannot keep up with the pace at which data is being gathered as it is constantly in motion. Self-service BI solutions allow users to gain access to the data faster for analysis and decision-making.

Table 11.1 Application Categories

Application Categories Aligned With Development Methodologies			
Application Category	*Application Features*	*Recommended Development Methodologies*	*Examples*
1.	• Provides back-end functionality • Services other applications • Linear in nature	• Waterfall • Iterative waterfall	• Relational DB • Operating systems
2.	• Provides service to an end user or end-user application • Encapsulates business logic or formats data • Combination of linear and iterative	• Unified process model	• Object-oriented code
3.	• Provides a front-end graphical interface (GUI) to an end user • Iterative in nature	• Scrum	• Data-driven apps • GUI

Each year, Gartner Research publishes a report entitled "Magic Quadrant for Business Intelligence and Analytics Platforms" which evaluates several BI software solutions into four distinct categories: niche players, challengers, visionaries, and leaders, based on the software's ability to execute and its completeness of vision (Sallam et al., 2017). See Figure 11.2. The BI platforms that are positioned further to the top right-hand corner, in general, are the disrupters in the industry who are creating more nimble platforms for data discovery. These platforms are often more suited for faster execution and rely less on a robust IT infrastructure to process data sets. As such, these platforms are more suited for agile development methodologies than those along the bottom third, which consist of larger well-recognized names in IT that have been slow to adjust to the changing demands of BI platforms. These stalwarts often rely on larger infrastructure requirements, complex ETL processes, and rely on centralized IT support and administration. Therefore, BI platforms

Figure 11.2 Gartner Magic Quadrant

more geared towards end-user development are more suited to apply agile development methodologies, such as scrum, for more effective development.

Specifically, the scrum process model was meant to be adaptable for different projects and situations (Schwaber and Sutherland, 2016). Using their model as a framework, the scrum process can be refashioned to build self-service BI solutions by end users more effectively. BI tools like Microsoft Power BI, Tableau, and QlikView are designed for the end-user desktop, use in-memory technology, and are compatible with multiple data sources (Sallam et al., 2017). Despite the availability of online training to learn the software product, these self-service BI solutions still require intentional thought to produce desired results around the questions the user wants to ask the data. Adapted from scrum and Dasgupta's work, scrum sprint teams can be organized in a manner that involves similar steps to building a back-end BI solution (Schwaber and Sutherland, 2016; Dasgupta and Vankayala, 2007). For example, the end user/developer still needs to think through issues related to: data requirements, data transformation, BI graphical user interface (GUI) development, testing and validation, and deployment, just as an IT developer would. Each of these phases, when translated into distinct sprint teams, according to scrum, would contain a master product backlog, each with its own set of requirements. See Figure 11.3. Each of the sprint teams would enable the end user/developer to gather the appropriate intellectual resources from various departments, including IT, if needed. Through each sprint, the team would build, design, and test at each fixed-duration sprint. While one could consider this entire process as one sprint team, team members could adjust over time and according to the required skill sets or knowledge. Conceptually, this model would enable self-service BI solutions to be developed with transparency, inspection, and adaptation. More importantly, validation occurs at every step to ensure accurate data results. When working with data, consumers of the data need assurance that the process can be audited, but without unnecessary red tape. However, following an adapted

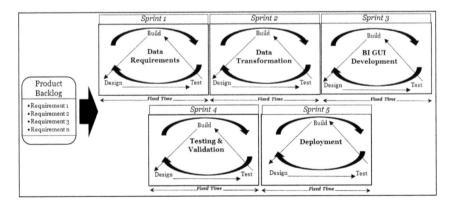

Figure 11.3 Agile Scrum for Self-Service BI

scrum model would give end users/developers the ability to mimic back-end BI development process using front-end tools with the ability to adapt and iterate as the data needs of the organization change at a frenetic pace.

Conclusions

This adapted scrum methodology exists conceptually and requires further research for testing its effectiveness. A real-world case study using scrum for end-user BI development in practice is necessary to understand the implications for viability of the aforementioned frameworks. While self-service BI tools allow non-IT staff to access data and transform it into knowledge, it remains incumbent to understand how the data will be used, its format and accuracy, and how best to create platforms for data discovery to make better decisions in a rapidly changing environment. As technology has allowed organizations to expand internationally, methodologies like scrum will enable end users to collaborate using a common language to aggregate data spanning the globe. This is especially important for multinational organizations that have data residing in multiple countries. End users along with technical specialists can benefit from implementing scrum in a BI context. Building agile development methodologies that are user friendly and adaptable will allow organizations to be just as agile and nimble. While Clive Humby referenced "data as new oil," businesses need to consider data as currency that can be used to gain a competitive advantage.

References

ANA Marketing Maestros. (2006, November 3). *Data Is the New Oil: Marketing Researcher Michael Palmer* [Blog post]. Available from: http://ana.blogs.com/maestros/2006/11/data_is_the_new.html

Baars, H. and Hütter, H. (2015). A framework for identifying and selecting measures to enhance BI-agility. In *48th Hawaii International Conference on System Sciences*. Washington, DC, USA. IEEE Computer Society. doi:10.1109/HICSS.2015.561

Benington, H.D. (1956). Production of large computer programs. In *Proceedings, ONR Symposium on Advanced Programming Methods for Digital Computers*, June 1956, (pp. 15–27). Los Alamitos, CA, USA. IEEE Computer Society Press.

Chaudhuri, S., Dayal, U., and Narasayya, V. (2011). An overview of business intelligence technology. *Communications of the ACM*, 54(8), 88–98. doi:10.1145/1978542.1978562

Codd, E. F. (1979). Extending the database relational model to capture more meaning. *ACM Transactions on Database Systems*, 4(4), 397–434. doi:10.1145/320107.320109

Cohen, J., Dolan, B., Dunlap, M., Hellerstein, J., and Welton, C. (2009). MAD skills: New analysis practices for big data. *Proceedings for the VLDB Endowment*, 2(2), 1481–1492.

Dasgupta, S. and Vankayala, V.K. (2007). Developing real time business intelligence systems the agile way. In *1st Annual IEEE Systems Conference* (pp. 1–7). IEEE Computer Society. Honolulu, HI, USA. doi:10.1109/SYSTEMS.2007.374652

Deighton, A. (2013). *Data and Organizational Issues Reduce Confidence.* Harvard Business Review: A report by Harvard Business Review Analytic Services. Available from: www.redmond.es/descargas/WP-HBR-Pulse-Survey-EN.pdf

Fowler, M. and Highsmith, J. (2001). *The Agile Manifesto.* Available from: http://dimsboiv.uqac.ca/8INF851/web/part1/introduction/The_Agile_Manifesto.pdf

Inmon, W.H. (1992). *Building the Data Warehouse.* New York: John Wiley and Sons.

Kimble, C. and Milolidakis, G. (2015). Big data and business intelligence: Debunking the myths. *Global* Business *and Organizational* Excellence, 35(1), 23–34. doi:10.1002/joe.21642

Krawatzeck, R., Dinter, B., and Thi, D.A.P. (2015). How to make business intelligence agile: The agile BI actions catalog. In *48th Hawaii International Conference on Systems Sciences* (pp. 4762–4771). doi:10.1109/HICSS.2015.566

Larson, D., & Chang, V. (2016). A review and future direction of agile, business intelligence, analytics and data science. *International Journal of Information Management,* 36(5), 700–710. doi:10.1016/j.ijinfomgt.2016.04.013

Mrdalj, S. (2007). Teaching an applied business intelligence course. *Issues in Information Systems,* 8(1): 134–138.

O'Leary, D. (2011). Building and evolving data warehousing and business intelligence artefacts: The case of Sysco. *Intelligent Systems in Accounting, Finance and Management,* 18, 195–213. doi:10.1002/isaf.330.

Rockart, J.F. (1979). Chief executives define their own data needs. *Harvard Business Review,* 67(2), 81–93.

Rotella, P. (2012, April 2). Is data the new oil? *Forbes.* Available from: www.forbes.com/sites/perryrotella/2012/04/02/is-data-the-new-oil/#2d6163e77db3

Royce, W. (1970). Managing the development of large software systems.In *Proceedings, IEEE Wescon,* August 1970 (pp. 1–9). The Institute of Electrical and Electronics Engineers, Inc.

Ruparelia, N.B. (2010). Software development lifecycle models. *ACM SIGSOFT Software Engineering Notes,* 35(3), 8–13.

Sallam, R., Howson, C., Idoine, C., Oestreich, T., Richardson, L., and Tapadinhas, J. (2017, February 16). *Magic Quandrant for Business Intelligence and Analytics Platforms.* Gartner.

Schlesinger, P. and Rahman, N. (2015). Self-service business intelligence resulting in disruptive technology. *The Journal of Computer Information Systems,* 56(1), 11–21.

Schwaber, K. and Sutherland, J. (2016). *The Definitive Guide to Scrum: The Rules of the Game.* Available from: www.scrumguides.org/docs/scrumguide/v2016/2016-Scrum-Guide-US.pdf#zoom=100

Scrum Alliance. (n.d.). *Why Scrum.* Available from: www.scrumalliance.org/why-scrum

Sircar, S. (2009). Business intelligence in the business curriculum. *Communications of the Association for Information Systems,* 24(1) 289–302.

Sprague, R.L., Jr. (1980). A framework for the development of decision support systems. *MIS Quarterly,* 4(4), 1–26.

Sutherland, J. (2014). *SCRUM: The Art of Doing Twice the Work in Half the Time.* New York: Crown Business.

Vanian, J. (2016, July 11). Why data is the new oil. *Fortune.* Available from: http://fortune.com/2016/07/11/data-oil-brainstorm-tech/

Watson, H.J. (2009). Tutorial: Business intelligence—Past, present, and future. *Communications of the Association for Information Systems,* 25(39), 487–510.

Zikopoulos, P., Eaton, C., deRoos, D., Deutch, T., and Lapis, G. (2012). *Understanding Big Data: Analytics for Enterprise Class Hadoop and Streaming Data.* New York: McGraw-Hill.

12 International Market Intelligence

Andrew Gross, Rajshekhar (Raj) G. Javalgi, and Nicholas Mathew

Beyond the Two-Fold View—A New Perspective

As a general rule, things can be classified into two categories: theory vs. practice, art vs. science, objective vs. subjective view, and macro- vs. microeconomics. Global business often makes a distinction in the same way: domestic vs. foreign markets, strategy vs. tactics, competition vs. collaboration, and emerging vs. mature economies. Marketing has an identical pattern: goods vs. services, consumer vs. industrial products, skim vs. penetration pricing, and transactions vs. relationships. And, in market research and analysis, reference is made to: short vs. long run, quantitative vs. qualitative forecasting techniques, information gaps vs. information overloads, and primary vs. secondary data sources (Gross, 2012).

Yet the important aspects are often in "the big middle." Thus, in global business there are many options between exporting and investment, for example licensing, franchising, joint ventures. In market segmentation there are several intermediate levels between macro and micro bases. When forecasting the size of markets, any combination of qualitative and quantitative techniques can be used; in distinguishing the origins of data, there are primary, secondary, and tertiary sources. By embracing "craftsmanship," a combination of art and science, business intelligence emerges as a blend of analysis, intuition, judgment, and new findings. The market research task is to build a "flight map" for navigating in a complex, multifaceted world for the assessment of the size, nature, and characteristics of diverse marketplaces. The best advice is to keep the initial scope narrow and segments to a select few. Through adjustments and feedback one can improve, learn, and perform better on all future assignments (Gleick, 2011; Gross and Solymossy, 2016; Stewart, 1997).

Key Challenges in Global Market Research

In going beyond the domestic scene, the first challenge is resource allocation. Regardless whether the marketplace is envisioned as a group, a city, several countries, or a region, a commitment has to be made on time horizon, labor, equipment, and funds. At the same time, a decision is needed on whether the investigation will be carried out in-house or outsourced to others. The second challenge is to delineate the task or linkage of "product-market interface." What good or service shall be offered, just when, how, and where to which customers? The third challenge is to design the appropriate research procedure of gathering the information for the goals set. Will surveys be coupled with observations? Select "born global" software and online companies do little or no market research, yet can succeed. On the other hand, makers of packaged consumer goods, vendors of machine tools, and providers of professional services often commission extensive research before entering select foreign markets or when expanding further on a regional or global basis (Cavusgil and Riesenberger, 2009; Craig and Douglas, 2005; Gross and Banting, 1993; Kuada, 2008; Kumar, 2000).

This chapter focuses on international *market* research rather than international *marketing* research. The former is a navigation tool in determining current market size, future dimensions, key characteristics, and likely constraints outside a domestic base; this task is really foreign market opportunity assessment with an emphasis on initial target countries and then select groups within (Cavusgil and Riesenberger, 2009; Kuada, 2008). The latter, on the other hand, focuses on strategies about the marketing mix in an international setting, after market research is completed (Kumar, 2000). Thus, once "on location" one has to deal with decisions about product, pricing, promotion, and distribution policies for ongoing operations and likely expansion. The latter topic is beyond the scope of this chapter. However, there is a definite overlap between the two, namely gathering data on diverse risks in select foreign settings. This involves looking at cultural, legal, and economic restraints, which must be done on an ongoing basis, both at the research stage and then in subsequent operations (Craig and Douglas, 2005; Ozturk, Joiner, and Cavusgil, 2015; Young and Javalgi, 2007). See Figure 12.1.

The Business Intelligence Hierarchy (or Knowledge Pyramid)

Since the 1950s, managers faced a bewildering range of business information, available as text or statistics, from numerous public and private sources, with the volume increasing exponentially each decade. Such information—portable, shareable, compressible—has to be managed, not because it is scarce, but because it is abundant. Indeed, quality of information is inversely correlated with quantity; volume must be reduced, so its value can increase. This is the central idea behind the business intelligence hierarchy shown in Figure 12.1. From billions of data bits and vast databases, we move to more concise forms, analytical reports, executive summaries, and intelligence that result in timely managerial decisions (Gross and Solymossy, 2016; Madhavaram, Gross, and Appan, 2016; Wolpert and Wolpert, 1986).

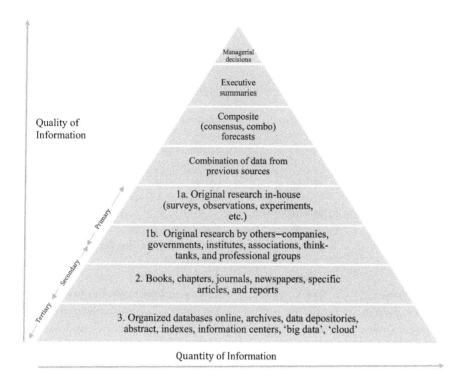

Figure 12.1 Business Intelligence Hierarchy

Sources: Wolpert and Weiss (1970), Wolpert and Wolpert (1986), Gross and Banting (1993), Gross, A.C. and Solymossy, E. (2016)

Note: This pyramid has been compared to the "Data, Information, Knowledge, Wisdom" pyramid (cf. Wikipedia, etc.), but the one here is modified for global business intelligence.

In decades past, one distinguished just between two kinds of information: secondary data available from others and primary data that was assembled based on surveys, observations, or experiments. Today, there are three levels of information that serve as foundation blocks of the hierarchy. Primary data can come from one's own surveys and observations; or the task can be outsourced to others. But governments and business firms also gather primary data via census surveys and the recoding of production/revenue figures, respectively. These statistics are condensed into public reports, press releases, journal articles, books, and other records, becoming secondary information. Finally, both sets are sorted into diverse abstracts, indexes, and digests, and into enormous databases, constituting tertiary information that can be readily accessed. All of the above can then be combined, sorted, and manipulated, usually via keywords, search terms, so-called Venn diagrams, and Boolean algebra. The number of online databases proliferated rapidly

Table 12.1 Major Online Business Databases

Database	Vendor	Primary Focus
ABI/Inform	ProQuest	Business news, articles, company profiles
Academic Source Complete	EBSCO	Academic, economic, and social topics
Business Source Complete	EBSCO	Business news, companies, case studies
Compendex (Ei Compendex)	Elsevier	Engineering and technical articles, data
Datamonitor	Informa	Industry studies, trends, economic data
Euromonitor-Passport	Euromonitor International	Business and market research reports
Hoover's	Dun & Bradstreet	Corporate data, profiles, industry news
IBISWorld	same	Industry studies, market data, competition
InfoTrac	Gale/Cengage	Academic, business, general references
Lexis-Nexis	RELX	Law cases, legal news, business trends
Marketresearch	MRDC	Industry studies, market data, trends
Mergent Online	same	Company data, economic, and financial news
OECD iLibrary	OECD	Economic, energy, industry data
Statista	same	Economic and business statistics
S&P NetAdvantage	Standard & Poor	Business, investment, financial news
SRDS	Kantar	Online and traditional media, rates
Westlaw/NEXT	same	Legal and business news, trends
WDI (World Devt. Indic.)	World Bank	Country demographics, economic data

Source: Berkeley College, Cleveland State U., Cornell U., Florida Institute of Technology, Harvard U., Ohio State U., St. Mary's U. (MN), U. of Chicago, U. of Michigan libraries

in the 1980s from 400 to 4,400; they are now estimated at over 10,000. However, in the world of business, 20 emerged as leaders, displayed here in Table 12.1. These databases should be the "starting blocks" in global market research. Each one has its unique format, guidelines, and fee structure researchers need to compare and contrast (Gross and Solymossy, 2016).

Creative Data Mining = Detective Work

In the past two decades advances in computer hardware, software, and networks brought easy access, high speed, and many search options in finding relevant statistics and text about specific markets in a nation, region, or around the globe. Much of the information is quickly available in digest or index form, as short abstracts, or even as full text and tables from the various online databases. But then comes creative work, through the judicious use of keywords and synonyms. Thus, as just one example, in case of the market for "water treatment chemicals" in "Eastern Europe," alternative phrases such as "water management chemicals" and the names of individual nations should be included. Capital goods are often labeled as machinery or equipment. Different national census bureaus have different codes for classifying engineering services; others combine the term with architectural services. Term such as "detergent" or "software" is an elusive concept, with numerous qualifications or variation. In sum, a given topic should be approached from several angles (Gross, 2012; Harrison et al., 2016; Hedin, 2011; Kotabe, 2009; Kuada, 2008; Malhotra, 2014).

How should one choose among the various databases and then the other sources? The choice should be dictated by the extent of holdings, fees charged, and desired output. Over time, users gain experience and confidence; shortcuts are often used. Databases beyond the Table 12.1 list can certainly prove useful; for example Dissertation Abstracts by ProQuest offers many, in-depth theses on highly specialized topics. GlobalEdge, a "knowledge portal" from Michigan State University, tabulates several key indicators on 25 emerging national markets on an annual basis. One's own organization is often a great source of data; since 2000, many large and small firms built up and now tap their own databanks ("if only HP knew what HP knows"). Innovative firms also solicit feedback from lead users, "beta sites," and foreign listening posts. Organizational learning is no longer an empty phrase! Both practitioners and academics have established informal networks and exchange information on an ongoing basis. Informal groups, with "fluid membership," have sprung up via e-communication on the internet/web, social media, and a variety of dedicated electronic exchanges (Katz, 2004; Madhavaram, Gross, and Appan, 2016; Pedersen, 2008; Silver, 2012; Surowiecki, 2004; Laudon and Traver, 2015).

Outsourcing and Contracting

Taking an in-depth look at the three levels of data sources as well as the underlying literature, gaps may be found and one may wish to go beyond their offerings, but still not conduct major in-house primary market research. In such a situation two major avenues are open. The first is to consider the offerings of market research firms; the second is to engage a provider of "software as a service." Table 12.2 shows the largest market research firms, all with global coverage, compiled by two US associations (Bowers and Brereton, 2016); another list, compiled by Greenbook (Murphy, 2016) shows "innovative" market research firms. The majority of firms on both lists focus their research on consumer goods, branding, and the use of social media. A third list, from igniteag.com, covers large firms doing business-to-business market research. Finally, there are market research firms in

Table 12.2 The Largest Global Market Research Firms

(US) Rank 2015	Global Rank 2012	Organization Name	Home Country	2015		2012	
				Global Revenue (in US$ millions)	% of Global Revenue Non-US	Global Revenue (in US$ millions)	% of Global Revenue from Outside of Home Country
1	1	Nielsen Holdings	US	$6,172.0	41.6%	$5,429.0	51.2%
2	2	Kantar*	UK	$3,710.0	73.8%	$3,338.6	72.2%
3	5	IMS Health	US	$2,921.0	61.4%	$775.0	65%
4	3	Ipsos	France	$1,608.7	65.7%	$2,301.1	93.2%
5	6	IRI Worldwide	US	$981.0	38.3%	$763.8	37.3%
6	8	Westat	US	$509.6	3.6%	$495.9	1.0%
7	4	GfK	Germany	$1697.7	79.6%	$1947.8	70.0%
8	11	ComScore Inc.	US	$368.8	27.3%	$255.2	28.1%
9	10	The NPD Group Inc.	US	$307.7	24.9%	$272.0	29.5%
10	15	J.D. Power*	US	$273.5	33.8%	$234.4	33.4%

Source: Honomichl, J. (2013); Bowers, D. and Brereton, M. (2016, Summer)

*Some or all figures are not made available by this company so instead are based upon estimations by the AMA report authors.

emerging nations that are familiar with their domestic setting; it is wise to seek their assistance as a complement or as replacement to a costly contract with one of the large global research agencies.

In the past 15 years several nimble organizations have been established that offer online survey platforms. They claim to be able to move clients from surveys to insights to actions in a rapid and flexible manner—in a matter of days, not weeks. These firms offer various panels whose members are qualified through interest and incentives; indeed, such collaborators are seen as forming a community where the participants are able and eager to respond to queries. The vendors formulate questions, organize panels, and collect data; they can provide product/concept testing, feedback on branding, and data analysis. Still, they function well in more developed countries so the question of representativeness and access must be raised. Many of these firms are under private ownership, with limited records on their accomplishments; however, their websites reveal their versatile offerings usually via case studies and testimonials from satisfied clients. The leading vendors are Qualtrics and SurveyMonkey; others are Confirmit, QuestionPro, Satmetrix, SnapSurveys, SurveyGizmo, and Vision Critical; for a long list and commentary, see trustradius.com.

In-House Primary Market Research

After tapping data from the various layers of the intelligence hierarchy and considering outsourcing possibilities, enterprises can embark on an investigation of their own, in-house. The process at this point has many similarities with its domestic counterpart: problem definition, methodology design, fieldwork, analytical reporting with visualization, and recommendations. However, major disparities are bound to arise that spring from social-cultural, political-legal, technical-sampling constraints, especially in emerging economies. When doing research in emerging nations, the cultural barriers, government regulations, and infrastructure deficiencies are some of the issues that need to be taken into account (Greenland and Kwansah-Aidoo, 2012). These issues can and do make market research more challenging in emerging markets nations. These challenges multiply as more countries are included and will affect comparability of results. Further, both marketplace and constraints are in a state of flux in any overseas setting; hence the research must be ongoing, carried out on a repeat basis.

Two preliminary steps prior to formal research are highly recommended at this juncture. First, consider attending one or more trade shows, fairs, or expos abroad where one can meet exhibitors, rival firms, and potential clients. These events are a century-long tradition in Europe and they are now popular in all other regions as well. For example, Aqua Expo has been a major show for water treatment equipment, held twice a year, once in Asia and once in Europe. In many nations there has been a tradition of holding a consumer goods show in spring and an industrial expo in autumn. A recent phenomenon, gaining in popularity is the virtual trade show on the Web; one can take an "electronic walkabout" and meet exhibitors. Such shows are gaining in popularity as travel becomes hectic and exhibit booths prove to be costly undertakings (Laudon and Traver, 2015).

A second step that yields primary information and insights prior to a formal market research is to attend professional society seminars aimed at practitioners. One of the largest and the most international of them all is ESOMAR, originally the European Society for Market and Opinion Research; it expanded from Europe and now has 5,000 members in 130 nations. There are other, older groups, but they are more focused in one nation, for example the American Marketing Association in USA and the Market Research Society of the UK. A list of selected websites are cited at the end of the bibliography. In addition, several industry associations hold international meetings and seminars, including so-called webinars, with opportunity to network and to gain insights on market potential in person or in "e-mode."

In undertaking the formal market research in house, solid guidelines have been suggested by academics and practitioners (Papadopoulos and Martin, 2011; Ozturk et al., 2015). The steps involve ascertaining major information needs related to macro issues such as cultural and legal constraints and micro issues such as sales potential, growth rate, and competitive intensity. Later on, there will be need to consider market expansion, coordination with other locales, and global rationalization, but that is the task for marketing research. In Figure 12.2 this chapter offers a framework or flow chart covering the major stages of primary international market research. In the first step, definitions and goals are tackled, especially the unit of analysis (local, regional, etc.). The next stages are designing the research methodology; the key considerations here are conceptual and translation equivalence, reliability, and construct validity. Sampling plays a major role in fieldwork

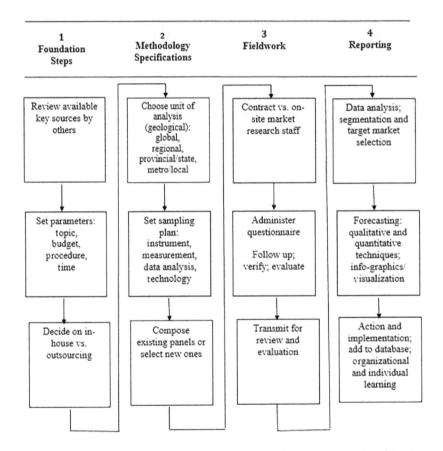

Figure 12.2 Framework for Primary Market Research in an International Business Context

Sources: primary research by the authors and a wide variety of books and journal articles (see citations in text and the complete bibliography at end of the chapter)

especially in developing countries. Finally, the assembled numbers must be analyzed, findings reported clearly along with visualization techniques. At each step, both the local constraints and complex comparability issues among the different sites must be considered (Cavusgil and Riesenberger, 2009; Papadopoulos and Martin, 2011; Young and Javalgi, 2007).

Design or methodology options and data collection in the field constitute two critical stages. In the former, there are choices among survey options, observations, experiments, and test markets; in the latter different cultural norms as well as language translation issues are tackled. The sampling plan and measurement equivalence concepts are more complicated by far when work is across national borders or possibly even within provinces or cities of a large nation with distinct differences in language and customs (e.g. Quebec vs. Ontario in Canada; Barcelona vs. Madrid in Spain). As a general rule, the selected sample must represent the large, underlying population to achieve external validity. Several authors recommend using a stratified random sample to mitigate this risk so as to assure relative representation. Familiarity of the good or service offered by the members of the eventual target markets will play a critical role in conducting the assignment (Kuada, 2008).

Consider the case of consumer packaged goods, such as processed food, toiletries, and non-alcoholic drinks, aimed at households versus the case of construction machinery, for example cranes and loaders for building contractors. In trying to ascertain the market for a new consumer good, the survey—be it focus group, mall intercept, or online—must be precise in general context and specific wording. Emphasis must be on probing consumer preferences, strength of existing brands, and ascertaining opportunities for entry. In contrast, in the case of machinery, the task is to reach contractors in person and probe how they perceive their desire for new equipment, often with better technical features. In this situation, security such as anti-theft devices and comfort such as air-conditioned cabs for the operator loom just as important as loading capacities. The research tasks in the two situations differ greatly, reflecting the distinct motives and buying habits of households vs. organizations. In other words, segmentation does matter for market research and later action.

Listening to the Numbers—Moving From Information to Intelligence

Enterprises, large and small, can choose among the three major possibilities of data acquisition outlined above—existing sources, outsourcing, and doing it in-house—but those that can afford time and expense are likely to decide on a combination. After the collection of statistics and text from the various sources and fieldwork comes the challenging task of "making sense" or "listening to the numbers." Such interpretation is a matter of "sifting and winnowing." The analytical task involves three complementary steps: (a) comparison and contrast of data from the various sources; (b) development of both cross-sectional and longitudinal statistics; and (c) formulating a framework for the product-market interface.

An informal survey by the authors conducted a few years ago showed that business economists and market researchers prefer to start with national data from government censuses, followed by statistics from their own industry/trade associations, and then the commercially available online databases. As for data available from regional or global nonprofit groups, users preferred the World Bank, the OECD, and Eurostat to UN agencies (such as FAO, WHO, ILO, and the UN itself) and to regional banks (e.g. ADB, IAB). Large firms are now likely to hire outside contractors with the choice based on online offerings and testimonials found on the websites of vendors. In-house primary research is more likely to be implemented by consumer goods firms than those in the industrial goods sector. With emphasis on transparency and collaboration across boundaries, enterprises now find that sharing some data and contacts are often a good solution, whether achieved at a large conference, small seminar, or various website chat-rooms (Katz, 2004).

Respecting the Past, Forecasting the Future

The goal of international market research is far more than attempting to forecast market size for a given product, in a given location (be it a metropolis, nation, or a region such as the Caribbean). To arrive at meaningful results, including long-run projections, past trends, relationships among key variables, and competitive intensity must be studied; and, how markets evolved over the past five to ten years must be analyzed. In addition, it is vital to consider whether projections made earlier have been achieved. Such "back-casting" about methods and results can be instructive. Back in the 1960s economists and marketers concluded that the range of error in national statistics was 10% for developed and 20% for emerging nations. During 1960–1980, market size forecasts made for ten years ahead were off by 5% to 35% for established products and in Western nations and much higher, at 35% to 550%, for high-tech goods and in emerging economies (Duncan and Gross, 1995).

In the 21st century, the situation improved, by utilizing thousands of time series from dozens of databanks, thereby easing comparison and analysis. Still, problems persist regarding reliability and validity of the underlying data; or the issue can often be one of definition, seldom a simple task. Thus, in attempting to estimate the European market for management consulting, the key association, FEACO, struggled with different terminology among member nations—just who is a management consultant? Adding to the problem, unemployed managers entered the field, declaring themselves as consultants. There were disputes regarding data collection techniques. No surprise that analysts' estimates differed often by 20% to 25%, making any projections even more challenging (Gross, 2012).

The major methods of forecasting have been known for decades, but newer and more sophisticated techniques have come to the forefront. The two major categories are "qual and quant" forecasting, that is qualitative and quantitative, both with subcategories. The "qual" usually includes: sales force estimates, users' expectations, executive judgment, and Delphi panels. These methods are useful for rough estimates of demand, but generally lack systematic analysis of cause and effect. The "quant" list includes trend fitting, moving averages, exponential smoothing, multiple regression, econometric models, and others. A more detailed description of each technique can be found in many business textbooks and specifically in the fundamental articles and books published by J. S. Armstrong and his colleagues (Armstrong, 2001; Armstrong, Kester, and Graefe, 2015; Duncan and Gross, 1995; Silver, 2012).

The authors' research and personal experience with market projections or product forecasts lead to the conclusion that there is much merit in: (a) developing composite or consensus forecasts for broad economic indicators; then (b) using a chain-ratio or break-down method by relating specific variables to broader ones; and (c) attempting a build-up method from producers' output or sales data. This conceptual idea, displayed in Table 12.3, shows the market for water treatment equipment in Brazil, from 2002 to 2022. Note the broad economic time series at the top of the page and then the subsequent, narrower product data. Doing such a study in the past, the first author of this chapter has found that many Western nations were able and willing to spend up to 1% of gross domestic product on pollution control in the late 20th century, then two-thirds of that amount for water and wastewater treatment. But beyond that, reluctance has set in on the part of both governments and enterprises. This is a notable finding and one that appears to hold in the 21st century as well.

The use of composite (also called combination or consensus) forecasts primarily has been done for general economic variables such as GDP, personal consumption spending, capital investment, etc., but it can also serve as a framework for doing the same at the level of estimating specific market sizes. Several authors have shown that forecasting accuracy can be improved by combining data from a variety of sources and both "qual" and "quant" techniques (Armstrong, Kester, Graefe, 2015; Silver, 2012) These experts suggest that such procedure is superior to any "single best" technique. The composite method simulates the real world wherein the diverse plans of many entities are converted into mutually consistent events. In this framework, one must consider both supplies and end uses. Thus for tires, supply is from natural and synthetic rubber, while demand is from both car and truck makers for new tires and millions of owners for the replacement units.

The authors conclude with these lessons for the art and science of forecasting: (a) work with a conceptual framework, rich in sources and diversity; (b) relate specific variables to broader indicators; (c) examine both the supply and demand side of the product line, noting viable alternatives (say synthetic vs. natural rubber; water treatment equipment vs. chemicals; full-time vs. part-time consultants); (d) consider the historical record of the industry,

Table 12.3 The Market for Water Treatment Equipment in Brazil, 2002–2022

Item	2002	2007	2012	2017	2022
Selected Indicators					
Population (million persons)	179.3	189.9	198.6	206.4	213.1
Gross Domestic Product (GDP) (bil 2011 $)	1,628	1,979	2,313	2,795	3,405
Water Use (bil meter^3)	16.7	27.0	29.9	32.5	35.3
Gross Fixed Capital Formation (GFCF) (bil 2011 $)	243.5	328.1	405.5	500.0	619.0
Water Treatment Equipment Demand (mil $)	350	500	680	950	1280
Selected Ratios					
GDP/capita ($)	9,080	10,420	11,650	13,540	15,980
GFCF as % of GDP (%)	14.9	16.5	17.5	17.9	18.2
Water Treatment Equipment/capita ($)	1.95	2.63	3.42	4.60	6.01
Water Treatment Equip./000$ GDP ($)	0.21	0.25	0.29	0.34	0.36
Water Treatment Equip $\times 10^3$/Water Use ($/m^3)	21.0	18.5	22.7	29.2	36.3

Source: World Water Treatment Equipment (Cleveland: The Freedonia Group, 2013). Used by permission. Copyright MarketResearch.com, Inc., 2014

Notes: In the original report, water treatment equipment demand is also shown by type of equipment and by type of major end-use segments.

This back-casting and forecasting layout has been labeled also as 'chain-ratio analysis or a 'break-down method' compared to a 'build-up' method of summing up producers' output.

competitive intensity, disruptive technical innovations, for example the case of disk drives; (e) be aware of overly optimistic forecasts by consultants; and (f) get to know the "key drivers" and the unique terminology of the sector studied. In the age of the internet, with easy access, high speed, search assistance, millions of websites, and billions of data bits, one must practice both retrospection and conceptualization to build a consistent picture of market knowledge and business intelligence.

Reporting the Findings, Visualizing the Data

Once the data have been compiled from diverse sources, the analyst must decide on how the material will be presented to the audience. Reporting can be in both oral presentations and written documents in print or electronic format; or it may even be in audio recordings. The recipients are likely to be not just fellow analysts and in-house business associates, but potential and actual clients, government agencies, foreign dignitaries, and academics such as professors and students. The report has to be sensitive in terms of the cultural-social background of listeners or readers as well as transparent in regard to sources and methods utilized during the research. Findings should be in the mixed form of both text and graphic exhibits, with an executive summary up front. Special attention should be paid to both results attained, compared to the original goals, and the limitations of the study. Finally, it is crucial to contrast the current findings with results from past studies.

In the case of a major global water pollution control equipment study of some years ago, the research consisted of personal and phone interviews with marketing managers of equipment vendors plus gathering of statistics from governments, industry associations, and already available corporate reports. Analysis involved a ten-year retrospective along with ten-year projections for equipment sales, by type and by end-use, for 25 key nations. Expenditures for equipment were related to broader indicators, showing both the rationale and the specific percentages. In addition, alternatives to such capital spending in the form of water treatment chemicals were also analyzed. The report was a "multi-client, off-the-shelf," 250-page report complete with numerous timeline, bar, and pie charts for readers.

Visual representation of information enhances reports by showing data in a clear fashion that complements and in many cases replaces the text. Tables are used mostly for time series, usually at one, two, five, or ten-year intervals, with absolute numbers and additional columns for growth rates. But it is charts of all kinds—graphs, maps, flow diagrams—that can aid even further to reveal patterns and trends. Data can be presented in the form of timeline, bar, and pie charts. Maps can indicate concentration of clients, actual and potential; flow charts reveal how sales shift from one location to another; and organization charts can indicate various distribution channels, hierarchies, vendor-buyer relationships. Computer software is now available for creating and manipulating graphic presentations in refined details (see Figures 12.3 and 12.4).

Both print and electronic media now offer visualization techniques via the use of "infographics." Key elements in information graphics are: appeal, comprehension, retention (Lankow, Ritchie, and Crooks, 2012; Laudon and Traver, 2015). A pioneer in visualization, Edward Tufte of Yale has written books suggesting many successful principles of design and practice (Tufte, 1983; Tufte, 2006). He espouses the notions stated above, and contends that the graphics must readily convey key patterns and trends in an incisive fashion. In Figure 12.3, a log-log chart shows the relationship between security expenditures for many countries versus gross domestic product, both on a per capita basis. Using such a chart readily reveals the pattern by the clustering of points around the trend line and showing situation between the two variables among different size countries. Figure 12.4 is a different

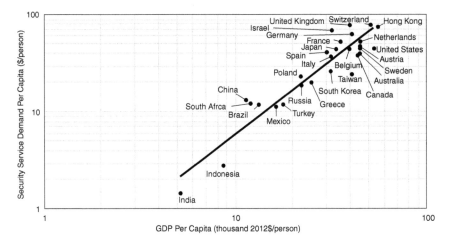

Figure 12.3 Relationship Between Security Equipment Demand Per Capita and GDP Per Capita, 2013 (logarithmic scale, both axes)

Source: World Security Equipment. (2010). Cleveland: The Freedonia Group. Used by permission. Copyright MarketResearch.com, Inc., 2015

global market opportunity diagram revealing both country clustering and market potential in the healthcare sector (Ozturk et al., 2015). This chart, as the previous one, can be easily updated for further timely comparisons and for "continuous improvement."

In the past decade visualization techniques have been refined even further and it is now possible to show "dancing data"—witness the TED talks which are now available free online on a number of economic and business topics. One of the most vivid displays has been showing economic progress, energy use, and healthcare expenditures during the past 100 years. A pioneer in this field was an eloquent "edutainer"—educator and entertainer—the late Hans Rösling of Sweden who developed "Trendalyzer" and established the Gapminder Foundation to promote understanding and visualization of many time series (see gapminder.org or Wikipedia for a detailed list).

Conclusions and Suggestions

The task for market researchers in reaching beyond the domestic scene is to build a "flight map" or navigational aids for estimating the size and characteristics of foreign marketplaces. In executing this assignment, the guidelines call for starting on a small scale, most likely in neighboring countries or even just select metro areas or well-defined target markets. Making constant adjustments and seeking feedback from potential or actual users should be paramount at all times. The challenges discussed include ascertaining the resources that are available, delineating the product-market interface, and then

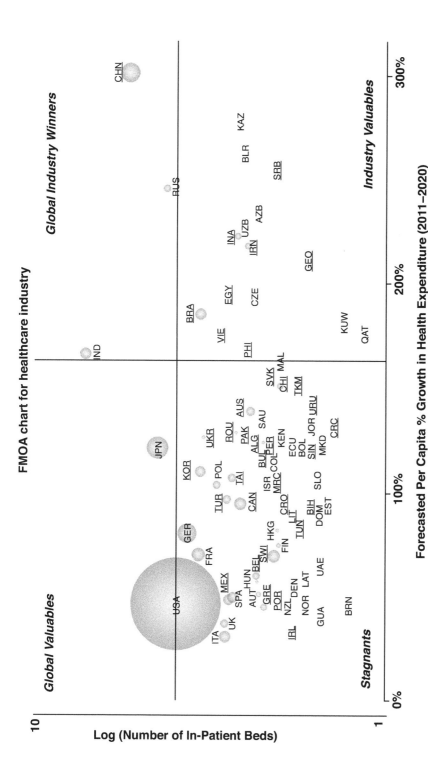

Figure 12.4 Foreign Market Opportunity Analysis (FMOA) for the Healthcare Industry

Source: Ozturk, A., Joiner, E., and Cavusgil, S. T. (2015). Delineating foreign market potential: A tool for international market selection. *Thunderbird International Business Review*, 57(2), 119–141

prescribing the procedures required for accomplishing the objectives. In short, marketing research and intelligence gathering are the foundation stones.

The first step is the mining of existing literature; this will serve as the first building block. There are three notable levels of information, though in practice all three are likely to be utilized jointly via keywords, search terms, Boolean algebra and Venn diagrams. After accomplishing this, the team members face several options—hiring a major or small vendor, engaging an online panel survey firm that has respondents already in place, or undertaking the primary research in-house. A combination of these options is a distinct possibility. The final choice will be based on resources of the firm, including the expertise of each individual on the team, the specific product-market interface, and the time horizon allowed for the assignment. Investigation of consumer goods will be sharply different from those of business or organizational products and services, with the former far more reliant on online panelists, emphasis on brands, and emotional buying motives.

In sizing up the market for a given consumer or industrial good, the development of time series back and forward is highly recommended. As a rule of thumb, such "back-casting and forecasting" for ten-year intervals are appropriate and afford insights on both underlying trends and patterns. It is also advisable to compute ratios between general economic variables and the specific product or service categories involved. When doing market research beyond the domestic scene, in another nation or a region, observing both social-cultural and legal-political restraints is imperative. In approaching panel members or potential buyers, the team should share its current data and promise future feedback.

When reporting the findings, the makeup of the audience is the first consideration. Tailor the presentation to the background of listeners or readers, provide the requisite highlights, emphasize the methods used, results achieved, and the limitations of the study. Information graphics are an excellent way to go beyond text, thereby identifying patterns and trends in tables, graphs, maps, and other visual displays. Current software programs make it easy to dazzle audiences, while also conveying insights on the basis of which managerial action can be taken. The concluding step to any given assignment is the integration of results into the information system of the enterprise, thereby providing the scale-up needed to go from information to intelligence and knowledge.

References

Armstrong, J. S. (2001). *Principles of Forecasting*. New York: Wiley.

Armstrong, J. S., Kester, C. C., and Graefe, A. (2015). Golden rule of forecasting: Be conservative. *Journal of Business Research*, 68(8), 1717–1731.

Bowers, D. and Brereton, M. (2016, Summer). *AMA Gold Report: Top 50 Market Research Firms*. Marketing News (pp. 1–12).

Cavusgil, S. T. and Riesenberger, J. (2009). *Conducting Market Research for International Business*. Business Expert Press. New York, NY.

Craig, C.S. and Douglas, S.P. (2005). *International Marketing Research* (3rd ed.). New York: Wiley.

Duncan, J.W. and Gross, A.C. (1995). *Statistics for the 21st Century*. Homewood, IL: Irwin.

Gleick, J. (2011). *The Information*. New York: Pantheon Books.

Greenland, S. and Kwansah-Aidoo, K. (2012). The challenges of market research in emerging markets: A practitioner perspective from Sub-Saharan Africa, *Australasian Journal of Market and Social Research*, 20, 9–22.

Gross, A. C. and Banting, P. (1993). Business marketing. Houghton Mifflin College Div.

Gross, A.C. (2012). Analyzing and forecasting business markets: Reflections and Recommendations. *ISBM Newsletter*, August, 4–7.

Gross, A.C. and Solymossy, E. (2016). Generations of business information, 1937–2012. *Information & Culture*, 51(2), 226–248.

Harrison, M. et al. (Eds.). (2016). *Market Research in Practice* (3rd ed.). Philadelphia: Kogan Page.

Hedin, H. et al. (Eds.). (2011). *Handbook of Market Intelligence*. West Sussex, UK: Wiley.

Honomichl, J. (2013). Honomichl global top 25. American Marketing Association (AMA).

Katz, R. (Ed.). (2004). *The Human Side of Managing Technological Innovation*. Oxford: Oxford University Press.

Kotabe, M. and Jiang, C. (2009). Contemporary research trends in international marketing. In A. Rugman (Ed.), *Oxford Handbook of International Business* (2nd ed.). Oxford: Oxford University Press, 447–501.

Kuada, J. (2008). *International Market Analysis*. London: Adonis-Abbey.

Kumar, V. (2000). *International Marketing Research*. Upper River Saddle, NJ: Prentice-Hall.

Lankow, J., Ritchie, J., and Crooks, R. (2012). *Infographics: The Power of Visual Storytelling*. New York: Wiley.

Laudon, K.C. and Traver, C.G. (2015). *E-Commerce* (11th ed.). New York: Pearson.

Madhavaram, S., Gross, A.C., and Appan, R. (2016). Knowledge needs of firms: The know-x framework. *AMS Review*, 4(4), 63–77.

Malhotra, N. (2014). *Basic Marketing Research* (4th ed.). New York: Pearson.

Murphy, L. (2016). The Top 20 Most Innovative Market Research Suppliers—Greenbook. Retrieved at March 01, 2017.

Ozturk, A., Joiner, E., and Cavusgil, S.T. (2015). Delineating foreign market potential: A tool for international market selection. *Thunderbird International Business Review*, 57(2), 119–141.

Papadopoulos, N. and Martin, O.M. (2011). International market selection and segmentation: Perspectives and challenges. *International Marketing Review*, 28(2), 132–149.

Pedersen, B. et al. (2008). Closing the knowledge gaps in foreign markets. *Journal of International Business Studies*, 39(7), 1097–1113.

Silver, N. (2012). *The Signal and the Noise*. New York: Penguin Press.

Stewart, T.A. (1997). *Intellectual Capital*. New York: Doubleday.

Surowiecki, J. (2004). *The Wisdom of Crowds*. New York: Anchor Books.

Tufte, E. (1983). *The Visual Display of Quantitative Information*. Cheshire, CT: Graphics Press.

Tufte, E. (2006). *Beautiful Evidence*. Cheshire, CT: Graphics Press.

Wolpert, S.A. and Weiss, W.M. (1970). Business Research Seminar. Cleveland: Predicasts, Inc.

Wolpert, S.A. and Wolpert, J.F. (1986). *The Economics of Information*. New York: Van Nostrand Reinhold.

World Security Equipment. (2010). Cleveland: The Freedonia Group. Used by permission. Copyright MarketResearch.com, Inc., 2015.

Young, R.B. and Javalgi, R.G. (2007). International marketing research: A global project management perspective. *Business Horizons*, 50(2), 113–122.

List of Select Websites

ama.org/publications/marketing news
gapminder.org/news/data-source, Data Sources used in Don't Panic—End Poverty
greenbook.org/market-research-firms
igniteag.com/top-b2b-market-research-firms, Top b2b Market Research Firms
marketingresearch.org
mrs.org.uk
trustradius.com

13 How Semiotic Analysis Generates Intelligence in Formulating Cross-Cultural Advertising Strategies

Satyendra Singh

Introduction

Culture influences clarity of communications. As such communications transmissions have noise, and the noise is even louder when crossing different cultures. It was a long-held belief among international marketing managers that standardizing advertisements should result in communication efficiency globally regardless of advertisement contents. Although managers may be forced by the globalization to be efficient and competitive, standardizing advertisements may not be any longer feasible because managers that maintain this perspective may miss businesses opportunities; consumers cannot simply comprehend products and advertisements that are inconsistent with their cultural beliefs. Thus, adaptation of advertisements to a country's culture is important as it impacts marketing decisions such as product, price, promotion, and most importantly demographics and psychographics segments of the target audience. Given, China and USA spend about $1 billion and $8 billion on advertisements, respectively, this chapter analyzes, using the semiotic technique, the four sets of advertisements from China and USA and recommends how cues (i.e. business intelligence) in advertisements can bridge the gap between the cultures by improving clarity in communications—visibly. To analyze the cues, we use the methodology based on semiotic reading, which interprets advertisements in their social, political, and cultural contexts. It is a suitable technique as it detects cues in advertisements and reveals how they make sense in relation to signs and symbols (Rose, 2007).

The purpose of the chapter is to illustrate how culture impacts business intelligence and marketing communications by using examples from two very different cultures—China and USA. The primary goal of business intelligence is to help managers make decisions, improve business performance, and promote the competitive advantage in the marketplace (Vitt, Luckevich, and Misner, 2002). Although it can be argued that technology makes a greater contribution to business intelligence in terms of collecting and converting large volumes of data into useful information for business managers, in our view, the basic technology-based definition of business intelligence is too narrow as it does not take into account the influence of culture on advertisement acceptance as business intelligence for communications. As such, people use cues for information in both personal and business settings. For the purpose of the chapter, we use cue and business intelligence interchangeably, the premise being effective cues lead to a superior business intelligence which in turn leads to a superior business performance. Culture is a programming of the mind distinguishing the members of one group or category of people from another. For example, individualistic (dimension of) culture such as in the USA highlights products' facts and features in their advertisements, whereas a collective culture such as China emphasizes situational and contextual relationships with people. China has been noted previously as being a collectivist culture and the USA as individualist (Emery and Tian, 2010). Collectivist cultures hold contextual cues more valid in accepting advertisements, while individualist cultures hold product-related thoughts toward advertisements. Given that globalization has contributed to time poverty and luxury consumption, it is relevant to consider Hofstede's latest dimensions of *long-term orientation* and *Indulgence vs. Restraint* and their impact on business intelligence across the Chinese and American cultures. These differences in cultures contribute to business intelligence and have implications for international managers; for example, it may be possible that in individualistic culture, customers may respond more enthusiastically to promotional deals than in collective culture. Hofstede's (1980) culture dimension is explained in the next section. This chapter is organized as follows: first culture is defined and cultural difference assessed, followed by a discussion on how culture impacts product, price, promotion, and market segmentation, leading to purchase decisions. Finally, the chapter concludes with recommendations for international marketing managers.

Hofstede's Culture Dimensions

Culture impacts cross-cultural communications and purchasing decisions. International marketing managers diagnose and bridge culture gaps between a seller and a buyer engaged in cross-cultural communications because sellers need to communicate about product features, price, and promotions, among others to the target culture (Hofstede, 1980). Indeed, culture may separate people from one another (Kale, 1991). However, Hofstede's original cultural dimensions are: the Power Distance (the extent to which the less powerful members of organizations and institutions accept and expect that power is distributed equally); Individualism (the degree to which individuals are integrated into groups); Uncertainty Avoidance (the extent to which individuals tolerate uncertainty); and, Masculinity (to the extent to which masculine or feminine values are dominant in a society). Recently, Hofstede presents a sixth dimension (Indulgence vs. Restraint) model that supersedes the fifth dimension (long-term orientation) model (for more dimensions, see www.geerthofstede.eu). These dimensions help marketing managers understand cultural differences across countries and their impacts on advertising strategies. Although Hofstede's cultural dimensions may be viewed as too broad, it is still relevant to assess their impacts on marketing practices in general and advertising in particular. These dimensions currently comprise the most comprehensive and widely used framework for the study of culture.

Business Intelligence, Culture, and Semiotic Assessment

To assess business intelligence through the cultural differences, the author draws upon the Semiotic analysis and presents a semiotic interpretation of the social and cultural meanings of consumer-related advertisements. Semiotics theory describes the use of cue and information for communications, and provides a model that justifies the complexity of information systems used in cultural contexts (Clarke, 2001). Based on existing wisdom, interpretation of semiotics theory is approached from social and cultural perspectives on the premise that a semiotic system offers at least three kinds of meanings simultaneously, though any one type of meaning may take precedence over another: (a) *Experiential* meaning that relates to presentations of advertisements; (b) *Interpersonal* meaning that relates to relationships through cues between consumers and firms; and, (c) *Textual* meaning that relates to how the text and images are structured to make meaning as a whole (O'Toole, 1994; Kress and van Leeuwen, 2006). Indeed, advertisements create structure of meaning, and the semiotic reading of it aims to deconstruct these meanings and locate cues within cultural codes and social contexts at specific times (Hackley, 2002). The author aims to provide interpretation of advertisements with respect to cultural meaning and its compatibility.

Methodology: The Case Studies

Four paired advertisements from China and the USA were chosen, ensuring that these advertisements communicated and reflected at least one dimension of Hofstede's culture in a most vivid manner so cues could be picked up. One of the features of advertisements is that it aims to generate new cultural meaning, attract customers, and boost business performance. For this reason, marketing can be seen as expropriating consumer cultural meaning and turning it to business intelligence (Goldman and Papson, 1996; Williamson, 1978). Being cognizant of the fact that advertising is an ideological strategy (Hackley, 2002), four advertisements from the global bands were selected—McDonald's, GAP, Mini Cooper, and Estee Lauder—following the method suggested by Yin (1984). Through the semiotics theory, these advertisements—a system of signs—contribute to the human grasp of reality, where meaning is not exclusively a property of books, computers, or any other means or source of knowledge, but is also a complex interplay of cues, codes, or conventions of which one is normally unaware (Chandler, 2007). Additionally, another advertisement of Tommy Hilfiger was chosen to illustrate some cross-cultural pitfalls while communicating intended messages. Although advertisements are directed at consumers who have cultural understanding of them, managers should acquire knowledge of consumers' symbolic meaning-systems when advertising in different cultures (Hackley, 2002). Specifically, based on the process of semiotic interpretation suggested by Koskela (2014), the following questions were researched: What is in the advertisements? How do the texts relate to the advertisements? What message do the advertisements try to communicate? How do the advertisements represent the culture? What kinds of references to time, space, or both do the advertisements contain?

Product-Related Business Intelligence

In today's fast-paced, competitive society, getting the attention of customers has become increasingly challenging. In this respect, semiotic-based advertisements have gained popularity in generating cultural meaning as a message. Cultural differences significantly influence the way a brand is received by consumers. A key factor in acceptance of a product often is the way it fits into the consumer's culture and lifestyle. For example, in some countries consumers take more risks than other countries due to the cultural differences. In assessing the connection between a culture and a brand by using Hofstede's uncertainty avoidance dimension, it can be found that China scores lower on this dimension than USA, meaning Chinese consumers should avoid risk associated with products or brands that are unfamiliar to them (Lin, 2001). However, as a country's ideology, social and political system changes, so does the risk-taking ability of its people. As China is emerging from a closed economy to a market economy, customers now may be willing to take more risks when purchasing products due to the change in the cultural values and attitudes brought by the market economy. By contrast, Americans are more risk tolerant and embrace uncertainty when buying products.

The link between a culture and a product acceptance can be demonstrated by comparing the fast food example in the context of the *time-orientation* dimension of Hofstede's culture across the Chinese and American advertisements. A study found that Americans are most accepting of convenience products due to their industrialized lifestyle and lack of time. That explains why fast food chains such as McDonald's are so successful in the USA and the Western countries. The advertisement (1a focusing on time-orientation) gives the impression of a sit-down traditional restaurant to Chinese customers. Naturally, cues such as cooks in their long caps and customers enjoying food using metal forks and knives are not immediately obvious to the mass public, but subliminally it works. Although it is true that McDonald's offers *speed-orientated* services in China also, they are generally characterized as an American lifestyle. Occasionally, Chinese families do enjoy such fast foods but it is not a routine occurrence like American consumers who are in love with fast food brands such as Starbucks, KFC, etc. A typical Chinese family ritual is to prepare three meals daily with fresh ingredients. Food advertisements in China exemplify food by stressing great taste over the amount of effort and time required for its preparation. These differences are evident in the McDonald's advertisements in China and the USA. In order for a message to be compatible with culture, many businesses use cues as business intelligence to examine its impact on business performance. In fact, these kinds of advertisements are common and designed to work semiotically (Bignell, 2002), creating a condition in which consumers can see the puppets but not the strings (Hackley, 2002). It is interesting to note how cultural differences are depicted semiotically in Chinese (1b focusing on freshness) and American (1c focusing on taste) to ensure that the same products are accepted effectively in different cultures (see Figure 13.1).

The Chinese advertisement (1b) for McDonald's uses brighter colors, and shows a greater product variety to display quality and freshness of their products. This advertisement is congruent with the Chinese cultural attitudes towards dining and focusing on quality and fresh products. In contrast, the American advertisement (1c) displays only a couple of different burgers and emphasizes the size of the burger as well as the incentive of receiving a free burger with the purchase of the initial one. This advertisement reflects American dining culture and the common American attitudes toward price sensitivity and quantity discount. Now, we discuss the impact of culture on price and promotion and how different advertisements are crafted for different cultures to gather business intelligence.

Price- and Promotion-Related Business Intelligence

Price consciousness is dramatically lower in societies with comparably higher power distance. The customers believe that they may better express their attachment to a certain class in society through the products they purchase and strive to associate themselves with their luxury (Hofstede's culture dimension of *indulgence*) consumption behaviors (Erdem, Swait, and Valenzuela, 2006). It is found that consumers in the collectivist culture have less tendency to seize promotional deals than individualistic culture (e.g. USA) because consumers may perceive that they may be labeled as cheap or low-class consumers (Dhar and Hoch, 1996). Studies also indicate that many African Americans (Green, 1995) and Hispanic Americans (Donthu and Cherian, 1992) have negative attitudes toward coupons, partly because coupons are a sign of a low class or may indicate an inability to pay full price, even if it is untrue. For the same reason, even Japanese consumers are embarrassed to redeem coupons (Kashani and Quelch, 1990). Clearly, the power distribution dimension of the culture is intertwined with the consumer decision-making process while purchasing products or services—ordinary or luxury.

Advertisement 1a

Advertisement 1b

Advertisement 1c

Figure 13.1 Cultures and Products

From the price sensitivity point of view, China is a less developed country than the USA and therefore Chinese advertisements are more likely to emphasize basic product benefits than American advertisements. A traditional American advertisement tends to emphasize facts about products through the use of experts and celebrities for product endorsements. In contrast, Chinese advertisers tend to base their strategy on emotional appeals. For example, American appliances almost always demonstrate the product's superiority using fact, statistics, and "proven" anecdotes; their emphasis is on *value for money* and results. In comparison, Chinese appliances advertisements may show how the product makes a good gift for your soon-to-be married daughter or your loving mother; they may not emphasize price much. Also, Chinese advertisements do not appear to mention the product merits, but focus semiotically on the contextual emotions involved in the purchase (e.g. mother-daughter post-marriage emotional relationship). In the next section, links between culture and segments is explained.

Segment-Related Business Intelligence

To be successful in international marketing, managers need to segment their customers carefully. Broadly, there are two approaches: demographics and psychographics. Some scholars believe that they influence each other, though some argue against it. Demographics are the makeup of a segment's average age, sex, family structure, income, level of education, social class, and religious beliefs (McCarty and Shrum, 1993). Scholars suggest that demographics affect psychographics which may influence emotional appeal, brand perception, and brand acceptance or resistance to a product. Psychographics is defined as the study of activities, interests, and opinions of segmented consumer groups (Dutta-Bergman, 2006). Psychographics are important in advertising as it appeals to emotion, and thus making semiotic cues effective. In fact, cross-cultural marketing success is dependent on the understanding of cultural differences because consumers grow up in their own culture and experience the same social behaviors that influence their value systems, beliefs, and perceptions (Emery and Tian, 2010). In the next section, age and gender aspects of demographic segment, emotion, perception, and brand acceptance and rejection aspects of psychographic segment in the context of Chinese and American advertisements for gathering business intelligence are explained.

Age- and Gender-Related Intelligence

Demographic factors such as age, gender, and family structure shape an individual's attitude and lifestyle choices. Gender display in advertisements may influence the credibility, differentiation, and competence of brands in certain cultures. Gender differences are fostered by a culture and are influenced by values and lifestyles (psychographics) (Gupta and De, 2007). When comparing demographics and psychographics in the semiotic advertising context, some scholars conclude that personal values from psychographics serve as a better determinant of consumer segmentation than demographics because psychographics still concern some aspects of age, income, and

Advertisement 2a (China)   Advertisement 2b (USA)

Figure 13.2 Cultures and Demographics

education of target segments. Although some researchers are reluctant to consider demographics for advertisement evaluations (McCarty and Shrum, 1993), a comparison of advertisements may illustrate how demographic differences such as age and lifecycle stages affect consumers' attitudes toward advertisements (Dutta-Bergman, 2006). This is evident in the following set of Chinese (Advertisement 2a) and American (Advertisement 2b) advertisements for GAP (see Figure 13.2).

The Chinese GAP advertisement contains both a male companion and a white dove, which could symbolize stability and practicality that are not usually conveyed in American advertisements. Further, the Chinese GAP advertisement evokes a sense of family in comparison to the American GAP advertisement that portrays a sense of individuality. The American advertisement can be interpreted as a young, free, more rebellious advertisement in comparison to the conservative Chinese version of this advertisement. These differences in the advertisements reflect the values and lifestyle differences present in each culture. Indeed, the semiotics presence in advertisements disarm consumers, resonate with their fantasies and aspirations, and normalize consumption practices (Hackley, 2002).

Emotion-Related Business Intelligence

Emotional appeal of a brand is defined as the feelings and thoughts an image or text evokes. Advertisements can evoke emotional feelings such as happiness, sadness, and connectedness, among others. Thus emotional appeals need to be managed carefully in advertisements as customers from different cultures react to emotions in different ways. For example, Chinese advertisements display connectedness through nature or harmony, whereas the use of group consensus as a business intelligence tool is usually unseen

Advertisement 3a (China)   Advertisement 3b (USA)

Figure 13.3 Cultures and Emotions

in American advertisements. The following two advertisements from China (3a) and USA (3b) that use emotions to attract customers are discussed (see Figure 13.3).

In the Chinese version of the Mini Cooper advertisement, the emotional appeal of the advertisement incorporates a collectivist culture as shown by many people in the Mini Cooper car at a time; that is, people like doing things and working together. The slogan "Be Mini" represents the compact product, meaning small and efficient car for the Chinese target segment. The emotional appeal of the product in this advertisement should attract the Chinese consumers whose cultural values are based on needs and wants. The Chinese culture also stresses the popularity of a product in their advertisements; for example, having many people in the car or wanting to be in the car shows the appeal of the popularity of the product. Having the emotional appeal of collectivism and popularity of a product represent what the Chinese culture looks for in an advertisement. Clearly, the social code of a particular group of consumers (the young consumers as depicted in the car in the featured case) can have influence on how the images can be semiotically encoded to have a priori agreed and understood business intelligence (Rose, 2007).

By contrast, the American version of the Mini Cooper advertisement is completely different from the Chinese one. The American version of the advertisement focuses on the look of the product overall. It does not just inform the customer about one style of the Mini Cooper; it rather shows them the four different styles they can choose from. The slogan "Collect Them All" stresses to American consumers that instead of having one style of the Mini Cooper, they should have multiple. Because Americans are focused on materialism and consumerism, having a few or all four styles of Mini Coopers would appeal to these kinds of customers. This is why the four models of Mini Coopers allow managers, who are gathering business intelligence, to target the four desirable segments. This advertising strategy gives each customer a choice to satisfy its needs of having a vehicle and emotionally connect to the product, brand, and advertisement. The customers should feel in control of their purchase decisions, ensuring satisfaction in the process. The emotional appeal of this advertisement stresses consumerism prevalent in the American culture. The Mini Cooper advertisement presented here is one of many examples of how the level of emotional appeals in different cultures relates to business intelligence that can be used to design effective advertisements.

Perception-Related Business Intelligence

Perception is defined as the process by which sensations are selected, organized, and interpreted. A customer's perceptions of brands are formed by associating it to their memory. Customers distinguish the psychological aspects of brand associations, such as thoughts, feelings, images, experiences, beliefs, and attitudes, among others, and link them to their memory. A product's physical qualities, packaging, price, advertisement, promotion, and merchandising also contribute to customers' perceptions of specific brands. Brand perception varies across culture because perception of a brand is dependent on the culture of the customer. Thus, advertisements should be consistent with the culture of the target market to get across the intended message and receive business intelligence as evidenced by effectiveness of advertisements. Different countries and cultures perceive messages and symbols in different contexts. Semiotically, a comparison is made with the following two Estee Lauder cosmetic advertisements prepared for Chinese (4a) and American (4b) cultures, respectively (see Figure 13.4).

The Chinese advertisement (4a) focuses on the product only; perhaps detailed product information was left intentionally, so that Chinese customers could perceive it as a popular product, and thus would want to have it. The perception is that the Chinese customers should associate the image of the advertisement with the physical product they own. By contrast, in the American advertisement, the perception is that the customers should associate with the model's appearance and the results. The focus of the American advertisement is on the beautiful model. Indeed, the physical product is less noticeable and thus presented at the bottom corner of the advertisement. Further, this advertisement ensures customers about their satisfaction with

Advertisement 4a (China)

Advertisement 4b (USA)

Figure 13.4 Cultures and Perceptions

the results of the product, a promise which is very important in American culture (time-orientation dimension of the culture). The promise that consumers will see results within a certain period of time contributes to the consumer perception, and confirms that they have made a right purchase decision. Furthermore, managers have designed this advertisement in a way that American consumers should perceive the products results as similar to the model's appearance. Because this is a skin product advertisement and the model has beautiful skin, the consumer should associate the model's skin with the product, and should perceive the product as effective. The differences in consumer perceptions in these cross-cultural advertisements demonstrate the importance of culture in international marketing. It is understandable that the reality of advertisements is a social product rather than a mere description, and that the perception of interpretations can be complex, as interpretations of advertisements can have both deliberate and unintended consequences in various ways (Koskela, 2014). In the next section, some of the cross-cultural pitfalls relating to interpretation and how to avoid them when designing advertisements are discussed.

Brand-Related Business Intelligence Acceptance or Resistance

Brand-related business intelligence acceptance or resistance is defined as consumers' reactions to risks involved in purchasing and consuming products. Products and brands benefit from associations with countries whose image is positive, and are harmed by associations with countries whose image is negative (Balbanis, Mueller, and Melewar, 2002). Having a positive country image contributes to attitudes and beliefs toward the products which were made in such countries. For example, if Coca-Cola is made in the USA and if China does not believe that the USA has a positive image, the brand perception of Coca-Cola should inherently be negative. Further, product and brand acceptance can directly relate to culture in which an advertisement is placed. Thus, the text of the advertisement should convey the intended message and should be sensitive to the target culture. This is explained semiotically by citing the Tommy Hilfiger's global advertisement campaign in Advertisement 5 (see Figure 13.5).

Signs and symbols are interpreted in relation to other signs, texts, and images in a social and cultural contexts. Although businesses try to direct customers semiotically to their messages through cues in advertisements, marketing efforts relating to business intelligence can be still ineffective (Goldman and Papson, 1996; Rose, 2007). To illustrate the point in advertisement 5's global campaign, Tommy Hilfiger used the semiotic concept of freedom by including a motorcycle that depicts a handsome man riding the motorcycle in the desert. In the USA, this advertisement is extremely effective in conveying the message of freedom relating to the cologne. If one semiotically analyzes the advertisement further, it is noticeable that it consists of a vintage motorcycle, speed, a ruggedly handsome alone man, and personal satisfaction. When this global standard advertisement for Tommy Hilfiger was released in China, it did not bode well with the Chinese target audience due to its incongruity with the Chinese culture. Indeed for the advertisement to be effective in China, perhaps a different emotional appeal technique would have allowed for a greater acceptance of the brand. Chinese culture does not favor individualism; it rather favors collectivism (i.e. family and traditional values). Thus, in Chinese culture, a motorcycle may be considered dangerous and may be a sign of low status. Possibly showing a car instead of a motorcycle would have been more effective in getting acceptance for this advertisement. Further, this advertisement shows only one man. In China, this may not be effective in gaining brand acceptance because it reflects more westernized culture like the USA. China's culture does not favor individualism, and thus including more than one person in this advertisement perhaps

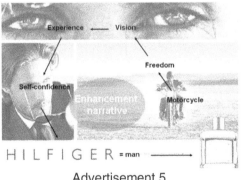

Advertisement 5

Figure 13.5 Cultures and Pitfalls

would have been much more effective. In addition, the Chinese advertisement should be based on status, and not personal satisfaction as the American advertisement depicts. If the Tommy Hilfiger advertisement was sensitive to these cultural aspects, the brand would have a greater acceptance rate in Chinese culture. Therefore, it is crucial that firms use appropriate semiotic advertising context to make their brands acceptable to the target segments in foreign cultures. Tommy Hilfiger's failed global advertising campaign and business intelligence suggest that the acceptance of a brand is related to advertising contexts applicable in that particular culture.

Conclusion

International marketing manages should realize the cultural differences in the context of advertising and be sensitive to the ever-changing cultures and adapt their advertisements for products and services accordingly to target customers in different countries. Based on the discussions in this chapter, it is concluded that the advertisements should be congruent with the consumers' culture and their own values. Accordingly, it is recommended that managers use co-branding strategies when entering a foreign country. Co-branding strategies consist of identifying a foreign product and associating it with an existing product which has a positive emotional appeal in the host country. Managers can use this strategy to incorporate psychographic characteristics to design semiotic advertisements that create a positive emotional appeal and lead to quality business intelligence. For example, if an international firm decides to introduce a new luxury Coach product, they could associate the Coach product with another luxury product with a positive emotional appeal in China or a country of interest.

As semiotic analysis relates to studying traditional signs and symbols of a certain culture, the use of this analysis enables international marketing managers to effectively link cultural values and lifestyles to brand acceptance of products (i.e. resulting in a purchase decision). By being sensitive to semiotic aspects of a culture and cues, firms can assess whether or not their advertisements will be effective in a given culture. Indeed, semiotics can aid managers in designing a campaign more tailored to brand acceptance in different cultures.

Finally, it is recommended that managers form strategic alliances which involve building an association of one product with a complementary product. The use of an alliance allows managers to gain perspective on emotional appeal in a similar industry, and build emotional trust for the new brand as it is associated with the reputation of an existing brand. For example, Heinz is a reputable brand in the USA. If a foreign manager wishes to enter the American market with their premium frozen French fries, they might consider partnering with Heinz to build a positive emotional appeal for the brand. This strategy allows managers to enter in a new market and new culture with a new product.

Acknowledgement

The author gratefully acknowledges the University of Winnipeg, Canada grant (# GT4279) for its support in this research project.

References

Balbanis, G., Mueller, R., and Melewar, T. C. (2002). The relationship between consumer ethnocentrism and human values. *Journal of Global Marketing*, 15(3/4), 7–37.

Bignell, J. (2002). *Media Semiotics: An Introduction*. New York, NY: Palgrave Macmillan.

Chandler, D. (2007). *Semiotics: The Basics*. New York: Routledge.

Clarke, R. (2001). Social semiotic contributions to the systemic semiotic work practice framework. *Sign Systems Studies*, 29(2), 587–605.

Dhar, S. K. and Hoch, S. J. (1996). Price discrimination using in-store merchandising. *Journal of Marketing*, 60(1), 17–30.

Donthu, N. and Cherian, J. (1992). The Hispanic coupon usage: The impact of strong and weak ethnic identification. *Psychology and Marketing*, 9(6), 501–510.

Dutta-Bergman, J. (2006). The demographic and psychographic antecedents of attitude toward advertising. *Journal of Advertising Research*, 10(10), 102–112.

Emery, C. and Tian, K. (2010). China compared with the US: Cultural differences and the impacts on advertising appeals. *International Journal of China Marketing*, 1(1), 43–59.

Erdem, T., Swait, J., and Valenzuela, A. (2006). Brands as signals: A cross-country validation study. *Journal of Marketing*, 70(1), 34–49.

Goldman, R. and Papson, S. (1996). *Sign Wars: The Cluttered Landscape of Advertising*. New York: Guilford Press.

Green, C. L. (1995). Differential responses to retail sales promotion among African-American and Anglo-American consumers. *Journal of Retailing*, 71(11), 83–92.

Gupta, A. S., and De, S. (2007). Changing trends of cultural values in advertising: An exploratory study. *Psychology Developing Societies*, 19(1), 113–123.

Hackley, C. (2002). The panoptic role of advertising agencies in the production of consumer culture. *Consumption, Markets & Culture*, 5(3), 211–229.

Hofstede, G. H. (1980). *Culture's Consequences: International Differences in Work-Related Values*. Beverly Hills: Sage Publications.

Kale, S. H. (1991). Culture-specific marketing communications: An analytical approach. *Journal of International Marketing Review*, 8(2), 18–30.

Kashani, K. and Quelch, J. A. (1990). Can sales promotion go global? *Business Horizons*, 33(3), 37–43.

Koskela, H. (2014). "Capture every moment"—The profane semiotics of surveillance advertisements. *Social Semiotics*, 24(3), 324–344.

Kress, G. and van Leeuwen, T. (2006). *Reading Images: The Grammar of Visual Design*. London: Routledge.

Lin, C. A. (2001). Cultural values reflected in Chinese and American television advertising. *Journal of Advertising*, 10(4), 83–94.

McCarty, J. and Shrum, L. J. (1993). The role of personal values and demographics in predicting television viewing behavior: Implications for theory and application. *Journal of Advertising*, 22(4), 77–101.

O'Toole, M. (1994). *The Language of Displayed Art*. London: Leicester University Press.

Rose, G. (2007). *Visual Methodologies: An Introduction to the Interpretation of Visual Materials*. London: Sage.

Vitt, E., Luckevich, M., and Misner, S. (2002). *Making Better Business Intelligence Decisions Faster*. Washington: Microsoft Press.

Williamson, J. (1978). *Decoding Advertisements: Ideology and Meaning in Advertising*. London: Marion Boyars.

Yin, R. K. (1984). *Case Study Research: Design and Methodologies*. Beverley Hills: Sage Publications.

14 Networks as Catalysts of Technological Intelligence

Cases of Chinese Small- and Medium-Sized Enterprises

Zongqiang Ren and Wiboon Kittilaksanawong

Introduction

Firm boundary has increasingly opened and extended with the influence of globalization and transformation into a knowledge-based economy through innovation networks (Chesbrough, 2003; Laursen and Salter, 2006). Innovation networks could create business intelligence that allows organizations to flexibly coordinate and integrate their scattered resources more efficiently. These networks can be built internally within the firm's boundary and externally through other organizations including universities, research institutes, and intermediaries. Therefore, the business intelligence could flow within and between the organizations. Achieving the synergy between such inter-firm and intra-firm innovation networks is thus the main challenge of organizations in building up innovation capability.

Based on case studies (Eisenhardt, 1989) of three manufacturing SMEs in China's Zhejiang province, this study explores strategic pathways, mechanisms, and dynamics of innovation capability building through external and internal innovation networks. Innovation capabilities in terms of an exploratory and an exploitative type are embedded in the innovation networks (Guan and Liu, 2016). The exploratory type involves the discovery of new knowledge that brings about long-term profitability and growth opportunities, whereas the exploitative type refers to the improvement of products and services based on existing knowledge and skills, aiming for near-term performance.

This study provides several implications. First, the complementarity between the internal and external networks simultaneously promotes exploratory and exploitative type of innovation capability, which is necessary for sustainable organizational performance. Second, the construction of internal network infrastructure allows firms to adopt and absorb advanced knowledge from external networks more effectively. Third, organizations can reduce the adverse effect of environmental turbulence through the synergy between external and internal innovation networks.

Profile and In-Depth Analysis of Representative Companies

EYG Company

EYG was established in 1984 as a small business with the output value of only 300,000 RMB in Zhejiang province. It had grown into a large professional integrated manufacturer and supplier of electrical appliances, cables, and intelligence units with its own in-house R&D, production, and sales. During early days, the company mainly increased production and management efficiency through reorganizing and integration of internal resources. With a relatively solid foundation, the company then entered in external collaborations to acquire new resources and best practices to upgrade its products.

The reform began in the late 1980s when EYG improved product quality by strengthening the internal production process and control. During the increasing industry competition and market demand heterogeneity in 1990s, the company experienced great competitive pressure because of limited product varieties. EYG thus extended product lines and developed new markets by diversifying into related businesses.

However, such diversification through the existing internal resources was not sufficient to catch up with the rapid change in market competition and technology advancement. After 2003, EYG began to collaborate with external organizations and intermediaries including universities and research institutes. Such collaborations enhance its internal basic research and absorptive capability.

After such accelerated reforms, the company realized a rapid sales growth. In 2008, the annual sales reached 800 million RMB with electrical appliances and smart home wiring systems occupying the largest market share in the industry. Since then, it increasingly used external networks as an expansion strategy and innovation capability building.

EYG had then transformed into a conglomerate of integrated product lines. It was committed to the discovery and application of high technology to upgrade the whole industry. The company won the award as being a pioneer in CIMS application from the National 863 Program. It had also been recognized as a key high-tech enterprise in Zhejiang province. The strategy for innovation capability building was summarized as follows.

Internal Resource Integration as Foundation for Building Innovation Capability

EYG focused on internal corporate restructuring and personnel adjustment, aiming to create a customer-oriented matrix organizational structure. The new organizational structure was relatively flat to increase operational efficiency. It began a major reform in 2005, which included the introduction of a modern management system, and the optimization of internal resource allocation in headquarters and subsidiaries.

Efficiency and Learning Through Implementation of
Corporate-Wide Information Technology System

EYG implemented a corporate-wide IT system to facilitate allocation and use of enterprise resources, while increasing management and operational efficiency. IT not only helped in product development, marketing, manufacturing, technology transfer, and other activities in the supply chain, it also facilitated virtual manufacturing and distribution facilities. EYG was able to integrate upstream suppliers and downstream distributors to ensure a more reliable product and service delivery. Further, it implemented a knowledge management system in 2008 as an integral part of becoming a learning organization.

Open Innovation and Innovation Capability Building Through
External Collaboration

From the mid-1990s, EYG began to collaborate with limited reputable universities in the province such as Zhejiang University and Zhejiang Science and Technology University to promote the use of computer-aided design and to jointly develop advanced manufacturing systems. In 2002, the two sides jointly set up a laboratory for the development of new technologies, which later won the award from the National Science and Technology Progress Council.

The collaborations led to commercialization of the research outputs and the industrial upgrading. EYG continued to collaborate with other domestic and foreign product design institutes to increase value added to the products. In 1999, it formed a joint venture with a leading Germany electrical cable company to acquire advanced design and manufacturing technology. In 2009, it collaborated with a Taiwanese optoelectronics company to enter the emerging energy-saving market.

SYG Company

SYG was started in 1986 as a small Chinese sewing-machinery workshop in Zhejiang province. In early periods, it had very limited product varieties, lagging behind its competitors. These products were mostly sold in the domestic market and in other developing countries. The company aggressively entered in collaborations with many external partners to extend its product lines and markets since the very beginning.

During the Southeast Asian financial crisis in 1997, its profitability declined sharply mainly due to the over-diversification and internal resource constraints. SYG therefore refocused its business scope and introduced related high technology to upgrade existing sewing products. It set up R&D centers in the headquarters and branches in Beijing, Ningbo, and Japan to collaborate with external partners. The company also hired overseas technical talent and continuously adopted new cutting-edge technologies from outside while integrating them with existing products and technologies.

Since then, SYG had grown into a large export-oriented group of companies, utilizing the scientific and technological resources at home and abroad. It had successfully secured over 300 national patents, becoming a leader in supplying a complete series of sewing machinery in the international markets. The company had significantly upgraded the sewing industry in China, producing over 50 series and 500 varieties of sewing products with an annual output of over five million units of sewing machines, occupying over 50% of the world production. The strategy for innovation capability building was summarized as follows.

External Resource Acquisition as Foundation of Development

SYG aggressively enhanced its technologies through a variety of external collaboration. It carried out scientific research in collaboration with the Shanghai Institute of Sewing Machines, Shanghai University, and Beijing Institute of Electrical and Mechanical Research as well as other research institutes in developed countries. Over 20 universities and research institutes were working directly with SYG and indirectly through other institutions on many projects, resulting in the increase of 30% in the product design efficiency and the decrease of 80% in the product failure rates.

SYG also formed joint ventures with foreign companies to accelerate the adoption of advanced technologies and the internationalization of high-end products. The company entered a joint venture with Singapore Double Star Group to produce the first-class garment hanging system, with Germany ZSK Company to manufacture advanced multi-head computerized embroidery machine, and with Italy MIFRA to manufacture high-end computerized knitting machine.

Demand-Driven Integrated Innovation

SYG always aimed to meet the domestic and foreign market demands by providing a cutting-edge product globally. Apart from establishing research centers with its own personnel, the company also hired experts to strengthen the intellectual resources on sewing technology. Every year, SYG sent over 50 key personnel for training at home and abroad. The company was committed to integrating advanced mechanical, electronic, computer, and optics technology into the manufacturing of sewing equipment, which resulted in successful technology upgrading acceptable in the international market.

Acquisition and Joint Venture as Major Access to External Technology

In 1998, SYG acquired several foreign companies with the most advanced technologies. It acquired 50% of equity interest in an Italy knitting company to build the country's largest sewing-equipment production base. Through a joint venture with Singapore Double Star Group, SYG had successfully developed a computerized garment suspension system. However, its internal resources and management were not strong enough to support such an aggressive strategy. The company faced even more operating difficulties when the financial crisis began in 2008.

CTG Company

Founded in 1987 as a small Chinese workshop-style factory in Zhejiang province, CTG aspired to be a leading company with its own innovation since the establishment. Since the early 1990s, it had entered scientific collaborations with external partners to develop a series of fiber optic products.

Based on the technology adoption through such collaborations, CTG continued to learn and internalize those technologies concurrently. The adoption, integration, and learning allowed CTG to be successful in developing a technology breakthrough in optical fiber preform in 2001. After 2005, it successfully developed a variety of fiber optic cable and optical fiber preform, thereby increasing its competitiveness in the industry.

CTG had grown to become a large enterprise with over 20 affiliates and subsidiaries providing a complete series of optical fiber products. Aspiring to be a competitive global company, it had set up its own technological and R&D center, which were recognized at the national level. The company had been regarded as one of the national high-tech enterprises, national innovative enterprises, top 100 Chinese private enterprises, and top 100 Chinese electronic and information enterprises. CTG emphasized the sustainable development through technological innovation and corporate social responsibilities. The strategy for innovation capability building was summarized as follows.

Technology, Equipment, and Management as the Core Elements in Technological Innovation

During the early period, CTG's technical resources were relatively weak. In 1995, it entered a joint venture with Japan Showa Electric Wire & Cable Company to access the cable technology. The company had entered in a number of joint ventures in the field of metal cables, optical cable, and other related communication equipment. In 1998, it adopted a new technology in optical communication equipment and testing from the United States, the United Kingdom, and Finland and became one of a few private enterprises engaging in the manufacturing of optical communication equipment.

Since 2008, CTG had increased the level of international collaboration to draw more foreign technological expertise and to expand in overseas markets. It entered in a joint venture with Sumitomo to develop optical fiber preform and cables in Tianjin, Chengdu, and Hong Kong. The company had transformed from a family business to a diversified professional company through a joint venture with Japanese enterprises that allowed the management from both sides to participate in the strategic decision-making.

Collaboration With Universities and Research Institutes to Enhance Basic Research and Absorptive Capacity

Early in 1993, CTG collaborated with China Research Institute of Posts and Telecommunications to develop three kinds of fiber optic cable. It extensively collaborated with domestic research institutes, including University of Electronic Technology and Zhejiang University, resulting in many Optoelectronics Technology Joint Research Laboratories and many key upstream and downstream technologies. CTG had been certified as the national technical center and post-doctoral research institute in the field of optical communication.

Technological Breakthrough Through Simultaneous Exploration and Learning

To overcome foreign technological barriers and achieve the breakthrough, in 2000, CTG initiated a major research project to acquire the technologies from abroad, learn them, and based on its knowledge foundation, build its own second technological innovation on the original equipment. After a year, the company mastered all core technologies, securing its own intellectual property rights, which were followed by a series of other supporting products and services. During 2002–2003, the company then scaled up its domestic production, overcoming a long-time foreign technological blockade, while increasing localization of equipment production.

Enterprise-Employee Co-Development as the Key to Organizational Sustainability

CTG tried hard to enhance its personnel's technical and management capability through an education and training system, career planning, professional work environment, attractive remuneration and promotion. The company learned and adopted the Japanese style of management. The employees at all levels were provided with an opportunity to develop themselves and to participate in the future development. Over 60% of the proposals for projects were initiated by different levels and groups of employees and they were supported and implemented.

Cross-Case Analysis of Representative Companies

The earlier in-depth analysis demonstrates how the three technology SMEs formulate and implement the open innovation strategy through the external and internal networks of collaboration. This section further analyzes the evolution of their network development strategy and network characteristics as well as the influence on innovation capability.

Organizational Network Development Strategy

The network development during early periods of EYG Company had relied mainly on the restructuring of internal organizational structure, which included the integration of resources and the introduction of information technology to increase operational and management efficiency. The company also diversified into closely related products to learn new technologies and markets. Such diversification through internal resources, however, did not allow the company to develop any substantial breakthrough technologies. The company mostly received profits from low-end new products.

The company realized such constraint in internal resources. It therefore subsequently extended relationships with external partners that were able to provide advanced technologies. This external network development successfully extended the company's business scope into five different industries.

SYG Company had aggressively established external networks of collaboration for acquisition of more advanced and higher value-added technologies since early periods of the establishment. These external networks provided access to necessary resources, including high-quality personnel, funding, and technical knowledge for new product development. The company was able to survive from the Southeast Asian financial crisis in 1997 largely due to the competitiveness derived from such new product development.

However, during the 2008 financial crisis when the credit market was contracted, the company's sales had declined sharply along with its rapid and excessive investments in new technologies and overseas markets. Lacking absorptive capacity, the company was not able to assimilate these new technologies and market knowledge to strengthen its core competency. The imbalance between internal absorptive capacity and external knowledge acquisition strategy had resulted in a significant rise of overall costs of products in the fragile market.

CTG Company had introduced the advanced technology from Japan during early periods of the establishment. Through several joint ventures with foreign companies, the company was able to access and learn new technologies from collaborative partners. The company did not have large external networks but these networks were very deep and strong. Importantly, through collaboration with universities and research institutes, the company was able to enhance its basic research capability necessary to digest and absorb new technologies.

The company tried hard to learn the original technology to strengthen its internal foundations. Based on such knowledge accumulation, the company later was able to successfully develop independent breakthrough innovations. Through simultaneous technology acquisition and learning, the company had become an industry leader by successfully developing core technologies that completed the industry's value chain. The balance between knowledge and resources acquired externally and learned and assimilated internally significantly contributed to this success.

Characteristics of Organizational Innovation Networks

EYG Company set up a central research unit (CRU) as the sole gateway within the company to collaborate and exchange with external partners. CRU was responsible for coordinating all basic research with universities and research institutes. Meanwhile, CRU also coordinated with other R&D subdivisions and R&D teams within the company to adopt external technology resources and facilitate to absorb them within the company. Based on research outputs from internal and external collaboration networks, CRU was a critical unit that made decisions on new product developments. The scope of collaboration with external partners was limited but the strength of the collaboration was high. This type of network interactions increased the efficiency of collaboration, particularly in the upgrading of the company's existing technologies.

SYG Company set up an independent research institute (IRI) to be responsible for searching new technology information and product R&D. Meanwhile, the company also established a technology center (TC) to collaborate research with universities, research institutes, and other technology companies. The joint research output from the TC was then used for the company's new product development. The company's headquarters was responsible to enter joint ventures or acquisitions to acquire and internalize needed technologies for TC. Overseas subsidiaries in each country were responsible for monitoring global technology trends and feeding back information to the headquarters. The headquarters, IRI, and TC worked together closely to access as many technology channels as possible to ensure fast adoption and absorption of new technologies.

CTG Company established joint ventures (JVs) to acquire and learn new technologies. The company established internal flexible research teams (FRT) to expedite learning and internalizing new technologies. Importantly, the company also set up a technology center (TC) to collaborate with universities and research institutes for all basic research discovery and absorption. FRT worked closely with the JV and the TC to ensure simultaneous acquisition and learning of new technologies.

Propositions Development

External Network Development

External networks where an organization is embedded have become an important source of technological innovation. Organizations with a larger sized external network are likely to be more resourceful and thus are likely to attain better innovation outcomes (Lorenzoni and Lipparini, 1999). External networks promote knowledge sharing among the collaborative partners (Uzzi, 1996) while reducing risks and opportunistic behaviors in new product development (Ahuja, 2000). A larger external network also provides firms an opportunity to explore new knowledge through a greater number of channels external to the organization.

Importantly, a larger external network with greater diversity of network participants helps organizations increase the extent to which they are able to acquire new knowledge that goes beyond their existing knowledge domains (Ahujia and Katila, 2004; Ozman, 2009). A wider range of externally acquired knowledge from such heterogeneous network allows organizations to increase their absorptive capacity. This absorptive capacity allows organizations to better adapt to new ways of innovative thinking and implementation while extending their existing technological boundaries (Levinthal and March, 1993; Rosenkopf and Nerkar, 2003).

By focusing on external network development with universities and research institutions and diverse partners along the value chain since the early of establishment, SYG and CTG were able to quickly acquire and introduce new technologies into the company. Particularly in the case of SYG, the collaboration among IRI, TC, and the company's overseas subsidiaries significantly increased the size and heterogeneity of external networks, which further enhanced the exploratory type of the company's innovation capability.

Proposition 1. The extent to which an organization collaborates with partners in the external networks enhances its exploratory type of innovation capability.

The interaction between external networks and internal resources plays an important role in the success of innovations. This interaction is coevolution between the exogenous social, political, and industrial environment and the internal organization's strategy and actions (Volberda and Lewin, 2003). As the connectedness to external networks increases, the participation of actors within the organization also increases, while the external network is also gradually extended.

These reciprocal interfaces require that an organization obtain desired external complementary resources to enhance potential values of its internal resources. The social capital from external networks strengthens a firm's opportunity recognition ability, which further increases potential values of its internal resources (Shane, 2004). Importantly, diverse resources from external networks bring new ideas and creativities that help overcome organizational constraints and enhance values from the use of internal resources. External networks thus also enhance the exploitative type of innovation capability.

EYG built its innovation capability on strong accumulated internal knowledge and efficient internal resource integration through CRU during early periods of the establishment. When the company extended its external networks in a later stage, the company quickly adopted and absorbed new technologies from outside to complement its internal resources. This complementarity allowed the company to better exploit internal resources in upgrading existing products.

> *Proposition 2. The extent to which an organization collaborates with partners in the external networks enhances its exploitative type of innovation capability.*

Internal Network Development

Successful innovations require close coordination among different units within an organization. Innovations increase organizational complexity and thus require that employees in all levels participate in the organization's innovation activities. Networks created from such coordination facilitate the mobilization of resources necessary for new product innovation. Internal networks break away traditional functional boundaries, bringing together, for example, sales, finance, procurement, and logistics to form a corporate-wide innovation system. Internal networks thus promote coordination and transfer of internal resources and information across the organization's functional departments (Tsai, 2001).

Internal networking is important in knowledge management processes (Swan, 1999). The traditional hierarchical structure of organizations hardly facilitates the transfer of knowledge in current dynamic market competition and technological change. Unlike information that can be simply transmitted, knowledge requires a more interactive, dynamic, and informal social network to effectively transfer it within an organization. Such internal networks therefore increase efficiency of knowledge and resource integration and reduce costs and uncertainty in the innovation processes (Tsai and Ghoshal, 1998).

The quantity and strength of inter-departmental formal and informal contacts of employees within an organization also strengthen synergies among different resources within the organization (Subramaniam and Youndt, 2005). Internal communication and integration are important for internal capability development (Ritter and Gemünden, 2003). Such socialization creates mutual trust among organizational members and thus willingness of the members to share their knowledge, which results in more efficient use of internal resources (Adler and Kwon, 2002; Rowley, Behrens, and Krackhardt, 2000; Dyer and Nobeoka, 2000). Networks within an organization have a positive effect on innovation because these networks align the interests between the networked parties that enhance mutual trust for the party to exchange resources, thereby improving innovation performance (Tsai, 2001).

EYG Company established the matrix organizational structure and CRU to efficiently coordinate, integrate, and use resources within the organization. This matrix structure allowed the company to better use internal resources, thereby increasing their values for current product improvements.

Proposition 3. *The extent to which an organization collaborates within its own internal networks enhances its exploitative type of innovation capability.*

In an open innovation system, the complementarity between internal and external resources can create more value for resources from both sides (Shane, 2004). The synergy of resources within different internal departments enhances the company's capability to integrate external resources and further explore new ideas and actions. Internal communication increases an organization's absorptive capacity, which is the foundation for acquiring and integrating external resources (Ritter and Gemünden, 2003). Higher levels of absorptive capacity thus allow organizations to be more capable of identifying technology and market opportunities (Lavie and Rosenkopf, 2006). Such internal socialization thus also helps the exploration of new knowledge (Atuahene-Gima, 2003; McFadyen and Cannella, 2004).

EYG Company focused on internal network development during early periods of the establishment, which was the foundation for subsequent external network building. Through strong internal network and resource management, the company successfully extended its external networks to acquire new technologies and capabilities to compete in emerging technology segments and new markets. Similarly, CTG Company not only built up external networks to acquire new technologies in the very beginning, its internal FRT facilitated learning and internalizing these technologies. With successful internalization of external technologies, the company further extended its external networks in a virtuous manner.

Proposition 4. *The extent to which an organization collaborates within its own internal networks enhances its exploratory type of innovation capability.*

Environmental Turbulence

The delay or inadequate response to environmental turbulence can have negative effects on organizational performance (Benner and Tushman, 2002). In a stable environment, the exploitative type of innovation capability leads to higher profitability than the ambidextrous type of innovation capability, while the exploratory type of innovation capability yields the lowest profitability (Castañer and Campos, 2002). However, when the intensity of competition increases, innovation performance from the exploitative type of innovation capability will be worsened (Auh and Menguc, 2005). In such an increasingly uncertain environment, companies need to constantly develop new products and services in response to rapid changes in market demand, emerging new technologies, and shorter product lifecycles.

In particular, organizations need to restructure their internal resources to adapt to the new environmental opportunities or threats. The turbulent environment also motivates organizations to establish more external collaborations to acquire new resources and capabilities necessary for the new environment. Such environmental turbulence reduces values of existing technologies and increases uncertainty in innovation outcomes. Therefore, the company can increase opportunities to develop new capabilities to cope with the turbulence through external collaboration and internal restructuring.

EYG Company focused too much on the internal resources and network building and therefore could not catch up with changes in technology and market competition. Particularly, the company lacked the exploratory type of innovation capability to cope with such environmental turbulence. SYG Company had demonstrated that establishing external networks helped the company overcome several crises. During the financial crisis, the company was able to access other complementary resources and capabilities in the external network of collaboration, which mitigated risks and brought about mutual benefits.

> **Proposition 5. Environmental turbulence strengthens the effect of networks on the exploratory type of innovation capability.**
> **Proposition 6. Environmental turbulence weakens the effect of networks on the exploitative type of innovation capability.**

Discussion and Conclusions

This study analyzes pathways, mechanisms, and synergy between external and internal network development strategies of three representative manufacturing SMEs in building their innovation capability. These networks allow the flow of business intelligence within and between the organizations. Internal networks include coordination among different functional departments within an organization whereas external networks involve collaboration between the company and other organizations in the value chain including intermediary organizations such as universities and research institutes.

The case studies demonstrate the coevolution between external and internal innovation networks of organizations in building innovation capability. Internal and external networks enhance both exploratory and exploitative type of innovation capability. Such networks form a synergistic interaction that allows the company to concurrently achieve exploratory and exploitative types of innovation capability, which drive its profitability and growth. The environmental turbulence requires that the company stresses on building the exploratory type of innovation capability through both external and internal networks.

Organizations increasingly grow in size and global reach. Market competition and technological advancement have gone beyond the national border. Therefore, the network of innovation and collaboration increasingly play a vital role in competitive advantage of organizations. The external network construction and development should be well connected and coordinated with the internal infrastructure. To ensure the innovation performance, organizations have to realize synergies between external and internal networks and strike a balance between exploratory and exploitative types of innovation capability. Managers should understand the factors that impact the internal and external network characteristics to achieve such synergy and balance.

Acknowledgments

This work was supported by (a) the JSPS KAKENHI Grant Number 15K03694, (b) the Zhejiang Provincial Natural Science Foundation of China Grant No. LY16G020018, and (c) the Humanities and Social Sciences Foundation of China Ministry of Education Youth Project Grant No. 15YJC630104.

References

Adler, P. S. and Kwon, S. W. (2002). Social capital: Prospects for a new concept. *Academy of Management Review*, 27(1), 17–40.

Ahuja, G. (2000). Collaboration networks, structural holes, and innovation: A longitudinal study. *Administrative Science Quarterly*, 45(3), 425–455.

Ahuja, G. and Katila, R. (2004). Where do resources come from? The role of idiosyncratic situations. *Strategic Management Journal*, 25(8–9), 887–907.

Atuahene-Gima, K. (2003). The effects of centrifugal and centripetal forces on product development speed and quality: How does problem solving matter? *Academy of Management Journal*, 46(3), 359–373.

Auh, S. and Menguc, S. (2005). A test of strategic orientation formation vs. strategic orientation implementation: The influence of TMT functional diversity and interfunctional coordination. *Journal of Marketing Theory and Practice*, 13(2), 4–19.

Benner, M. J. and Tushman, M. (2002). Process management and technological innovation: A longitudinal study of the photography and paint industries. *Administrative Science Quarterly*, 47(4), 676–707.

Castañer, X. and Campos, L. (2002). The determinants of artistic innovation: Bringing in the role of organizations. *Journal of Cultural Economics*, 26(1), 29–52.

Chesbrough, H. W. (2003). *Open Innovation: The New Imperative for Creating and Profiting from Technology*. Boston, MA: Harvard Business School Press.

Dyer, J. and Nobeoka, K. (2000). Creating and managing a high performance knowledge-sharing network: The Toyota case. *Strategic Management Journal*, 21(3), 345–367.

Eisenhardt, K. M. (1989). Building theories from case study research. *Academy of Management Review*, 14(4), 532–550.

Guan, J. and Liu, N. (2016). Exploitative and exploratory innovations in knowledge network and collaboration network: A patent analysis in the technological field of nano-energy. *Research Policy*, 45(1), 97–112.

Laursen, K. and Salter, A. (2006). Open for innovation: The role of openness in explaining innovation performance among UK manufacturing firms. *Strategic Management Journal*, 27(2), 131–150.

Lavie, D. and Rosenkopf, L. (2006). Balancing exploration and exploitation in alliance formation. *Academy of Management Journal*, 49(4), 797–818.

Levinthal, D. A. and March, J. G. (1993). The myopia of learning. *Strategic Management Journal*, 14(S2), 95–112.

Lorenzoni, G. and Lipparini, A. (1999). The leveraging of interfirm relationships as a distinctive organizational capability: A longitudinal study. *Strategic Management Journal*, 20(4), 317–338.

McFadyen, M. A. and Cannella, A. A., Jr. (2004). Social capital and knowledge creation: Diminishing returns of the number and strength of exchange. *Academy of Management Journal*, 47(5), 735–746.

Ozman, M. (2009). Inter-firm networks and innovation: A survey of literature. *Economic of Innovation and New Technology*, 18(1), 39–67.

Ritter, T. and Gemünden, H. G. (2003). Network competence: Its impact on innovation success and its antecedents. *Journal of Business Research*, 56(9), 745–755.

Rosenkopf, L. and Nerkar, A. (2001). Beyond local search: Boundary-spanning, exploration, and impact in the optical disk industry. *Strategic Management Journal*, 22(4), 287–306.

Rowley, T., Behrens, D., and Krackhardt, D. (2000). Redundant governance structures: An analysis of structural and relational embeddedness in the steel and semiconductor industries. *Strategic Management Journal*, 21(3), 369–386.

Shane, S. A. (2004). *Academic Entrepreneurship: University Spinoffs and Wealth Creation*. Edward Elgar Publishing.

Subramaniam, M. and Youndt, M. A. (2005). The influence of intellectual capital on the types of innovative capabilities. *Academy of Management Journal*, 48(3), 450–463.

Swan, J. (1999). Knowledge management and innovation: Networks and networking. *Journal of Knowledge Management*, 3(4), 262–275.

Tsai, W. (2001). Knowledge transfer in intraorganizational networks: Effects of network position and absorptive capacity on business unit innovation and performance. *Academy of Management Journal*, 44(5), 996–1004.

Tsai, W. and Ghoshal, S. (1998). Social capital and value creation: The role of intrafirm networks. *Academy of Management Journal*, 41(4), 464–476.

Uzzi, B. (1996). The sources and consequences of embeddedness for the economic performance of organizations: The network effect. *American Sociological Review*, 61(4), 674–698.

Volberda, H. W. and Lewin, A. Y. (2003). Co-evolutionary dynamics within and between firms: From evolution to co-evolution. *Journal of Management Studies*, 40(8), 2111–2136.

15 Creating Value From Business Intelligence Systems Investments

Mohamed Z. Elbashir

Introduction

Both academics and practitioners have recognized the value of business intelligence systems (BI systems, hereafter) to enhance planning, control, decision-making, and organizational performance. This value stems from the ability of the several applications and technologies that BI systems comprise to interpret the big business event data saved in the data warehouse of the organization. Such capabilities enable BI systems to generate reports that support the organizations' operational and competitive activities, including production, customer service, competitors' moves, new technology, public policy, and market forces (Elbashir, Collier, Sutton, Davern, and Leech, 2013). Such capabilities have made BI systems one of the most critical strategic technologies for an organization's survival and success (Cottrill, 1998; Thomas, 2001).

The strategic importance of BI systems is clearly reflected in the increased spending by organizations around the world to acquire these technologies. For instance, the International Data Corporation (IDC) estimated that global spending on BI systems and related products in 2016 was $130 billion. Such spending is expected to reach a whopping $203 billion by the year 2020, representing an annual growth rate of 11% (King, 2016). The potential importance of BI systems and the scale of investment have raised some important questions regarding whether BI systems create business value to organizations. Early BI systems research was dominated by descriptive and qualitative studies and mainly focused on whether BI systems improve BI performance. Those studies indicated that organizations failed to use their BI investments effectively to exploit their big data (Williams and Williams, 2007). However, recent studies show a broad agreement among BI researchers about the positive link between BI investment and organizational performance. For instance, the findings of recent research indicate that BI systems provide significant contribution to organizational performance at different areas of the organization (Elbashir et al., 2013; Amani and Fadlalla, forthcoming).

Prior literature also reported a substantial variation in the level of BI payoff among organizations invested in the same or similar BI technologies (Elbashir et al., 2013). Thus, this phenomenon attracted a significant amount of research that seeks to explain why some organizations are successful with their BI investments while others are not. This challenge has now shifted the outstanding research question from whether BI systems create business value to "how" and "why" BI systems create value. Answering these questions requires deeper investigation of the association between BI investments and organizational performance that was reflected by the "basic research model" tested in prior studies. This basic research model proposes *a direct* relationship between BI investments and organizational performance. The basic research model which is also referred to in IS literature as the "black box" model has received significant criticism in relation to its design and simplicity that lacks the realism of how value is created from BI systems (Barua, Kriebel, and Mukhopadhyay, 1995; Hitt and Brynjolfsson, 1996; Sircar, Turnbow, and Bordoloi, 2000, Barua and Mukhopadhyay, 2000; Davern and Kauffman, 2000).

The author of this chapter has conducted a series of studies in collaboration with a group of international scholars with the aim to better understand how organizations create business value from their BI investments. These studies have enabled building and testing richer research models that contribute towards unlocking the "black box" model of IT/BI payoff studies. At least three limitations in prior IS studies were identified and used as motivational approaches to advance our BI payoff research framework. These limitations are: (a) failing to measure BI systems at the locus of value; (b) failing to capture the BI use as the conversion factor; and (c) a lack of differentiation between BI infrastructure and BI applications. In the following section, each of the three limitations will be referred to and discussed. Then, new approaches are used to build a richer research model of the BI systems payoff that can be used globally will be proposed.

BI Systems Business Value Creation

Three streams of literature yield key insights regarding the organizational performance attributed to BI systems: the process-oriented approach, the resource-based view, and the real option theory. This section starts with highlighting the distinction between IT/BI infrastructures and the BI applications. Subsequently, the three streams of literature are discussed and synthesized to build the theoretical framework of BI systems value creation.

Conceptualization of IT and BI Infrastructure

Information technology infrastructure is a multifaceted concept which includes two related but distinct components: technical (physical) IT infrastructure and human IT infrastructure (Broadbent and Weill, 1997; Byrd

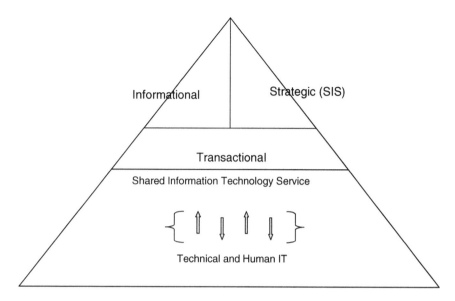

Figure 15.1 The Elements of IT Infrastructure
Source: adapted from Broadbent et al., 1997

and Turner, 2000). Each of the two concepts will be elaborated below and then linked to the process of BI systems deployment. Figure 15.1 presents the various elements of IT and BI infrastructure (Broadbent and Weill, 1997). Shared IT/BI infrastructure, as shown at the base of the pyramid, represents the IT foundation which enables organizations to implement IT applications including BI application software such as SAP crystal reports and Cognos analytics software (Broadbent and Weill, 1997; Broadbent, Weill, and Neo, 1999; Elbashir, Collier, and Sutton, 2011). At the top of the pyramid there are three types of IT applications that build on the organization's shared IT/BI infrastructure: transactional, informational, and strategic.

Technical IT/BI Infrastructure

Technical IT/BI infrastructure refers to the composites of platform technology (hardware and operating systems), network and telecommunication technologies, key data, core data processing, business applications, and services required for the existence, operation and management of an enterprise IT environment (Duncan, 1995; Broadbent and Weill, 1997; Weill and Broadbent, 1998; Bharadwaj, 2000; Lewis and Byrd, 2003; Byrd, Lewis, and Turner, 2004). IT/BI infrastructure allows an organization to deliver IT/BI solutions and services to its employees at different levels of the organization, as well as to its partners, customers, or both, and is usually internally deployed. IS researchers have identified IT/BI infrastructure as a critical resource that enables organizations to implement future IT/BI applications that support organizations' competitive strategies (Keen, 1991; Duncan, 1995; Broadbent and Weill, 1997; Broadbent, Weill, and Clair, 1999; Byrd and Turner, 2000; Weill, Subramani, and Broadbent, 2002). Executives' recognition of the contribution of IT/BI infrastructure to their organizations' competitiveness is reflected in the high spending (58% of the IT budget and about 4% of revenue) each year in IT infrastructure (Broadbent and Weill, 1997; Byrd and Turner, 2000).

Two types of technical IT infrastructures are considered as necessary conditions for successful deployment of BI applications: first of all, "generic IT infrastructure." The generic IT infrastructure includes the IT architecture, standards, security, servers, and the internal computer network. Moreover, it is a necessary condition for implementing and effectively using BI software. Generic IT infrastructure enables the organization to combine and integrate data from different sources and make it available for data analyses and reporting activities of BI systems. The second technical IT infrastructure is BI infrastructure which includes BI tools such as data warehouses, data marts, extract-transform-load (ETL), data mining, and reporting tools. They maintain and exploit the data provided through the IT generic infrastructure. Therefore, the generic IT infrastructure and BI infrastructure together provide the integrated and shared data environment that is necessary for successful implementation and use of BI systems (Elbashir et al., 2011).

Human IT Infrastructure

Human IT infrastructure comprises the managerial and technical IT knowledge, skills, and expertise which binds the IT components into a shared IT infrastructure service in order to support the whole organization. The deployment of IT/BI infrastructure is not usually achieved in one shot; rather, it is a long process involving IS people, management users, including line managers and executives. The level of managerial and technical IT knowledge, skills, and expertise affects the willingness as well as the ability of IT and line managers to work closely as partners. Such partnership will enable better understanding of the strategic intent of the organization signaled by the top management. Such partnership will also help in translating that intent into IT/BI infrastructure that supports a wide range of business activities within the organization (Sambamurthy and Zmud, 1999; Harrington and Guimaraes, 2005).

The Resource-Based View (RBV)

The resource-based view (RBV, hereafter) has been widely used in IT payoff studies as a theoretical foundation regarding the conditions that enable organizations to gain and sustain competitive advantages from their IT resources (Barney, 1991; Mata, Fuerst, and Barney, 1995; Bharadwaj, 2000; Wade and Hulland, 2004). The main underlying argument of the RBV in the IT context is that firms gain and sustain competitive advantages by creating and maintaining IT resources that are valuable, rare, appropriable, and difficult to imitate and substitute (Penrose, 1959; Wernerfelt, 1984; Barney, 1991; Grant, 1996). Resource attributes determine whether the resource helps only to create advantages, or both create and sustain competitive advantage (Wade and Hulland, 2004; Piccoli and Ives, 2005; Ray, Muhanna, and Barney, 2005). The ability of IT/BI infrastructure to be a source of competitive advantage is empirically challenged in prior IS literature. Both IT/BI infrastructures are a necessary resource of advantages, but they are not sufficient for a firm to create and sustain the advantages (Clemons and Row, 1991). This is because IT and BI tools and their services are commodity-like products as they can be easily purchased, duplicated, or both and are, therefore, not costly to imitate by competitors (Mata et al., 1995; Carr, 2003; Powell and Dent-Micallef, 1997; Ray, Barney, and Muhanna, 2004; Aral and Weill, 2004).

RBV falls short in relation to its explanatory power of the process of BI resources creation, how they are best applied, and the processes through which a competitive advantage from BI systems is gained, (Porter, 1991; Foss, 1997; Wade and Hulland, 2004; Melville, Kraemer, and Gurbaxani, 2004). Real options theory is used in our BI research as an additional lens to supplement the RBV in explaining how organizations can capitalize on IT/BI infrastructure to create unique and inimitable resources that generate competitive advantage in turbulent environments (Dos Santos, 1991; Foss, 1997; Amran and Kulatilaka, 1999; Kogut and Kulatilaka, 2001).

Real Options Theory

Real options theory has received increased attention in the IS literature as a framework for investigating uncertain investments in IT resources (Bowman and Hurry, 1993; Dixit and Pindyck, 1994; Benaroch and Kauffman, 1999; Sambamurthy, Bharadwaj, and Grover, 2003; Bardhan, Bagchi, and Sougstad, 2004; Fichman, 2004; Fichman, Keil, and Tiwana, 2005). This is due to the explanations provided by the theory which are consistent with the nature of IT/BI investments including its high uncertainty and irreversibility of the cost of IT/BI projects. The mixed results in prior IT payoff studies may be attributed to a failure to account for the various options created by IT/BI infrastructure which will be exploited in the future (Kambil, Henderson, and Mohsenzadeh, 1993). Therefore, overestimation of IT/BI investments without valuing the options they generate can lead IS researchers and executives to the conclusion that the BI systems payoff in the period does not justify the large amounts of resources invested in BI systems.

Analogous to financial options, real options refer to investing in necessary resources, such as IT/BI infrastructure, whose possession provides

managers with options or implicit contracts which will position the organization favorably to exploit available opportunities at different time points
in the future (Bowman and Hurry, 1993; Kambil et al., 1993). There are
three conditions that act as prerequisites for using real options theory to
structure the evaluation and management of IT investments or other uncertain investments (Fichman, 2004, pp. 134–135): (a) uncertainty in relation
to the net payoff of the investment, (b) irreversibility of the project cost, and
(c) managerial flexibility in structuring investment projects. These three conditions hold when the firm invests in IT/BI infrastructure (Fichman, 2004).
Regarding the first condition, payoff from IT/BI infrastructure is uncertain
and depends on many factors, including the effective implementation, integration, and use of the IT/BI tools to support future BI applications, the
ability of the firm to overcome the burden of learning how to use new BI
applications, the availability of big and integrated data that the BI applications can draw on, and the competitive environment of the firm. Investment
in IT/BI infrastructure also meets the second condition (irreversibility of the
project cost), as many types of spending in IT/BI infrastructure (such as the
cost of IT/BI tools implementations, staff training, consultants, and some of
the costs of the hardware and software) are not reversible and become sunk
costs. Investment in IT/BI infrastructure also fulfills the third prerequisite as
managers enjoy considerable flexibility related to the processes they follow
to deliver the new systems as well as the features, functions, and capabilities
of the new systems.

Investing in IT/BI infrastructure, whether the "technical" or the "human"
parts, is seen as a positioning investment which creates options through
enabling various follow-up IT/BI projects including the development and
implementation of BI applications (Taudes, Feurstein, and Mild, 2000;
Fichman, 2004). The options value is magnified when the firm utilizes these
business opportunities to generate competitive advantages compared to the
competitors (Taudes et al., 2000; Sambamurthy et al., 2003; Dai, Kauffman,
and March, 2006). Future opportunities which could be generated by
real options include future investments in additional IT/BI infrastructure
components, the development and implementation of value-generating BI
applications (such as BI software including dashboard and performance
management systems), and learning opportunities for follow-on IT/BI
investments (Hitt, Keats, and DeMarie, 1998; Weill et al., 2002; Dai et
al., 2006). The role of IT/BI can be referred to as *a digital options genera-
tor* which strengthens IT/BI-enabled capabilities in the form of digitized
enterprise work processes and knowledge systems, which in turn enable
organizations to seize emerging opportunities (Sambamurthy et al., 2003).
Four types of digital options have been identified in prior literature. These
are digitalized process reach, digitized process richness, digitized knowledge reach, and digitized knowledge richness (Sambamurthy et al., 2003).
Therefore, developing the technical and human IT/BI infrastructure will
increase the flexibility of the organization and provide options that enable

the exploitation of any future BI investment opportunity that relate to the organization's business strategies and activities (Sambamurthy et al., 2003).

Based on the above discussion, it is concluded that technical and human IT/BI infrastructure enhances an organization's ability to implement new BI systems applications when they become available and use them to enhance business strategies through developing new products and services (Duncan, 1995; Broadbent, Weill, and Neo, 1999; Weill et al., 2002; Sambamurthy et al., 2003; Fichman, 2004; Fichman et al., 2005). Drawing on real options theory, it is argued that investing in the human and technical IT/BI infrastructure creates strategic options and enables organizations to strategically capitalize on those options (Bowman and Hurry, 1993; Armstrong and Sambamurthy, 1999). This is because building high-quality IT/BI infrastructure is path dependent and socially complex as follow-on IT/BI projects are built on previous investments and prior learning (Sambamurthy et al., 2003; Dai et al., 2006). Linking the real options argument to the RBV, we also argue that the options generated in IT/BI infrastructure are valuable, rare, appropriable, and difficult to imitate and substitute and, when exploited, will enable organizations to use their BI applications effectively to create and sustain competitive advantages (Bowman and Hurry, 1993).

The Process-Oriented Approach

Barua and colleagues (Barua et al., 1995; Barua and Mukhopadhyay, 2000), among others, attribute the mixed results in early IT payoff research to Production Economics approach research methodologies followed in prior studies. The PE approach posits that IT input provides positive contributions to organizational outputs by combining inputs according to a specific functional form (Brynjolfsson and Hitt, 1993; Barua and Mukhopadhyay, 2000). As the distance between the immediate effects of IT (first-order) and organizational performance (high-order) increases, the probability to capture the impact of IT will decrease (Weill, 1992; Barua et al., 1995). This is because unrelated factors may confound the effect of IT on organizational performance (Melville et al., 2004). For example, a firm may generate competitive advantage from one BI-enabled activity (e.g. increased profit). But some stakeholders such as executives may obtain the increased profit performance in the form of a high bonus before they affect organizational performance (Ray et al., 2004). Therefore, using "high order" performance measures (such as profitability, share price, ROI, etc.) to measure the BI systems payoff and ignoring the effect on business processes can lead to a misleading conclusion regarding the business value of BI systems (Elbashir, Collier, and Davern, 2008; Davern and Kauffman, 2000). Few prior studies suggest that the organizational performance impact of IT can be best measured through its immediate (business process) level contribution (Mooney, Gurbaxani, and Kraemer, 1995; Barua et al., 1995; Tallon, Kraemer, and

Gurbaxani, 2000; Sambamurthy et al., 2003; Devaraj and Kohli 2003; Melville et al., 2004; Ray et al., 2005). Failure to capture the business processes dimension of IT performance will reduce the ability to explain effectively *how* and *why/why not* IT value is created.

Responding to the call made in prior research, the process-oriented approach is followed in BI payoff studies. In doing so the author made two distinct contributions: (a) tested research models that explicitly consider the BI systems assimilation which capture the locus of BI systems value creation, namely the business process activities and strategies (Mooney et al., 1995; Barua et al., 1995; Tallon et al., 2000; Davern and Kauffman, 2000). BI systems assimilation is the extent to which an organization uses BI systems to support business strategies and activities (Armstrong and Sambamurthy, 1999; Chatterjee, Grewal, and Sambamurthy, 2002). BI systems assimilation also represents the ability of the organization to convert BI investment into business applications and competencies (Armstrong and Sambamurthy, 1999; Barua and Mukhopadhyay, 2000). Adding the assimilation factor to the business value model represents an important step towards developing and testing a richer model of business value creation. This suggests that the significant value from BI will not be fully realized until its implicit functionalities are assimilated into an organization's strategy and business activities. Such a model will provide the possibility to test whether the assimilation is the missing link between IT investment and organizational performance.

(b) Based on an understanding of the characteristics of BI systems the author developed a measure of business value of the BI systems that is specific to the systems and capture the business value at two levels: business process and organizational levels (Elbashir et al., 2008). The business process dimension of the measure captures the three main business process benefits: internal processes benefits, customer relation benefits, and suppliers relations benefits. While the organizational dimension of the measure captures the business value at the firm level and mainly uses financial measures such as profit and ROI. It is argued that the organizational-level measure is an evaluative tool as it shows managers whether the organization has realized the financial performance benefits. While the process-level performance measures act as a diagnostic tool to help management on why/why not organizational performance is improved. In doing so, the business process measures point to which of the value chain activities are not performing effectively and therefore have negative impact on the expected organizational benefits (Elbashir et al., 2008). Then the relationships between the two performance levels were examined and the results show that they are positively related. This indicates that a failure to capture the value of the BI systems at the two levels will provide misleading conclusions regarding the economics value of BI systems.

Figure 15.2 presents the high-level model that depicts the BI value creation model. The model highlights two sets of IT/IS infrastructures, technical and human, as the antecedents and drivers of BI systems assimilation

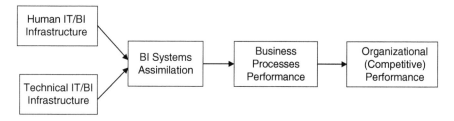

Figure 15.2 Conceptual Model of the Business Value of Strategic Information Systems

and organizational performance. *IT/IS infrastructure* is motivated by real options theory and the resource-based view of the firm literature (Wernerfelt, 1984; Barney, 1991; Sambamurthy et al., 2003; Fichman et al., 2005; Dai et al., 2006). Drawing on the process-oriented view, BI systems are expected to enhance business processes and organizational performance through *BI systems assimilation* (Armstrong and Sambamurthy, 1999; Chatterjee et al., 2002; Ranganathan, Dhaliwal, and Teo, 2004). BI systems assimilation is depicted in the business value creation model as a mediating factor that captures the process of converting BI investment into organizational performance. The BI systems business value creation model and the underlying relationships is elaborated upon in the following subsection.

BI Systems and Business Value Creation

There are at least two perspectives, resource-based view and strategic positioning, used in prior literature to explain why BI systems are critical sources of competitive advantage (Ray et al., 2004). These two perspectives are elaborated below. Despite the different premises on which each of the perspectives is based, strategic management researchers have recognized the complementarity of the two perspectives, which suggests that both perspectives can co-exist and can be used to explain the organization performance (Spanos and Lioukas, 2001; Rivard, Raymond, and Verreault, 2006).

From the resource-based perspective, although BI systems have unique capabilities and functions that make them valuable, these technologies cannot be a source of competitive advantages on their own. This is because BI systems can easily be procured in factor markets by all organizations. However, through assimilation of the systems, organizations will be able to enhance their business activities and create core competencies that are necessary for the organization to remain competitive. Hamel (1994) suggests three categories of core competency: market-access, integrity-related, and functionality-related competencies. Typical BI systems should be able to support organizations to build each of these three groups of competencies. For instance, BI systems enable organizations to segment their customer base and target the right customers with offers that match their demands. BI systems can also support various production activities which enable efficiency and high-quality products and services. Moreover, BI systems can also support R&D activities which enable organizations to design, produce, and deliver unique products and services to their customers in a shorter period. Organization competencies are path dependent, socially complex, and require longer periods of time to build (Ravichandran and Lertwongsatien, 2005). Therefore, competencies developed through the assimilation of BI systems are inimitable and heterogeneously distributed, and therefore, will enable organizations to maintain competitive positions and performance.

From the strategic positioning perspective, an organization is described as a collection of discrete but interrelated activities (Porter, 1985, 1991). *Activities* are actions (such as serving customers or ordering supplies) which organizations undertake to achieve their objectives or purposes. On the other hand, *strategy* relates to a unique and valuable position that an organization creates relative to its competitors (Porter, 1991). Strategy determines the way the organization integrates different activities across different functional departments to achieve its objectives. Organizations will be able to achieve operational effectiveness when they use their BI systems to support their various business activities. Moreover, organizations are able to create competitive advantages when BI systems are used to support their business strategies and to establish differences that they can sustain: for example delivering greater value to customers, or creating comparable value at a lower cost, or both (Porter, 1996).

The two perspectives have important implications to BI payoff studies. Using common ground between the two perspectives, the following argument can be made (Ray et al., 2004): the quality of the BI systems that organizations control will significantly influence the ability of organizations to support their business activities and strategies. However, organizations' BI systems and their capabilities will only have an impact on organizational performance when they are assimilated into business activities and strategies.

In addition to organizational (competitive) performance, BI systems also support organizations to create benefits across their *value chain activities* (Barua et al., 1995; Tallon et al., 2000; Melville et al., 2004; Subramani, 2004). Example of business process benefits include improved efficiency of internal processes, improved decision-making processes, and improved efficiency of inventory management. Most prior IT payoff studies, especially those that draw on RBV, examine the performance impact of IT resources at the organizational level. The RBV logic can also be applied to explain the performance variation at the business process level (Ray et al., 2004). Competencies developed through the assimilation of BI systems are valuable when they enable an organization to improve the *absolute* performance of its business processes such as increased efficiency and effectiveness (Ray et al., 2005). However, improving the business process performance of an organization as compared to its competitors will depend on how rare and costly to imitate these BI systems-enabled competencies are (Wernerfelt, 1984; Barney, 1991; Ray et al., 2005).

First-order business processes benefits of BI systems are leading indicators for organizational competitive benefits. An organization's overall performance depends on, among other factors, the effectiveness of these business processes in supporting its business strategies (Ray et al., 2004). However, some external factors beyond the control of an individual organization are likely to moderate the relation (such as competitive response, general economic conditions, and environmental changes). Organizations which generate greater benefits from their BI systems investments, relative to competitors across large number of business processes, will be able to gain a competitive advantage. Consistent with the two-stage model of benefits suggested in prior literature (Mukhopadhyay and Kekre, 2002; Melville et al., 2004; Subramani, 2004), our studies show that business processes benefits from BI systems enhance the organizational-level performance (sales growth, profit margin, ROI).

Conclusion and Implications

The chapter synthesizes perspectives from the process-oriented, real options, and resource-based view literature in order to propose an integrated model of the business value of BI systems. Drawing on the real options literature, the model suggests that IT infrastructure sophistication enhances the assimilation of BI systems. BI systems assimilation is a necessary condition for an organization to achieve enhanced payoff at both business processes and organizational level. Therefore, BI assimilation is the mediator between IT infrastructure sophistication and business value from BI systems

Several implications can be deduced from the BI systems value creation model. First, the series of studies summarized in this chapter represent an important attempt to open the "black box" of BI systems investments and explain why some organizations are able to leverage their BI investments and generate higher competitive advantages than others. BI systems assimilation in business strategies and activities, which has not been examined adequately in IT literature, is the major driver of the business value of BI systems. This implies that future IT/BI payoff studies should include the assimilation factor in the research model.

Second, IT/BI infrastructure is an important antecedent for successive deployment of BI systems by organizations. However, organizations can no longer rely solely on technical IT infrastructure to achieve competitive performance. Investment in human infrastructure is equally important and crucial for the success of BI investments. This includes hiring the right IT people, providing the necessary training and mentoring, forming partnerships between IT and businesspeople, and top management support.

Third, the chapter bridges the two bodies of literature by presenting a research model that predicts a relation between assimilation of BI systems and business value of BI systems. In doing so, it is argued in this chapter that acquiring and developing high-quality IT/BI infrastructure, software applications, or both is not necessarily sufficient for organizations to create business value. Business value from BI systems is determined by how the technology is used by organizations to support business strategies and value chain activities.

Fourth, the study provides some insights on some of the skeptical views which claim "IT doesn't matter" (Carr, 2003). Such view is seen as discouraging organizations to invest in IT and innovations. As the research model suggests, IT infrastructure is the enabler of BI systems assimilation which in turn provides the explanation as to how organizations are able to create benefits from their BI systems investments. Therefore, failure to differentiate between IT/BI infrastructure, BI systems as applications/software, and the organization's ability to exploit its IT investments is a fundamental flaw of the skeptical views regarding IT. High-quality IT/BI infrastructure is path dependent and takes a longer time to develop. Therefore, organizations should continue investing in IT/BI infrastructure coupled with developing managerial/human IT knowledge and skills that convert BI systems investments into capabilities which are fundamental for successful business strategies.

Finally, the current global diffusion of BI systems, which is reflected by the huge spending on BI systems and related products by both private and public sector organizations all around the world, is reflective of their growing strategic importance. Such development entails the need for global attention and joint efforts by academics and practitioners to be directed towards enhancing the performance of the current and new BI systems. To date there are few empirical studies on the performance impact of BI systems. The extant BI systems literature is dominated by qualitative and descriptive studies. The research presented in this chapter extends the IT business value literature to the business intelligence domain and summarizes some of the outcomes of the series of research projects that the author has conducted, in collaboration with international scholars, on the performance impact of BI systems. A valuable contribution of this research is the extension of the business value of IT literature through the investigation of IT payoff model using BI systems as a context.

References

Amani, F. and Fadlalla, A. (2017). Data mining applications in accounting: A review of the literature and organizing framework. *International Journal of Accounting information Systems*, 24(1), 32–58.

Amran, M. and Kulatilaka, N. (1999). *Real Options: Managing Strategic Investment in an Uncertain World.* Boston, MA: Harvard Business School Press.

Aral, S. and Weill, P. (2004). IT assets, organizational capabilities and firm performance: Asset and capability specific complementarities. *CISR Working Paper* 356.

Armstrong, C. P., and Sambamurthy, V. (1999). Information technology assimilation in firms: The influence of senior leadership and IT infrastructures. *Information Systems Research*, 10(4), 304–327.

Bardhan, I., Bagchi, S., and Sougstad, R. (2004). Prioritizing a portfolio of information technology investment projects. *Journal of Management Information Systems*, 21(2), 33–60.

Barney, J. (1991). Firm resources and sustained competitive advantage. *Journal of Management*, 17(1), 99–120.

Barua, A., Kriebel, C. H., and Mukhopadhyay, T. (1995). Information technologies and business value: An analytic and empirical investigation. *Information Systems Research*, 6(1), 3–23.

Barua, A. and Mukhopadhyay, T. (2000). Information technology and business performance: Past, present, and future. In R. W. Zmud (Eds.), *Framing the Domains of IT Management: Projecting the Future Through the Past* (pp. 65–84). Cincinnati, OH: Pinnaflex Education Resources.

Benaroch, M. and Kauffman, R. J. (1999). A case for using real options pricing analysis to evaluate information technology project investments. *Information Systems Research*, 10(1), 70–86.

Bharadwaj, A. S. (2000). A resource-based perspective on information technology capability and firm performance: An empirical investigation. *MIS Quarterly*, 24(1), 169–196.

Bowman, E. H. and Hurry, D. (1993). Strategy through the option lens: An integrated view of resource investments and the incremental choice process. *Academy of Management Review*, 18(4), 760–782.

Broadbent, M. and Weill, P. (1997). Management by maxim: How business and IT managers can create IT infrastructures. *Sloan Management Review*, 38(3), 77–92.

Broadbent, M., Weill, P., and Clair, D. (1999). The implications of information technology infrastructure for business process redesign. *MIS Quarterly*, 23(2), 159–182.

Broadbent, M., Weill, P., and Neo, B. S. (1999). Strategic context and patterns of IT infrastructure capability. *Journal of Strategic Information Systems*, 8(2), 157–187.

Brynjolfsson, E. and Hitt, L. (1993). Is information systems spending productive? New evidence and new results. Degross, J., Bostrom R., and Robey, D. eds. Proceddings In *The Proceedings of the 14th International Conference on Information Systems*, New York, NY: The Association of computing Machinery, 47–64.

Byrd, T. A., Lewis, B. R., and Turner, D. E. (2004). The impact of IT personnel skills on IS infrastructure and competitive IS. *Information Resources Management Journal*, 17(2), 38–62.

Byrd, T. A. and Turner, D. E. (2000). Measuring the flexibility of information technology infrastructure: Exploratory analysis of a construct. *Journal of Management Information Systems*, 17(1), 167–208.

Carr, N. G. (2003). IT doesn't matter. *Harvard Business Review*, 81(5), 41–49.

Chatterjee, D., Grewal, R., and Sambamurthy, V. (2002). Shaping up for e-commerce: Institutional enablers of the organizational assimilation of Web technologies. *MIS Quarterly*, 26(2), 65–89.

Clemons, E. K. and Row, M. C. (1991). Sustaining IT advantage: The role of structural differences. *MIS Quarterly*, 15(3), 275–292.

Cottrill, K. (1998). Turning competitive intelligence into business knowledge. *The Journal of Business Strategy*, 19(4), 27–30.

Dai, Q., Kauffman, R., and March, S. (2006). Valuing information technology infrastructures: A growth options approach. *Information Technology and Management*, 8(1) 1–17.

Davern, M. J. and Kauffman, R. J. (2000). Discovering potential and realizing value from information technology investments. *Journal of Management Information Systems*, 16(4), 121–143.

Devaraj, S. and Kohli, R. (2003). Performance impacts of information technology: Is actual usage the missing link? *Management Science*, 49(3), 273–289.

Dixit, A. K. and Pindyck, R. P. (1994). *Investment Under Uncertainty*. Princeton, NJ: Princeton University Press.

Dos Santos, B. (1991). Justifying investments in new information technologies. *Journal of Management Information Systems*, 7(4), 71–90.

Duncan, N. B. (1995). Capturing flexibility of information technology infrastructure: A study of resource characteristics and their measure. *Journal of Management Information Systems*, 12(2), 37–57.

Elbashir, M., Collier, P., and Davern, M. (2008). Measuring the effects of business intelligence systems: The relationship between business process and organizational performance. *International Journal of Accounting Information Systems*, 9, 135–153.

Elbashir, M., Collier, P., and Sutton, S. (2011). The role of organisational absorptive capacity in strategic use of business intelligence to support integrated management control systems. *The Accounting Review*, 86(1), 155–184.

Elbashir, M., Collier, P., Sutton, S., Davern, M., and Leech, S. (2013). Enhancing the business value of business intelligence: The role of shared knowledge and assimilation. *Journal of Information Systems*, 27, 87–105.

Fichman, R. G. (2004). Real options and IT platform adoption: Implications for theory and practice. *Information Systems Research*, 15(2), 132–154.

Fichman, R. G., Keil, M., and Tiwana, A. (2005). Beyond valuation: "Real Options thinking" in IT project management. *California Management Review*, 47(2), 74–96.

Foss, N. J. (1997). The resource-based perspective: An assessment and diagnosis of problems. *DRUID Working Paper* No. 97–1. Available from SSRN: http://ssrn.com/abstract=43626 or doi:10.2139/ssrn.43626.

Grant, R. M. (1996). Toward a knowledge-based theory of the firm. *Strategic Management Journal*, 17(S2), 109–122.

Hamel, G. (1994). The concept of core competence. In G. Hamel and A. Heene (Eds.), *Competence-based Competition* (pp. 11–33). New York: Wiley and Sons.

Harrington, S. J. and Guimaraes, T. (2005). Corporate culture, absorptive capacity and IT success. *Information & Organization*, 15(1), 39–63.

Hitt, L. M. and Brynjolfsson, E. (1996). Productivity, business profitability, and consumer surplus: Three different measures of information technology value. *MIS Quarterly*, 20(2), 121–142.

Hitt, M. A., Keats, B. W., and DeMarie, S. M. (1998). Navigating in the new competitive landscape: Building strategic flexibility and competitive advantage in the 21st century. *The Academy of Management Executive*, 12(4), 22–42.

Kambil, A., Henderson, C. J., and Mohsenzadeh, M. (1993). The strategic management of information technology investments: An options perspective. In R. Banker, R. Kauffman, and M. Mahmood (Eds.), *Strategic Information Technology Management: Perspectives on Organizational Growth and Competitive Advantage*. Pennsylvania: Idea Group Publishers, 161–178.

Keen, P.G.W. (1991). *Shaping the Future: Business Design Through Information Technology*. Boston: Harvard Business School Press.

King, R. (2016). *Business Intelligence Spending Report*. Accessed June 28, 2017. Available from: https://blog.rainkingonline.com/blog/2016-business-intelligence-spending-report

Kogut, B. and Kulatilaka, N. (2001). Capabilities as real options. *Organization Science*, 12(6), 744–758.

Lewis, B. R., and Byrd, T. A. (2003). Development of a measure for the information technology infrastructure construct. *European Journal of Information Systems*, 12(2), 93–109.

Mata, F. J., Fuerst, W. L., and Barney, J. B. (1995). Information technology and sustained competitive advantage: A resource-based analysis. *MIS Quarterly*, 19(4), 487–505.

Melville, N., Kraemer, K., and Gurbaxani, V. (2004). Information technology and organizational performance: An integrative model of IT business value. *MIS Quarterly*, 28(2), 283–322.

Mooney, J., Gurbaxani, V., and Kraemer, K. L. (1995). A process oriented framework for assessing the business value of information technology. In *Sixteenth Annual International Conference on Information Systems*, eds DeGross, J., Ariav, G., Beath, C., Hoyer, R. and Kemerer, C. (pp. 17–27), Amsterdam, The Netherlands, 10–13 December.

Mukhopadhyay, T. and Kekre, S. (2002). Strategic and operational benefits of electronic integration in B2B procurement processes. *Management Science*, 48(10), 1301–1313.

Penrose, E. (1959). *The Theory of the Growth of the Firm*. London: Basil Blackwell.

Piccoli, G. and Ives, B. (2005). IT-dependent strategic initiatives and sustained competitive advantage: A review and synthesis of the literature. *MIS Quarterly*, 29(4), 747–776.

Porter, M. E. (1985). *Competitive Advantage: Creating and Sustaining Superior Performance*. New York: Free Press.

Porter, M. E. (1991). Towards a dynamic theory of strategy. *Strategic Management Journal*, 12(S2), 95–117.

Porter, M. E. (1996). What is strategy? *Harvard Business Review*, 74(6), 61–78.

Powell, T. C. and Dent-Micallef, A. (1997). Information technology as competitive advantage: The role of human, business, and technology resources. *Strategic Management Journal*, 18(5), 375–405.

Ranganathan, C., Dhaliwal, J. S., and Teo, T.S.H. (2004). Assimilation and diffusion of web technologies in supply-chain management: An examination of key drivers and performance impacts. *International Journal of Electronic Commerce*, 9(1), 127–161.

Ravichandran, T. and Lertwongsatien, C. (2005). Effect of Information systems resources and capabilities of firm performance: A resourced-based perspective. *Journal of Management Information Systems*, 21(4), 237–276.

Ray, G., Barney, J. B., and Muhanna, W. A. (2004). Capabilities, business processes, and competitive advantage: Choosing the dependent variable in empirical tests of the resource-based view. *Strategic Management Journal*, 25(1), 23–37.

Ray, G., Muhanna, W. A., and Barney, J. B. (2005). Information technology and the performance of the customer service process: A resource-based analysis. *MIS Quarterly*, 29(4), 625–652.

Rivard, S., Raymond, L., and Verreault, D. (2006). Resource-based view and competitive strategy: An integrated model of the contribution of information technology to firm performance. *Journal of Strategic Information Systems*, 15(1), 29–50.

Sambamurthy, V., Bharadwaj, A., and Grover, V. (2003). Shaping agility through digital options: Reconceptualizing the role of information technology in contemporary firms. *MIS Quarterly*, 27(2), 237–263.

Sambamurthy, V. and Zmud, R. W. (1999). Arrangements for information technology governance: A theory of multiple contingencies. *MIS Quarterly*, 23(2), 261–290.

Sircar, S., Turnbow, J. L., and Bordoloi, B. (2000). A framework for assessing the relationship between information technology investments and firm performance. *Journal of Management Information Systems*, 16(4), 69–97.

Spanos, Y. E. and Lioukas, S. (2001). An examination into the causal logic of rent generation: Contrasting Porter's competitive strategy framework and the resource-based perspective. *Strategic Management Journal*, 22(10), 907–934.

Subramani, M. (2004). How do suppliers benefit from information technology use in supply chain relationships? *MIS Quarterly*, 28(1), 45–73.

Tallon, P. P., Kraemer, K. L., and Gurbaxani, V. (2000). Executives' perceptions of the business value of information technology: A process-oriented approach. *Journal of Management Information Systems*, 16(4), 145–173.

Taudes, A., Feurstein, M., and Mild, A. (2000). Options analysis of software platform decisions: A case study. *MIS Quarterly*, 24(2), 227–243.

Thomas, J. H. (2001). Business intelligence-why? *eAI Journal*, 2001(July), 47–49.

Wade, M. and Hulland, J. (2004). The resource-based view and information systems research: Review, extension, and suggestions for future research. *MIS Quarterly*, 28(1), 107–142.

Weill, P. (1992). The relationship between investment in information technology and firm performance: A study of the valve manufacturing sector. *Information System Research*, 3(4), 307–333.

Weill, P. and Broadbent, M. (1998). *Leveraging the New Infrastructure: How Market Leaders Capitalize on Information Technology*. Harvard Business School Press, Boston.

Weill, P., Subramani, M., and Broadbent, M. (2002). Building IT infrastructure for strategic agility. *Sloan Management Review*, 44(1), 57–65.

Wernerfelt, B. (1984). A resource-based view of the firm. *Strategic Management Journal*, 5(2), 171–180.

Williams, S. and Williams, N. (2007). *The Profit Impact of Business Intelligence*. Cambridge, MA: Morgan Kaufmann Publishers.

16 Advanced Analytics
Moving the Needle of Business Performance*

Jason Balogh

Introduction

Digital transformation is fully upon today's organizations. The advent of cloud computing, social media, advanced analytics, the Internet of Things (IOT), mobile computing, artificial intelligence (AI), and robotic process automation (RPA) have not only led to a bevy of new business acronyms, but also to fundamental changes to the way organizations do business. And, with this dawn of digital change comes business disruption. Even the most staid, traditional companies are finding that their core business models are being disrupted in ways that were not foreseen even two years ago. There are new ways to engage customers and new ways to transact with partners. There exist shifting value models that replace asset intensity with IP development and monetization and customer focus. The Hackett Group's data illustrates these disruptive changes in the following graphic, which breaks down "digital" into core technology components and their expected business impact today and in two to three years. The spikes are significant and material (see Figure 16.1).

These are placing unprecedented stress on business models and professionals themselves. Think of how Uber replaced a traditional taxi model and created a multi-billion dollar business in a matter of years—all without owning a single car. Disruption will result in a new set of winners and losers, perhaps even greater than the change experienced in the Industrial Revolution.

When one thinks of the disruptions that the digital age presents to today's companies, one must contemplate new risks associated with digital business as well. Each day, newspapers provide evidence of the challenges and risks that the blossoming interconnected environment presents to the business world. The Hackett Group's empirically derived benchmarking and research database shows that executives are exceptionally concerned with areas such as cyber/information security (67%), intensified competition (58%), and disruptive innovation (56%). Clearly the changes to business models are increasing the nature and intensity of risk and the need to manage it carefully

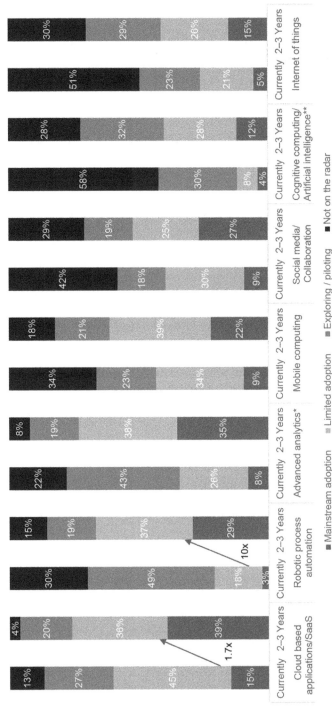

Emerging Technology Adoption—Finance

■ Mainstream adoption ■ Limited adoption ■ Exploring / piloting ■ Not on the radar

	Currently	2–3 Years
Cloud based applications/SaaS	13% / 27% / 45% / 15%	4% / 20% / 36% / 39%
Robotic process automation	30% / 49% / 18% / 3%	15% / 19% / 37% / 29%
Advanced analytics*	22% / 43% / 26% / 8%	8% / 19% / 38% / 35%
Mobile computing	34% / 23% / 34% / 9%	18% / 21% / 39% / 22%
Social media/ Collaboration	42% / 18% / 30% / 9%	29% / 19% / 25% / 27%
Cognitive computing/ Artificial intelligence**	58% / 30% / 8% / 4%	28% / 32% / 28% / 12%
Internet of things	51% / 23% / 21% / 5%	30% / 29% / 26% / 15%

1.7x   10x

Figure 16.1 Emerging Technology Adoption in Finance

Source: Key Issues Study—The Hackett Group—2017

and thoughtfully. See the following graphic for how dramatic the new age of technology has become. The Hackett Group's maturity model outlines where organizations were with technology even ten years ago (Platform 1.0) and then continued to make dramatic investments in data and system integration (Platform 2.0), only to find that predictive insights and advanced analytics were still not at their fingertips. In Platform 3.0, organizations have begun to shed the complexities of internal technology residence in replacement with cloud adoption, but equally, if not more importantly, have begun to be open to broader sets of data and new tools "on top" of the stack to help make sense of the numbers (see Figure 16.2).

So, with these dramatic business changes and a more tenuous risk climate, how ready are today's organizations to navigate the impacts on their businesses? The short answer: not very. Many organizations are poorly positioned to seize on the opportunities that the digital age is fast-presenting (Figure 16.3). The Hackett Group's research reveals that executives across the business overwhelmingly agree that digital age change will fundamentally change the way business will be done, but only a minority appear to be prepared for this shift.

When contemplating the net impact of these changes, one message becomes increasingly clear: a major determinant for winning and losing in the digital age will be an organization's ability to capture and enrich data, and leverage information as an asset in the market. Successful firms are moving from "those with the assets and scale win" to "those with the information and insights win."

Rather than thinking in far-flung visionary terms, it is grow increasingly clear that these capabilities will be largely evident in the marketplace survivors by 2020, and with others left far behind. The Hackett Group thinks of this as the "2020 Analytic Firm of the Future," which will be characterized by a service delivery model of highly nimble systems meshing internal and external data to support analysis and insights by the analytic professional; all held together with newly emerging organizational and governance constructs.

Advanced Analytics Defined

What exactly are advanced analytics? In some ways, advanced analytics is easier to define by articulating what it is not. Its characteristics are largely different from more traditional analyses done by mainstream organizations.

Characteristics of Advanced Analytics

Velocity vs. Exactitude

The first area of differentiation from more traditional analysis is the importance of speed. Speed is the priority at the expense of the typical precision that entails a financial, operational, or sales analysis. Executive questions

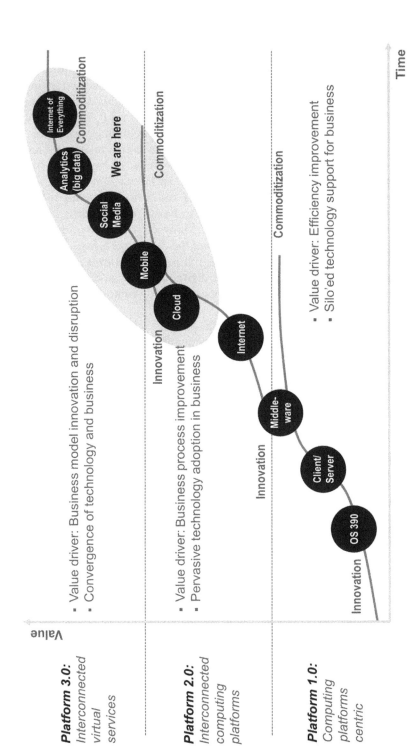

Figure 16.2 The Hackett Group's Maturity Model

Source: Key Issues Study—The Hackett Group—2017

Believe digital transformation will **fundamentally change** the way business services are delivered in their function over the next 3-5 years

91%

86%

92%

84%

92%

... but only

36% **Finance**

34% **HR**

32% **IT**

25% **Procurement**

26% **GBS Organizations**

report having **resources and competencies** in place to execute a digital transformation strategy

Figure 16.3 Digital Transformation Impact and Readiness
Source: Key Issues Study—The Hackett Group—2017

are usually at the core of these, in which a query is launched regarding a spending category, a product, or a customer, for instance. What typically results from these is one to two weeks of work by 10–15 staff pulling data from multiple, highly invested technology tools, pushing this data through various email chains and ultimately being aggregated in a spreadsheet and painstakingly formatted into a presentation deck. Advanced analytics breaks this vicious cycle. In the new paradigm, hypotheses are set and nimble methods to prove or disprove them are launched, often in significantly fewer cycles and with far more importance attached to absolute precision of the numbers. Advanced analytics seek to interpret and inform trends, not pinpoint the variances between one account and another. This presents one of the first major cultural shifts to the future analytic professional (about which more later).

Direction vs. Precision (or the "Fear of Failure" Paradigm)

The next concept associated with advanced analytics is the employment of the 80/20 rule when completing an analysis. In a typical setting, analysts respond to their natural desire for perfection, the direction of those around them, or both to focus on very high levels of precision in the work that they prepare. This is completely counter to the advanced analytic model: run enough analysis to see the patterns and then make recommendations and act upon them. In fact, The Hackett Group has proven with empirical data that less depth in analysis produces a more statistically valid forecast than otherwise (Figure 16.4). In this case, the company's analysis proves that spending less time and going into less detail tends to yield better accuracy in forecasted earnings.

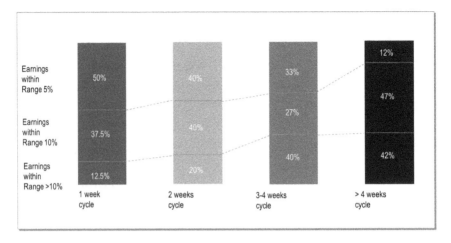

Figure 16.4 Relationship Between Cycle Time and Accuracy
Source: Performance Study—The Hackett Group—2010

Deployed vs. Centralized

There are many opinions on this topic, ranging from the organizational adoption and deployment of Centers of Excellence (COE) in a more centralized model to the self-service concept of a more widely deployed and decentralized model of accessing and analyzing the various components of the business. High performers utilize both COEs and self-service models, and in the 2020 future state, one would expect a much more capable analytics professional who partners with the business to not only interpret, but predict and influence performance. The COE will house the data scientists for the highly developed analytics as well as do the critically important yet painful work of data management, data governance, technology harmonization, and deployment. Executive sentiment and technology trends suggest that the idea of limited information availability is going to be quickly replaced with a model of dissemination of vast amounts of data to the masses, who have the tools and training to navigate and analyze in new, simple, and effective ways.

Fewer vs. More in the Analysis

Here is the next paradoxical shift in the rationale: with advanced analytics, as the speed of end-to-end analysis increases, combined with the analytic IQ of the deployed analytics professional, one could conclude that even more people will be involved in the analytic process. This is a very likely scenario, but in a much nimbler model. More people will be involved in analytics, but there will be far fewer "reviewers and checkers" among them. Layers of approvals, validations for non-value-added adjustments based upon the "gut instinct" of midlevel management will be replaced with small groups of multifunctional people proving and disproving hypotheses, interpreting data, and feeding the results to the organization. These "analytics pods" will become the new normal and even begin to challenge the traditional hierarchical models of business today.

Predictive vs. Historical

Another big shift in advanced analytics again relates to the cultural dynamic found in many organizations today. Traditionally, executives urgently want to know why something happened, which spins the analytic functions into numerous cycles of research and explanation, but only with data available internally, which only further impairs the true visibility of root causes and external factors for performance variances. Additionally, the traditional model launches these explorations at the quarter-end business review, making any efforts to use the resulting analysis to influence or redirect past decisions impossible. The advanced analytic model fundamentally shifts the questions that an executive would ask, from "Why did that happen?" to "What would happen if. . .?" and therefore challenge the analytics professional to leverage historical data, external data, tools, and analytic methodologies to inform and influence future business decisions.

Correlations vs. Spreadsheets

Statistics or decision support has tended to be an arcane set of activities that only a small group of people in the organization are permitted to conduct. Those days are over. Companies do not need to create large communities of data scientists within the hallways of industry, but firms need to develop individuals who can leverage the power of statistical analysis, driver data, and correlations to interpret and predict performance without the overlay of human instinct. Over time they will be able to deliver far more predictable and reliable bands of expected performance outcomes.

Impact vs. Content

This shift might seem trite, but is responsible for vast amounts of hours spent by analysts in the traditional model. In the new model, 100-page PowerPoint decks will be replaced with one-page "analytic pull sheets," five-page analytic justifications and ten-page executive/board briefings in a standard format. Furthermore, these artifacts will be augmented by vast amounts of information deployed to decision makers daily via their preferred channel. Interactive "war rooms" of offices with machine learning and AI will focus executives on emerging or urgent topics in a way that supports decisive action.

The Hackett Group's Value Performance Framework and Analytic Methodology

The table is set for the strategic rationale for advanced analytics as well as the characteristics and how they have changed the game from a more traditional analytic assignment. What is the next step? Through the company's research and work with clients, it is clear that a Value Performance Framework is required before tactical analytics can be pursued (Figure 16.5).

While many frameworks exist in today's business marketplace, the point is to anchor on one that aligns the organization's mission, vision, and values with the set strategic objectives. After that, the cascade can occur from objectives to targets, measures, and ultimately, prioritized analytics. Why is this important? Because as firms pivot to the analytic enterprise there is a need to acknowledge that it will not happen with dramatic increases in functional budgets; rather, it will have to happen with savings achieved from efficiency gains. Thus, analytic advancements must be directly aligned with the objectives of the company and how these objectives will be achieved going forward.

The cascade is critical (Figure 16.6). For instance, if an organization aspires to grow revenue through new product launches, how should this be measured? Does everyone understand these targeted growth areas? And are the organization and the various functions involved aware and directly responsible for those performance levels at a tactical level?

The other tier of the framework that is essential is that of key performance indicators (KPIs). Chapter 10 describes these in detail, but in terms of advanced analytics, they are again essential to the cause. When firms execute analyses using internal and external data sources, statistical mechanisms and correlations, and advanced tools, there is a need to deliver meaningful insights on the KPIs that matter to the business. Often, this is a combination of predicted KPI results that balance across efficiency and effectiveness metrics. This creates an environment that allows realization of the opportunity of advanced analytics.

The Analytic Toolkit and Methodology

There is a vast array of methods at the disposal of the analytic professional. Part of the challenge facing organizations today is building institutional and individual knowledge of these methods and, most importantly, knowing when and how each should be applied. Figure 16.6 presents a list of analytic and data collection methods.

Many opportunities are arising for education courses that can help develop these skills. One thing that is vitally important prior to jumping into an analytic exercise is to appropriately frame the situation. Simply stated, firms need to ask better questions if better answers are intended.

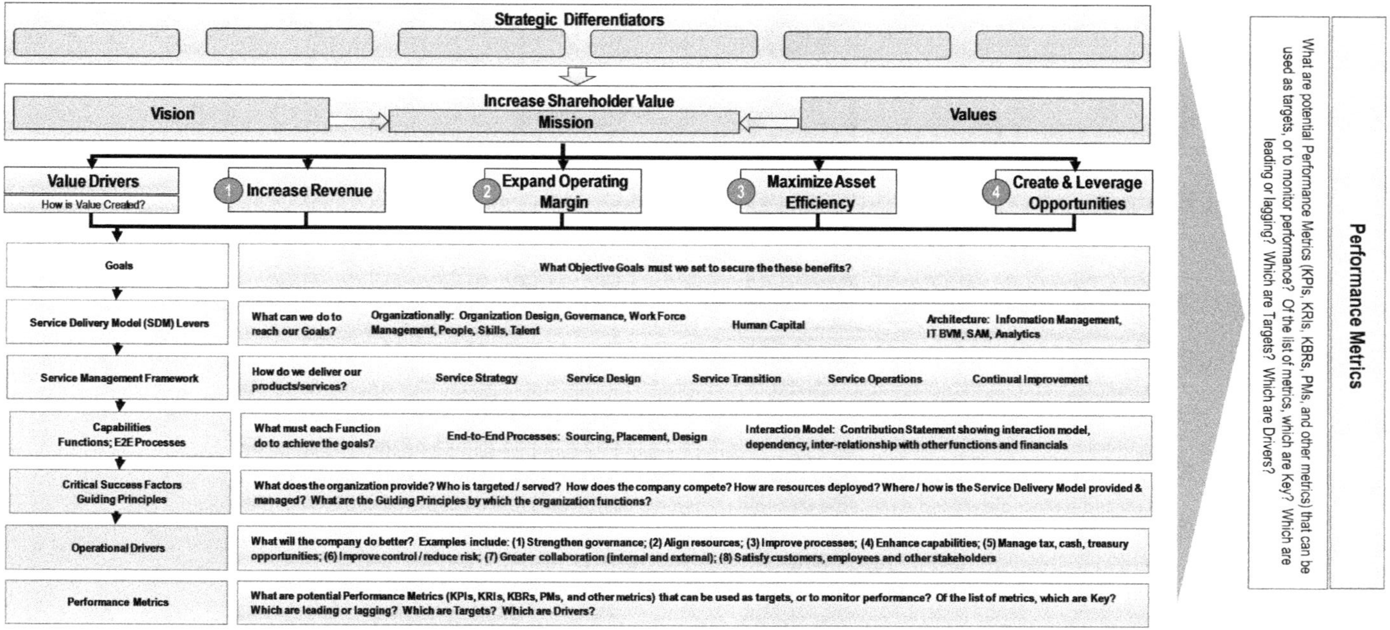

What are potential Performance Metrics (KPIs, KRIs, KBRs, PMs, and other metrics) that can be used as targets, or to monitor performance? Of the list of metrics, which are Key? Which are leading or lagging? Which are Targets? Which are Drivers?

Strategic Differentiators

Vision

Increase Shareholder Value

Mission

Values

Value Drivers
How is Value Created?

1 Increase Revenue

2 Expand Operating Margin

3 Maximize Asset Efficiency

4 Create & Leverage Opportunities

Goals
What Objective Goals must we set to secure the these benefits?

Service Delivery Model (SDM) Levers
What can we do to reach our Goals?
Organizationally: Organization Design, Governance, Work Force Management, People, Skills, Talent
Human Capital
Architecture: Information Management, IT BVM, SAM, Analytics

Service Management Framework
How do we deliver our products/services?
Service Strategy
Service Design
Service Transition
Service Operations
Continual Improvement

Capabilities Functions; E2E Processes
What must each Function do to achieve the goals?
End-to-End Processes: Sourcing, Placement, Design
Interaction Model: Contribution Statement showing interaction model, dependency, inter-relationship with other functions and financials

Critical Success Factors Guiding Principles
What does the organization provide? Who is targeted / served? How does the company compete? How are resources deployed? Where / how is the Service Delivery Model provided & managed? What are the Guiding Principles by which the organization functions?

Operational Drivers
What will the company do better? Examples include: (1) Strengthen governance; (2) Align resources; (3) Improve processes; (4) Enhance capabilities; (5) Manage tax, cash, treasury opportunities; (6) Improve control / reduce risk; (7) Greater collaboration (internal and external); (8) Satisfy customers, employees and other stakeholders

Performance Metrics
What are potential Performance Metrics (KPIs, KRIs, KBRs, PMs, and other metrics) that can be used as targets, or to monitor performance? Of the list of metrics, which are Key? Which are leading or lagging? Which are Targets? Which are Drivers?

Figure 16.5 The Hackett Group's Value Performance Framework

- Benchmarking
- Business Cases
- Business Activity Modeling
- Constraints Analysis
- Cultural Analysis
- Data Flow Diagrams
- Data Modeling
- Financial Analysis
- Impact Analysis
- Interviews
- Lessons Learned
- Metrics and Key Performance Indicators (KPIs)
- Mind Mapping
- Observations
- Organizational Modeling
- Process Analysis
- Process Modeling
- Prototyping
- Record Sampling
- Risk Analysis and Management
- Roles and Permissions Matrix
- Root Cause Analysis
- Data Samplings
- Survey or Questionnaire
- System Event Analysis
- SWOT Analysis
- Use Cases and Scenarios
- Value Chain Analysis
- Work Measurement
- Workshops

Figure 16.6 Analytic and Data Collection Methods

Figure 16.7 Problem Decomposition Framework

The following problem decomposition framework (Figure 16.7) provides a structure to assist in that framing activity.

1. Problem Decomposition: It is often difficult for organizations, let alone individuals in those organizations, to define the issues needing to be addressed, but this early step is essential to avoid misguided work efforts.

   a. A problem statement should be articulated and be as clear and concise as possible.
   b. Expanded problem statements should delve into areas such as "who, what, where, when, and why" characteristics.

2. Rationale: What is the reason for addressing this issue?

   a. What are the impediments to achieving strategic objectives and value creation?
   b. Problems are likely to have upstream, downstream, and external consequences within the organization.

3. Evidence: When and where does the problem occur and how does it manifest itself in the business?

Guiding Principle	Considerations
Use analytics to find and address root causes rather than symptoms	Ask the 5 whys to be sure you are addressing root cause
Use analytics to improve business capabilities (process, data, people and technical) rather than just focus on technical	Analytics is not a tool or "big data", but a set of techniques, technologies and skills that can be leveraged to improve capabilities and decision making
Use analytics to find the creative solutions rather than prescribed or predefined solutions	Oftentimes the value of analytics is the discovery of new opportunities "on the margin". Key mantra – "Think Differently"
Use analytics to drive for feasible solutions rather than all possibilities	Brainstorm possibilities then leverage hypothesis to test analytics of highest speed to value or success outcomes that optimize use of limited resources
Use analytics across the full lifecycle rather than focusing on one of the areas	Focusing on only one aspect of the analytics lifecycle will limit outcome achievement. Different techniques will be needed across the full spectrum
Use analytics to drive discussions for negotiation, issue resolution and decisions rather than conflict avoidance	Using analytics to drive an improved outcome will and should cause conflict. Techniques will need to be utilized to turn the conflict, often negative, to positive and constructive tension
Use analytics to improve business agility rather than perfection	Focus on feasible and probable...80/20 rule is always in play...quicker, better, faster...

Figure 16.8 Effective Analytics Guiding Principles

  a. Understand the scope of the analysis: in what ways is the problem confined?
  b. Stress the need to seek data without forming a preconceived notion of the root causes.

4. Business model/process impacts: Articulate the issues within the taxonomy of the business.

  a. What are the activities and tasks that are affected?
  b. Where are the handoffs across functional groups, external parties, or both?
  c. What are potential root causes?

5. Stakeholders: Who is being affected by this issue and in what ways?

  a. Identify impacts to functions and individuals.
  b. Gather insights and perspectives as to root causes, but as hypotheses—not as facts.

The problem decomposition framework can be very effective in helping to set the analytic journey up for success, but it is only the start. When broadly considering the end-to-end cycle of a value-added analytic exercise, there are several guiding principles that are proven guardrails for effective analysis (Figure 16.8).

Technological Implications

It is important to note some rather dramatic shifts in the technology landscape that need to be factored into a company's analytic plans. The technologies have become so much more functional and integrated that they must be addressed and considered as a key strategic enabler to a high-performing analytic environment.

Data, Data, Everywhere. . . .

The architectures of enterprise data warehouses and the means to implement and maintain these behemoths have been recently changed—not abandoned in many cases, but augmented with additional architectures that can vastly speed up analysis. Data lakes are challenging the paradigms of the non-technical businessperson, but the concept is simple: gather all relevant internal and external data, as is, and apply analytic tools "on top" to gain insights.

Now, data is still data. Everyone has challenges of data quality and definitional integrity. Again, while the fight needs to be waged for common account, product, customer, and service masters, the analytic world cannot wait. The 80/20 rule kicks in and decisions get made and margins get influenced, using the data available, however imperfect.

More Effective Governance

Some of The Hackett Group's Fortune 500 clients have found themselves at some point with a "data governance council" that has managed to convince executives that very little can be done until data standards are fully unwoven and rewoven. To facilitate advanced analytics, firms need to create an environment in which analysts know: who owns what data, how they can access it, who has responsibility for data quality/validation, and whether definitions require updating. Companies need to treat analysis like the financial closing process and rigorously execute, as opposed to engaging dozens of people in conference rooms monthly in an exercise with ultimately little value.

Virtualization and Information Delivery

The author has assisted clients for 30 years on these topics and the idea of an "executive cockpit" has always been out there. Historically, the difficulties of technology and architecture alignment have left those executives largely underserved and dissatisfied, but they have been a patient group. The technology available today has nearly eliminated these barriers. CXO cockpits can now have dynamic feeds to various systems and find correlations with external data. They can refocus the executive on areas with high variances, and can "learn" along the way via AI so that the summary information delivered is the most relevant for the time and consumer. All of this can now be done and delivered via every available channel and mechanism.

Rapid Deployments, Agile Developments, Yet Gentle Care in Broad Adoption

With the advent of cloud and new delivery models, it is important to note that any organization that wants to embrace an improvement in advanced analytics can do so without a three-year, $100M broad-based systems integration initiative. It is proven through The Hackett Group's client work that great pilots can be executed in a 4 to10-week timeframe that prove or disprove the hypotheses mentioned earlier in the chapter. But, the high performers think carefully about broad-based adoption of these analytics— "What analytics should be done daily? weekly? monthly? ad hoc?" This has prevented the institutionalization of new analyses that are not yet required or have limited value added.

The 2020 Analytic Professional

Where does the reader go from here? Best practice suggests that one does not go and seek new IT solutions, but rather, reflect on the capabilities of the professionals in their respective organizations and say, "How do we raise our individual and collective analytics IQ?"

The analytic professional is a core component to this sea of change in business operations. Rather than be replaced with automated results, the resource needs to become the true "handyman" of analysis—tapping into tools and data and methods that can allow him or her to approach predicted financial outcomes from potential operational or sales decisions that can help maximize the profit of the enterprise. It may be easier to think of this in terms of "from" actions and "to" actions as it relates to the analytic professional of 2020:

From (less of these skills and activities):

- Data collection
- Data reconciliation and bridging
- Report creation
- Rote budget and forecast preparation and bottom-up plan creation for mature parts of the business
- Period-end slideware creation
- Spreadsheet maintenance and management

To (more of these):

- Solution hypothesis development
- Correlations and business driver analysis
- Versioning and scenario modeling of potential outcomes
- Interactions with business partners proactively to scope and shape analytic needs consultatively
- Use of methods and tools that stretch past the spreadsheet dogma

- Situational/ad hoc analysis to prove or disprove root causes of variance or future performance
- Governance over data changes and expanding data needs across the enterprise

Let us translate these statements into a relevant talent model for the new analytic professional (Figure 16.9).

Business drivers: the new model requires professionals to not only hear about business pressures, but understand them in the context of the strategic objectives of the organization and where the critical inflection points are that will make or break performance.

Technology drivers: the new model also requires analytic professionals to demonstrate a distinctively new acumen for how tools can be leveraged to support business insight. They will understand the organization's current and directed technology strategy and will be ambassadors for the journey. They will enthusiastically seize on every mechanism at their disposal to advance analytic insights.

Functional drivers: the analytic professional of 2020 needs to bring a consultative mind-set and delivery model to their role in the business. This requires the development of skills such as internal "client" engagement to explore and understand challenges and scope out specific analytics that can meet those needs; an ability to operate in an unpredictable environment and create value through "mini-projects," as opposed to repeated tasks; and a "bedside manner" that helps the business leader grasp the realities of

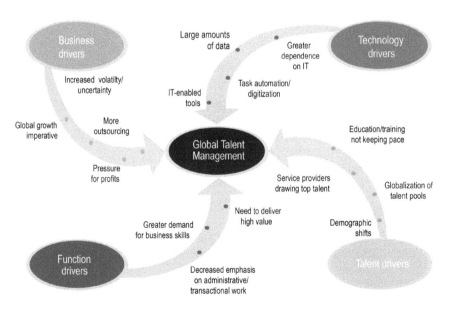

Figure 16.9 The Hackett Group's New Analytic Professional Talent Model

the digital era without overwhelming them along the way. Certainly, a new functional set of disciplines is emerging.

Talent drivers: as it relates to talent, the 2020 analytic professional needs to demonstrate a comfort level with the new modes of conducting business such as virtual teams, conference calls, video conference, social platforms, global engagement models, and so on. The new analytic professional needs to be comfortable with ambiguity, dealing with global resources, and interactions with business partners who are not traditionally evident in today's model.

What Does Analytics 2020 Hold for Us?

With all the ground that was covered in this chapter and the book overall, the question that emerges is, "What does the future hold?" Many executives are asking themselves this question and are trying to balance the "art of the possible" with the practical, pragmatic realities of how their business has traditionally worked, served customers, and created value for stakeholders. The Hackett Group's numerous client engagements, performance studies, and empirical research has shown that the future is going to be quite different from business as usual.

One can expect to see large swaths of highly manual, traditional bodies of work replaced and enhanced with AI; machine learning applied to ever-larger segments of data; broader, more integrated end-to-end decision platforms; and cross-platform robotics solutions. For instance, given all the newly available technologies and analytic methodologies, why shouldn't at least 80% of the thousands of hours dedicated to business planning and forecasting be automated, limiting the need for human intervention to interpretation (a "hands-free forecast")—while simultaneously delivering predictions that are far more accurate to gauge and shape business direction. Similarly, why can't these same technologies automate the thousands of hours spent collecting, reconciling, and creating reports and slideware to explain historical results? Automating these manual efforts is not constrained by technology, but rather by enterprise culture and the lack of integration and alignment of tools and data already resident in the business. The winners will be the organizations willing to change their cultural norms and embrace analytics as a driver of competitive advantage.

To secure this advantage, The Hackett Group recommends three immediate steps:

1. Establish an analytic road map: complete an honest assessment of the organization's current capabilities across the organizational structure, functional model, and comprehensively across the service delivery model components (people, technology, information, governance, process, etc.). Work with executives to clarify potential future capabilities and prioritize where value can be created and develop a phased journey map over a three-year period with numerous delivery points along the way.

2. Launch analytic pilots: as described, these solutions are more agile than traditional efforts, so seek areas where controlled hypotheses can be developed and leverage tools and methods to run pilots in a four-to-eight-week window for each. Establish executive access and governance to the results and course correct from learnings from each, as well as publish the successes and value created along the way.

3. Assess and address the organization's "analytic IQ": the human component of analytics is critical in the future state. What and where are the current organization's capabilities? Where are the gaps? How well do today's development/learning plans and competency models reflect the analytics skills desired by the organization, and how should they be enhanced? What vehicles are available to develop analytic skills efficiently? Exploring these questions will lead to a journey map for the professionals that will create the path to improving skills in the area and benefits to the business along the way.

Case Studies

Building Materials Company—Data First: Analytics to Identify and Exploit Efficiencies

The company had grown for decades through acquisition in a multi-business unit model with decentralized decision authority, resulting in over 500,000 performance reports and over 150 ERP/reporting systems across the footprint. This resulted in below-peer efficiency and effectiveness levels in finance and IT functions.

Challenge

Lack of capability to efficiently and effectively conduct exploratory analysis at a large scale within a multitude of data sources, helping analytics to identify and exploit efficiencies on the bottom line within various operational areas, and to grow revenues and markets for the top line.

Solution

Business and IT teams agreed on a pilot to understand the impact of sale value of homes with their products and ROI from the investment.

- IT team deployed big-data technology capabilities to efficiently and effectively conduct exploratory analysis at a large scale within a multitude of data sources.
- Business team leveraged The Hackett Group's business insights framework, conducted exploratory analysis, and discovered analytic evidence driven by data that showed.

- Company products increase the value of a home, and make consumers feel safer and more secure with their residence.
- The value of certain products is known to increase the value of an address in its resale value, and more than other competitive providers.

Benefits

- Higher close rate and shortened sales cycle.
- Mobile-ready field sales analytics tool with near real-time data and capabilities to show the measurable increase in value of sold homes providing evidence on what the local ROI is for a given marketplace from the investments.
- The average homes in your neighborhood, saw an average increase of 10% more closed sale value when Product XYZ was part of the home.
- The rep can select on the mobile device the defined territory to bring back the results.

Large Mobile Telecom—Data-Driven, Evidence-Based P&L Forecasting

Challenge

Complexity in its driver-based planning process, specifically related to the model used to forecast the corporate P&L. Inability to determine which of the 170-plus drivers used for forecasting bore any resemblance to what was being forecasted and supported by evidence. At issue was the inordinate amount of time and energy spent in the forecasting process to arrive at forecasts that were not known to be accurate or reliable.

Solution

An evidence-based approach to driver identification on this project by determining which drivers share variability with what is being predicted. Without sufficient shared variability, forecasting is guesswork. The team reduced the number of evidentiary drivers from over 170 to approximately seven, while at the same time improving the accuracy of the actual forecast.

Benefits

- Vastly reduced complexity in the forecasting model.
- Automated modeling to allow analysts to examine anomalies instead of spending time specifying the model.
- Reduction in forecasting errors of more than 5%+ ($100 million+).

Large Industrial Manufacturer—Self-Service Analytics and a Digital Data Storefront

Challenge

The company determined that an analytics platform would place the power of data availability in a user's hands, relieving the data-request burden on various internal IT processes. It would also make certain data more readily available for the user to navigate irrespective of where, what, and when the data is accessed.

Solution

The company is building an analytics platform that leverages Hadoop as a back-end solution to store the data. It chose Denodo as a data-virtualization layer to define the data structure and map relationships. The two are joined in a way that is masked to end users, yet allows them to select the data they want to use to conduct analytics. The team further extended this solution to include natural language processing and Tableau for presentation and simulations that supported users' inquiries into the data without technical SQL language coding or modeling skills. Natural language processing was also leveraged for navigation so that users only have to speak to the application and tell it to what screen to navigate next.

Benefits

- "Storefront" effectively and efficiently delivers data as self-service.
- Simulation capabilities allow for prescriptive analytics; it is expected to instill a data-driven decision-making culture.
- Analyst access to data without burdening IT; reducing costs and improving delivery of data and analytics for decision-making.
- CFO "cockpit" view that focuses on actionable data.
- Machine learning to present data based on the user's role, updated daily.

Consumer Packaged Goods Company—Determining Where Products and Customers Make (or Lose) Money

Challenge

Contributors to the company's situation included its own network over-capacity, poor fill rates and service levels, and challenges in understanding the real underlying profitability of their product/customer portfolio. In response, the company launched a transformational program to address these challenges and reposition itself to enhance its financial performance within a challenging market.

Solution

S&OP tools and analytics further exposed a disconnect between overall sales volume (which was correct in totality) and the split by customer and product, which precluded the company from taking definitive actions on specific products or customers. To solve this challenge, a strategic business model was implemented that allowed the organization to review existing product and customer profitability easily. The model also allowed the company to generate pro forma modeling of the impact of common business scenarios such as price increases, higher costs of raw materials, competitive deal reviews, and so on. This multidimensional tool sourced data from disparate systems to paint a complete picture of company performance.

The diagram below illustrates how all the components work together.

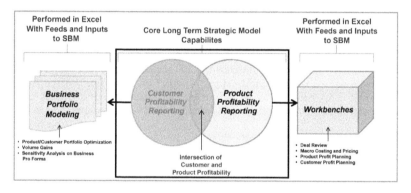

The enhancements to the pricing and profitability analysis capabilities enabled the company to more accurately interpret shifts in the marketplace and respond with decisions that enhanced profit margins and economic returns. By focusing on a sustainable platform, the solution's tools and capabilities may be used daily by the organization to plan, react, and influence decisions based on facts.

Keys to Implementing Sustainable Change

Designing and deploying the tools and processes within these areas was a significant effort, but the organization was determined to ensure that the changes were fully, widely, and permanently adopted. This required attending to all aspects of managing and adopting the new capabilities by the legacy organization. Some of the most successful tactics used are described below:

- **Executive engagement**—When the program was initiated, the executive team dedicated time every week to ensure that the effort was appropriately focused and scoped. They participated in numerous workshops to evaluate designs, continually driving the message to the organization that this is critically important, and will fundamentally change the way the business operates.

- **Ongoing focus on the target**—The business situation and the targeted performance levels were determined at the start of the transformation, widely communicated, and continually reinforced throughout the effort. As such, the targeted performance levels (both financial and operational) served as guardrails to support decision-making and issue resolution during the effort.
- **Introducing new talent to the table**—While the transformation largely relied on adoption of changes by the legacy resource base, the executive team honestly assessed where the strengths and gaps existed in these key functional areas, and introduced new hires who brought a fresh point of view and greater levels of expertise with the targeted future-state operating model.
- **Iterative "develop and adopt" methodology**—The analytic tools and workbenches to support daily pricing decisions and assess performance were not developed in the traditional sense of formally completing a design phase, then moving into build/test. Rather, after the core model and logic were developed, several iterative working sessions were held with future users to present, refine and validate functionality, with actual business situations simulated for relevance.
- **Use of "start-stop-continue" models**—To make the changes "stick," the teams developed detailed, tactical lists of specific activities for each affected functional area that should "start," "stop," or "continue" in the future model. This process led to meaningful discussions as individuals interpreted these changes in relation to their current work activities.

The Net Result: Improved Business Performance

The 12-month transformation program was a difficult effort for the entire organization, one requiring a high level of resources and attention. The results were significant and positive, however. The company built a new, foundational S&OP process that better aligns demand, supply, and economic performance, thereby enhancing service levels and managing cost. The organization also enhanced its pricing and profitability analysis capability, which allows it to better interpret and respond to the marketplace in a way that protects and enhances margins.

The net result is a business in a tough industry segment that has reset its EBITDA performance after the 2008–2009 economic downturn, with embedded capabilities to better plan, react, and guide business decisions in years to come.

Note

* Noting significant contributions from The Hackett Group's Advisory, Enterprise Analytic Institute, and Advanced Analytic practices.

17 Conclusion

J. Mark Munoz

Global Business Intelligence and Corporate Changes

Global Business Intelligence will likely define the nature of corporations in the coming years. Companies would need to rethink, restructure, and reinvent themselves in order to adapt to market changes that are taking place.

In the technological realm, the following trends are emerging: increase in usage of self-service business intelligence; advancement in customized visualization, enhanced device and system compatibilities; expansion in the use of "software as a service"; conflicts on data access and usage; growth in the application of the Internet of Things; competitive prices on big-data analytics; increase in usage of mobile analytics; and the breakthrough in power, speed, and flexibility of data analytics, and heightened competition among business intelligence (Marvin, 2015). Trend Micro (2017) revealed in a research article that 20% of global companies consider cyber-espionage as the most serious business threat.

In business research, the trends include: instant research using mobile devices, deeper examination of customer values and motivation, heightened consideration of return on investment, increasing use of automation, interest in neuromarketing research, research convenience and data race, more online tools and social analysis, data storytelling, engagement and sentiment analysis, use of real-time research, humanization of big data, emotional research tools, increase in demand for graphical information, examination of what drives customer choices, and sustainable research solutions (Schmidt, 2016).

These trends suggest that companies need to refine their strategies in order to respond to consumer expectations, competitive activities, and the quest for operational excellence.

Strategic Refinements

The chapters in this book, along with academic literature indicate that certain strategies lead to the effective implementation of business intelligence. Corporations need to operate in a particular way to overcome challenges and reap benefits associated with business intelligence. In this section, Organization Structure, Information Management, and Strategic Imperatives are discussed and considered as pathways towards effective global business intelligence.

Organizational Structure

In this section, organizational structure refers to the way an organization needs to configure itself in order that it can optimize the process of business intelligence. Key considerations include the following:

> *Goal mutuality and alignment.* A company would benefit from having clear business intelligence goals that are understood and appreciated by the entire organization. Moreover, a firm's business intelligence strategy needs to be aligned with its goals and priorities (Gonzales, 2011).
>
> *Structure for results.* When coaching a sports team, it makes sense to position the best players where they can score the most points. Similarly, in an organization individuals that have the talent and customer proximity to gather critical information should be relied upon to gather business intelligence. Salespeople are an excellent source of competitive intelligence because of their proximity to the customer. (Marshall, Moncrief, and Lassk, 1999).
>
> *Supportive leadership team.* Organizational leadership and culture factors into the success of a business intelligence strategy (Kiron, Shockley, Kruschwitz, Finch, and Haydock, 2012). A leadership team that cultivates the appropriate environment for business intelligence to thrive would likely be met with success.
>
> *Organizational teamwork.* The effective gathering of business intelligence is not the responsibility of one person, but rather the entire organization. Effective competitive intelligence is often a result of a collective effort (Crossan, Lane, and White, 1999). An organization that shares the business intelligence load and operates as one unit would be in a position to manage information well. Cross-operational collaboration is essential in business intelligence (Wagner and Weitzel, 2012).

Information Management

In this section, information management refers to the gathering, processing and analyzing of information in order that the organization can make effective business decisions. Important considerations are as follows:

> *Consider ease of usage.* Organizational members have different attitudes, intelligence, education, and skills. Having an information gathering,

processing, and evaluating platform that can be easily used by every-one increases the odds of the work getting done right. Catering to a whole-brain thinking approach can be beneficial (Spreng and Grady, 2010). Usefulness and ease of usage are often considered by end users (Legris, Ingham, and Collerette, 2003).

Attention to data security. Given that it has become exponentially easier to gather information worldwide, businesses ran the risk of leaking out confidential information. There is merit in network pruning, graft-ing, and closing to manage risk of knowledge leakages (Hernandez, Sanders, and Tuschke, 2015). In a Trend Micro (2017) report, it was revealed that almost two-thirds of businesses experienced a form of cyberattack in the past 12 months, and ransomware attacks resulted to about $1 billion in business losses worldwide.

Reliable data storage and management. Integral to the practice of busi-ness intelligence is the storage and management of all collected data. With huge volumes of data collected, organizing and safekeeping the information in a sensible manner can be a challenge. Investment of time and resources in planning and managing risk would be resources well spent. Knowledge configuration and storage is an important con-sideration (Baars, 2006).

Action orientation. Information gathered need not be done simply to impress or for prestige. It has to serve an important need and set the stage for decision-making and action. Information gathered are strategic tools (Pottruck, 1988). It provides the momentum for task implementation.

Use multiple data points. Best research practices typically suggest the validation of information by examining different sources. Objectiv-ity in the approach is important (Buchanan and O'Connell, 2006). Cross-checking information across different levels and platforms would be beneficial. Diverse information sources improve perspec-tive (Fiol, 1994). There is value in considering firm goals and mar-ket environment in the analysis (Short, Ketchen, Palmer, and Hult, 2007).

Analysis and reflection. Critical to the business intelligence process, is analysis of information gathered and ensuring that it leads to sound management decisions. Educational institutions and business organizations tend to reward logical and analytical left-brain think-ing rather than the innovation-driven right-brain thinking (Pink, 2005). Being accustomed to a particular style of thinking may lead to incorrect analysis. Combination of quantitative and qualitative approaches can be beneficial (Wallenius et al., 2008). Taking on a reflective approach can prevent the overlooking of important issues. The use of reflection utilizing the context of past, current, and future on actions and decisions can be useful (Jordan, Messner, and Becker, 2009).

Strategic Imperatives

Strategic imperatives in this section refers to actions that organizations take to achieve their set goals and advance global business intelligence. Relevant approaches are:

> *Effective management.* The best business intelligence in a poorly managed organization would likely not have much of an operational impact. Business intelligence needs to be integrated with sound management approaches (Wells, 2008).
>
> *Leverage strengths.* Companies differ in their operational strengths. Using the best talent and resources to obtain the best business intelligence can yield important benefits. Inimitable BI systems differentiate organizations and can optimize performance (Teece, Pisano, and Shuen, 1997). It is important to note that business core competencies need to be anchored on markets, integrity, and functionality (Hamel and Prahalad, 1994).
>
> *Plan for operational diversity.* Managing business intelligence, especially in a global context poses significant challenges. Diversity in a work setting impacts the way information is processed (Van Knippenberg, De Dreu, and Homan, 2004). Organization leaders have to deal with issues such as different skill levels, cross-cultural biases, and diverse operational systems across geographic regions. In this scenario, intelligence could benefit from balancing the task with diverse factors and approaches (Davis, 2002).
>
> *Timeliness of action.* Business intelligence needs to be acquired, processed, and analyzed at the right time in order for the best decisions to be made. As an example, competitive intelligence needs to be timely and actionable with clear insights on the organization as well as the competitive terrain (Boncella, 2003).

Figure 17.1 below demonstrates how organizational structure, information management, and strategic imperatives relate to global business intelligence.

Figure 17.1 highlights the fact that global business intelligence constitutes at least three important functions. The findings further suggest the following about the practice:

1. **Multifaceted**—global business intelligence is not a single action step or one that only requires the involvement of a single business unit. It requires multiple activities and several operational units operating in tandem.
2. **Holistic Approach**—in order to be effectively implemented, global business intelligence requires top management support and the cooperation of the entire workforce. Its planning requires an all-inclusive perspective and method.

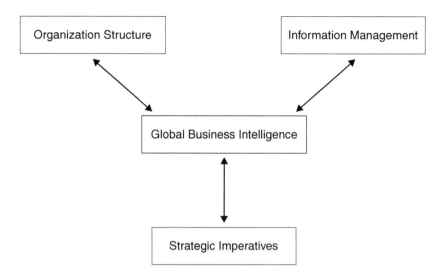

Figure 17.1 Drivers of Global Business Intelligence

3. **Resource Commitment**—given the significant commitment of organizational time and talent, along with required investment in relevant technologies, global business intelligence requires a substantial resource commitment. Careful planning needs to accompany its implementation.

4. **Inconsistently Utilized**—differences in workforce abilities and available technologies mean that there is a huge diversity in the way that business intelligence is implemented nationally and internationally. This disparity presents an opportunity for a company to distinctly set itself apart from its competitors.

5. **Management Reliant**—the success of a global business intelligence practice is anchored on sound management practices and effective strategies. Managerial efficiencies in structure formation, management of information, and strategy formulation are anchors for success.

Global business intelligence can be a complex practice. However, careful planning can help overcome obstacles and lead to the discovery of niche opportunities that will lead to success.

Recommended Path Forward

This section highlights action steps to enhance global business intelligence in organizations. Based on the noted findings, Table 17.1 presents an Operational Checklist with key questions designed to help the reader think through the business intelligence process.

Table 17.1 Global Business Intelligence Operational Checklist

Organization Structure	
Goal mutuality and alignment	What are your current business goals and priorities? How does business intelligence help you address your goals? What changes need to take place?
Structure for results	Does your current organizational structure allow you to optimize gains from business intelligence? Why or why not? Where are the loopholes? What needs to change?
Supportive leadership team	Is the top management team supportive of business intelligence? What are the areas for improvement?
Organizational teamwork	How is business intelligence gathered and shared in your organization? Is everyone involved? Does everyone have a role to play? How can collaboration be enhanced?
Information Management	
Consider ease of usage	What technology and tools do you currently use for business intelligence? Is everyone proficient? Who needs training? How will this be done and by when?
Attention to data security	How secured are corporate data? Who is accountable? Where are areas of weakness? Is there a contingency plan? Has risk assessment been made? How can data security be improved?
Reliable data storage and management	How are data stored and managed? Who is accountable? Where are the areas of weakness? Is there a contingency plan? Has risk assessment been made? How can data storage and management be improved?
Action orientation	What does the path of data collection, processing, and analyzing look like? How is collected business intelligence translated into actionable business decisions? Who are involved and are responsible? How long does the process take? How can the process be improved?
Use multiple data points	What types of cross-checking and validation is done on gathered information and intelligence? Who does the validation? Who is accountable? How can the process be improved?
Analysis and reflection	Who does the analysis and reflection on business intelligence? How is it done? What is done to ensure there are no biases? How can the process be improved?

Strategic Imperatives	
Effective management	Have managers been trained on business intelligence? Has an assessment been made? Where is the management strong and where is it weak? What are potential areas for improvement?
Leverage strengths	What are the organization's strengths with regard to business intelligence? How can this be best leveraged? Are there strengths the company needs to develop internally? How can this be done and by when?
Plan for operational diversity	How is the company managing operational diversity? Who is accountable? How can the process be improved?
Timeliness of action	What is the timeline from business intelligence gathering to decision-making? Who is involved? Who is accountable? Does this timeline suit the organization's needs? How can the process be improved?

The list of questions listed in Table 17.1 is by no means exhaustive. The questions are conversation starters that can stimulate further organizational discussions on the subject.

Aside from utilizing an Operational Checklist to get started, the following are recommended:

1. **Assess Your Organization's Intelligence Capability**—it would be beneficial to understand how an organization conducts its business intelligence. Understanding its strengths and weaknesses would be helpful in determining future plans and directions.
2. **Invest in the Right Technology**—software development in business intelligence is growing rapidly. It makes sense to use these tools to capture the best business intelligence. It will help in gathering top quality information in the fastest and most accurate manner.
3. **Provide Appropriate Training**—research has pointed out a large disparity in knowledge, know-how, and competencies in business intelligence across organizations. Training can help narrow the skills gap in the workforce and provide the foundation for optimum performance. Developing employee skills in research, listening to customers, and market analysis can enhance business intelligence.
4. **Create a Culture of Intelligence**—business intelligence needs to be a mind-set and a way of life. Making business intelligence a part of the culture and providing incentives for excellent achievements can be beneficial. Recognition and awards such as Business Intelligence of the Month and Business Intelligence of the Year can help drum up interest and commitment on business intelligence.

5. **Develop Specific Business Intelligence Policies**—many organizations take business intelligence for granted. Creating clear policies on business intelligence, along with specific goals and employee expectations would enhance its practice. Developing a "Business Intelligence Code" or "Code of Intelligence" might be beneficial.

6. **Organize for Success**—specify workforce roles in business intelligence and who is ultimately accountable for key tasks. Assigning leaders and organizational rainmakers to lead business intelligence efforts would be helpful. The overall business intelligence in a company can be headed by a person with a position title like Chief Information Officer, Chief Intelligence Officer, Chief Strategist, Head of Business Intelligence, Director for Business Intelligence, or Business Intelligence Coordinator.

7. **Link Business Intelligence to Strategy**—organizations need to close the loop of the entire business intelligence process. The flow of information from the gathering stage to the decision-making stage should be carefully planned and tracked. Given the importance of business intelligence in organizations, it makes sense to create a "Business Intelligence Strategic Plan."

8. **Have Intelligence Allies**—business intelligence need not be exclusively done within the confines of an organization. Companies can tap into suppliers, customers, and service providers to capture relevant business information. Developing strategic intelligence alliances can be beneficial.

9. **Integrate Business Intelligence**—across many organizations, business intelligence takes place in an uncoordinated manner. Important information gathered in one department may not get passed on to another department that could use it. Having an information portal where the workforce can post and access business intelligence on a daily basis might be helpful. Having an "Intelligence Circle" or "Intelligence Committee" that regularly meets to advance business intelligence could be beneficial. Organizations need to make an effort to effectively capture and integrate business intelligence.

10. **Review and Assess Progress**—after making organizational and operational changes to improve business intelligence, it will be worthwhile to review progress made. It would be helpful to determine which areas were successful and which ones need further attention. Review and assessment is important in future planning.

There are similarities between business intelligence and military field intelligence. Brei (1996) cited success measures for intelligence products in the military as: Readiness, Timeliness, Accuracy, Objectivity, Usability, and Relevance. These attributes are equally important in determining the quality of business intelligence. Lieutenant General Michael D. Maples of the USA Defense Intelligence Agency identified five strategies for intelligence excellence in the agency: (a) organizational agility for intelligence depth,

(b) strengthen human, analytic, and technological capabilities, (c) support unification of effort within the intelligence community, (d) recruit, develop, and retain a diverse workforce, and (e) establish high-quality support systems (DIA, 2007). These approaches would work well for a contemporary corporation looking to enhance its business intelligence.

Global business intelligence would be effective when carefully planned and executed. Strategic intelligence, or the gathering of relevant intelligence to advance an organization's goals is critical to its practice. Business intelligence will definitely grow in usage in the coming years. Firms that build on this expertise and leverage the skills well, will gain a definitive advantage.

References

Baars, H. (2006). Distribution von Business-Intelligence-Wissen—Diskussion eines Ansatzes zur Nutzung von Wissensmanagement-Systemen für die Verbreitung von Analyseergebnissen und Analysetemplates. In P. Chamoni and P. Gluchowski (Eds.), *Analytische Informationssysteme—Business Intelligence-echnologien und -Anwendungen* (3rd ed., pp. 409–424). Berlin: Springer.

Boncella, R. J. (2003). Competitive intelligence and the web. *Communications of Association of Information Systems*, 12, 327–340.

Brei, W. S. (1996). Getting intelligence right: The power of logical procedure. *Occasional Paper* No. 2. Washington, DC: Joint Military Intelligence College.

Buchanan, L. and O'Connell, D. (2006). A brief history of decision making. *Harvard Business Review*, 84(1), 32–41.

Crossan, M. M., Lane, H. W., and White, R. E. (1999). An organizational learning framework: From intuition to institution. *Academy of Management Review*, 24(3), 522–37.

Davis, J. (2002). Sherman Kent and the profession of intelligence analysis. *Occasional Papers, The Sherman Kent Center for Intelligence Analysis*, 1(5), 1–16.

DIA. (2007). *Strategic Plan 2007–2012. Leading the Defense Intelligence Enterprise.* Accessed June 23, 2016. Available from: www.hsdl.org/?view&did=474568

Fiol, C. M. (1994). Consensus, diversity, and learning in organizations. *Organization Science*, 5(3), 403–420.

Gonzales, M. L. (2011). Success factors for business intelligence and data warehousing maturity and competitive advantage. *Business Intelligence Journal*, 16(1), 22–29.

Hamel, G. and Prahalad, C. (1994). The concept of core competence. In G. Hamel and A. Heene (Eds.), *Competence-Based Competition* (pp. 11–33). New York, NY: Wiley & Sons.

Hernandez, E., Sanders, G.W.M., and Tuschke, A. (2015). Network defense: Pruning, grafting, and closing to prevent leakage of strategic knowledge to rivals. *Academy of Management Journal*, 58(4), 1233–1260.

Jordan, S., Messner, M., and Becker, A. (2009). Reflection and mindfulness in organizations: Rationales and possibilities for integration. *Management Learning*, 40, 465–473.

Kiron, D., Shockley, R., Kruschwitz, N., Finch, G., and Haydock, M. (2012). Analytics: The widening divide. *MIT Sloan Management Review*, 53(2), 1–22.

Legris, P., Ingham, J., and Collerette, P. (2003). Why do people use information technology? A critical review of the technology acceptance model. *Information & Management*, 40(3), 191–204.

Marshall, G. W., Moncrief, W. C., and Lassk, F. G. (1999). The current state of sales force activities. *Industrial Marketing Management*, 28(1), 87–98.

Marvin, R. (2015). *10 Business Intelligence Trends for 2016.* Accessed June 21, 2016. Available from: www.pcmag.com/article2/0,2817,2496370,00.asp

Pink, D. H. (2005). *A Whole New Mind: Moving From the Information Age to the Conceptual Age.* New York: Riverhead.

Pottruck, D. S. (1988). Turning information into strategic marketing weapons. *International Journal of Bank Marketing*, 6(5), 49–56.

Schmidt, S. (2016). *Predicted Market Research Trends for 2016.* Marketresearch. com. Accessed June 22, 2016. Available from: http://blog.marketresearch.com/predicted-market-research-trends-for-2016

Short, J. C., Ketchen, D. J., Jr., Palmer, T. B., and Hult, F.T.M. (2007). Firm, strategic group, and industry influences on performance. *Strategic Management Journal*, 28, 147–167.

Spreng, R. N. and Grady, C. L. (2010). Patterns of brain activity supporting autobiographical memory, prospection and theory of mind, and their relationship to the default mode network. *Journal of Cognitive Neuroscience*, 22, 1112–1123.

Teece, D. J., Pisano, G., and Shuen, A. (1997). Dynamic capabilities and strategic management. *Strategic Management Journal*, 18, 509–533.

Trend Micro. (2017). *Cyber Espionage Tops the List as Most Serious Threat Concern to Global Businesses in 2017.* Accessed March 29, 2017. Available from: http://newsroom.trendmicro.com/press-release/company-milestones/cyber-espionage-tops-list-most-serious-threat-concern-global-busine

Van Knippenberg, D., De Dreu, C.K.W., and Homan, A. C. (2004). Work group diversity and group performance: An integrative model and research agenda. *Journal of Applied Psychology*, 89(6), 1008–1022.

Wagner, H. T. and Weitzel, T. (2012). How to achieve operational business-IT alignment: Insights from a global aerospace firm. *MIS Quarterly Executive*, 11(1), 25–35.

Wallenius, J., Dyer, J. S., Fishburn, P. C., Steuer, R. E., Zionts, S., and Deb, K. (2008). Multiple criteria decision making, multi attribute utility theory: Recent accomplishments and what lies ahead. *Management Science*, 54, 1336–1349.

Wells, D. (2008). *Business Analytics—Getting the Point.* Accessed June 23, 2016. Available from: http://b-eye-network.com/view/7133

Index

Note: Page numbers in *italics* with an *f* denote figures. Page numbers in *italics* with a *t* denote tables.

For Product Safety Concerns and Information please contact our EU
representative GPSR@taylorandfrancis.com
Taylor & Francis Verlag GmbH, Kaufingerstraße 24, 80331 München, Germany

www.ingramcontent.com/pod-product-compliance
Ingram Content Group UK Ltd.
Pitfield, Milton Keynes, MK11 3LW, UK
UKHW020938180425
457613UK00019B/453